Salesforce.com For Dummies®

Cheat Sheet

Navigating the Salesforce.com Home Page

- **Tabs:** Click the tabs to navigate salesforce.com. When you click a tab, the tab's home page appears with sections for views, tools, and reports to help you manage your work.
- **Taskbar:** Click a link on the taskbar to perform common operations in salesforce.com such as creating accounts, contacts, and opportunities.
- **Recycle Bin:** Click the Recycle Bin link on the taskbar if you've deleted a record(s) in the last thirty days that you want to restore to keep your job.
- **Calendar:** Use the home page calendar to keep track of your schedule in salesforce.com. With the calendar view icons, you can jump to different time periods and view the calendars of other users or resources.
- **My Tasks:** Use the My Tasks section to stay up to speed on your to-do items.
- **Search:** Find information fast in salesforce.com by entering keywords and clicking Search. A search results page appears with lists of records that matched your search.
- **Recent Items:** Use Recent Items to open records that you recently visited.
- **Messages and Alerts:** View Messages and Alerts for important communications from your CRM project team or managers.
- **Web Links:** Click links in the Web Links section on the sidebar to quickly access important Web sites or corporate applications.
- **Personal Setup:** Click the Setup link in the top-right corner to go to the Personal Setup page and modify your personal settings. If you're an administrator, use Personal Setup to customize, configure, and administer salesforce.com.
- **Help and Training:** If you need help, click the Help and Training link in the top-right corner the see the tips in the following section.

Getting Help Fast

- Contact your system administrator. If you're the administrator, proceed to the next bullet.
- For reinforcement training, click the Help and Training link in the top-right corner, and then click the Training tab in the window that appears.
- For help documentation, click the Help link on most pages of salesforce.com page or the Help and Training link to access the help guide.
- For general support, click the Help and Training link, and then click the Support tab. On the Support tab, click the Find Solution button to search the knowledge base or click the Log a Case button to initiate a formal inquiry.

D1299649

Call 1-800-762-2974.

For Dummies: Bestselling Book Series for Beginners

Salesforce.com For Dummies®

Quick Answers on Common Everyday Operations

How do I . . .

✔ **Track a suspect?** Click the New Lead link on the taskbar, fill in the record, and click Save.

✔ **Track a company?** Click the New Account link on the task bar, complete the record, and click Save.

✔ **Set up parent/child relationships?** Create records for parent and child accounts. Click the Edit button on a child account and use the Lookup icon next to the Parent Account field to associate the parent. Click Save to reunite the family.

✔ **Track a person?** Go to an Account detail page where the person is employed, and then click the New Contact link on the taskbar. Fill in the record and click Save.

✔ **Establish org hierarchies?** Create records for contacts of an account. Click the Edit button on a contact record and use the Lookup icon next to the Reports To field to associate the manager. Click Save.

✔ **Add a deal?** Go to an Account detail page for the related customer, and then click the New Opportunity link on the taskbar. Complete the fields including the Stage and Close Date fields, and then click Save.

✔ **Link a partner?** Create an account for the partner first. Then go to the related customer Account or Opportunity detail page and click the New button on the Partners related list. Complete the fields to link the partner account, and then click Save.

✔ **Track competitors?** Go to the relevant Opportunity detail page and click the New button on the Competitors related list. Complete the fields and click Save.

✔ **Track contact roles?** Add contacts first. Then go to the related Account or Opportunity detail page and click the New button on the Contact Roles related list. Complete the fields to associate contacts, and then click Save.

✔ **Schedule a meeting?** Click the New Event button on your home page, complete the record, and click Save.

✔ **Look at my calendar?** From the home page, click the calendar view icons to find your desired view.

✔ **Set up a to-do?** Go to a related record detail page (such as a contact or account) and click the New Task link on the task bar. Complete the fields and click Save.

✔ **Log a call?** Go to a related record detail page and click the Log A Call button on the Activity History related list. Complete the fields and click Save.

✔ **Send an e-mail?** Go to a related record detail page (such as a contact or lead) and click the Send An Email button on the Activity History related list. Complete the fields and click Save.

✔ **Access sales collateral?** Click the Documents tab and in the Find Documents section, enter keywords to search for sales collateral.

✔ **Manage a campaign?** If you have campaigns and the proper permissions, click the New Campaign button on the taskbar. Fill in the fields and click Save.

✔ **Initiate a customer service inquiry?** Go to a related record detail page (such as an account or contact) and click the New Case link on the taskbar.

✔ **Create a reusable focus list?** Click a relevant record tab and click the Create New View link in the Account Views section. Complete the settings for the view and click Save.

✔ **Create a report?** Click the Reports tab and then click the Create New Custom Report button. Follow the steps through the wizard and click the Run Report button when ready.

✔ **Export a report?** Go to a report and click the Export to Excel button. Follow the steps to export the report.

✔ **Merge duplicate records?** On a Lead detail page, click the Find Duplicates button. For merging accounts, click the Merge Accounts link in the Tools section on the Accounts home page. For merging contacts, go to an Account detail page and click the Merge Contacts button on the Contacts related list. In each situation, follow the steps in the merge wizard to complete the operation.

✔ **Transfer a record?** Assuming you have transfer rights, go to a record detail page and click the Change link in brackets next to the Owner field. Complete the fields and click Save.

For Dummies: Bestselling Book Series for Beginners

Salesforce.com®
FOR
DUMMIES®

by Tom Wong

WILEY

Wiley Publishing, Inc.

About the Author

Tom Wong claims he is the number one fan of salesforce.com. He keeps a picture of the Web site on his desktop and a Team Edition football in his car. He sends his wife salesforce.com meeting invitations. His friends say he can't talk about anything else.

Prior to writing this book, Tom was vice president in charge of CRM solutions for Theikos, a leading salesforce.com partner. And before then, he held several senior management positions at Gomez, another satisfied salesforce.com customer. He is a certified salesforce.com partner and has been involved in over thirty implementations impacting thousand of users.

Now that Tom has finished this book, he will try to return to a more normal life. He has an amazing and highly patient wife; a son who is a talented drummer; and a daughter aspiring to be a ballerina. They try not to discuss salesforce.com.

Tom has just launched a weblog devoted to salesforce.com at his new Web site, www.clientology.net. Tom's mission is to build an online community of business users and administrators seeking to network, share ideas and extend the value of salesforce.com. If you share his vision, join the community at www.clientology.net or send him an email at twong@clientology.net.

Dedication

To my wife and family. I asked Lorraine to believe in me, and she has always been there for me. She has been my emotional support throughout the entire writing process. She, JT, Phoebe, and the rest of the Wong clan have been a constant source of inspiration.

Author's Acknowledgments

This is not the Academy Awards, but this book couldn't have gotten done without the support of many people. I promise to keep my credits to a minimum and to stop when the orchestra begins to play.

I want to thank my editors at Wiley: Bob Woerner for believing in me; Beth Taylor in particular for her great patience and insight in guiding me through this first book; and Virginia Sanders for her smart comments and sense of humor.

I want to thank my friends at salesforce.com. In my professional life, I've used many applications. Most of them I've either deleted or sit in boxes in my basement. I have never, ever come across an application and a company that so outperformed my expectations. It isn't hard to be passionate about something you so believe in, and I know I'm not alone. What you might not know is that behind the application and the company is a set of incredible people who have provided me both knowledge and support prior to and during this book. I want to express a special note of gratitude to Tien Tzuo and his team.

I also want to thank my customers and just about every employer I ever worked for. I couldn't have written this book without a context for sales, marketing, and customer service. I've had the fortune of working with many companies, some small and some large, but all have shared a common interest in serving the customer. I've learned as much from them as they from me.

Finally, I'd like to thank my friends who have listened quietly as I've ranted and raved the last several months. High fives all around to the Krafts, Finellis, and "friends of Gomez" (you know who you are). I've benefited in particular from Alan Alper, who as a salesforce.com user and an author has provided both perspective and a sanity check for me.

Publisher's Acknowledgments

We're proud of this book; please send us your comments through our online registration form located at www.dummies.com/register.

Some of the people who helped bring this book to market include the following:

Acquisitions, Editorial, and Media Development

Project Editor: Beth Taylor

Senior Acquisitions Editor: Bob Woerner

Copy Editor: Virginia Sanders

Technical Editor: Tien Tzuo

Editorial Manager: Leah Cameron

Editorial Assistant: Amanda Foxworth

Cartoons: Rich Tennant (www.the5thwave.com)

Composition Services

Project Coordinator: Maridee Ennis

Layout and Graphics: Andrea Dahl, Joyce Haughey, Barry Offringa, Jacque Roth

Proofreaders: Leeann Harney, Jessica Kramer, TECHBOOKS Production Services

Indexer: TECHBOOKS Production Services

Publishing and Editorial for Technology Dummies

Richard Swadley, Vice President and Executive Group Publisher

Andy Cummings, Vice President and Publisher

Mary Bednarek, Executive Acquisitions Director

Mary C. Corder, Editorial Director

Publishing for Consumer Dummies

Diane Graves Steele, Vice President and Publisher

Joyce Pepple, Acquisitions Director

Composition Services

Gerry Fahey, Vice President of Production Services

Debbie Stailey, Director of Composition Services

Table of Contents

Introduction

*T*his book is for users of salesforce.com, including those users who have Enterprise, Professional, Team, or Personal Edition. It's for salesforce.com users who want to know how to use this browser-based service without wasting time. Don't look in this book to find out how salesforce.com works. Look in this book to find out how you can manage your customers and your teams and close more business by using salesforce.com.

- ✔ **If you're a sales rep,** this book can help you use salesforce.com to manage your leads, accounts, contacts, and opportunities. You can spend less time doing administrative work and more time focused on making money.

- ✔ **If you're a sales manager,** you find out how to utilize salesforce.com to track team activities, realign territories, shorten the ramp-up time on new hires, and pinpoint critical sales opportunities that require your involvement.

- ✔ **If you're in marketing,** I show you how to use salesforce.com to make an immediate and measurable impact on your sales organization. Manage campaigns, track leads, measure return on investment (ROI) — I cover each of these areas. And this book shows you how to use salesforce.com for traditional marketing issues such as products, pricing, positioning, and promotion.

- ✔ **If you're in customer service,** know that this book is almost entirely focused on how to use salesforce.com for sales productivity and effectiveness. Don't look here for how-to's on supportforce.com.

- ✔ **If you sit on the executive team,** this book shows you how to use salesforce.com to measure your overall business.

- ✔ **If you're and administrator or involved in your company's customer relationship management (CRM) initiative,** this book gives you practical knowledge for customizing, configuring, and maintaining your solution. Plus, I raise issues that you need to address to implement salesforce.com successfully. If I were in your shoes, I would flip through the sales and marketing chapters in Parts II and III to understand how salesforce.com is commonly used by end users. Then I would use that to guide me in administering salesforce.com in Parts III and IV.

- ✔ **If you're my wife,** buy this book so you can prove to your parents that I haven't been slacking off these last several months.

I show you everything you need to know to manage the lifecycle of your customer relationships in salesforce.com from qualifying leads to closing opportunities to handling customer service inquiries. On the way, you have a laugh or two. And this book can expose you to useful features and functionality that you might not have even known existed.

Although this book applies to users of all salesforce.com editions, be aware that not all portions of this book necessarily apply to your edition. Different editions have varying degrees of feature and functionality. I make sure to point this out where it's relevant.

About This Book

This book is jam-packed with instructions, advice, shortcuts, and tips for getting the most out of salesforce.com. Here's a bare outline of the parts of this book:

- ✔ **Part I: Salesforce.com Basics** — Part I gives you the big picture on salesforce.com. I show you the best ways to navigate the system, where to go for help, and how to personalize salesforce.com for your individual needs.

- ✔ **Part II: Driving Sales** — Part II shows you how to use salesforce.com for every facet of your sales process. I explain how you can use salesforce.com for prospecting leads, managing accounts, working with partners, pursuing opportunities, and more.

- ✔ **Part III: Optimizing Marketing** — If you're in marketing, Part III is your friend. Marketing in salesforce.com and your business is much more than campaign management. You discover how to use salesforce.com to standardize communications, extend your brand, control sales collateral, and analyze your products and prices.

- ✔ **Part IV: Measuring the Overall Business** — Part IV shows every rep, manager and senior executive how to use salesforce.com to measure and analyze their business. This book doesn't tell you how to improve your business (that's largely up to you), but Part IV helps you place the data at your fingertips.

- ✔ **Part V: Designing the Salesforce.com Solution** — Salesforce.com is great out of the box, but you can get more out of it when you customize it to meet your corporate objectives. Part V is for system administrators and the CRM project team. You get to know the important steps for configuring, customizing, and maintaining your system.

✔ **Part VI: The Part of Tens** — In Part VI, you get lists that are guaranteed to catch your attention. I cover some of the newest features from the latest salesforce.com release, plus some great — but sometimes overlooked — productivity tools. I also summarize some best practices for successfully implementing salesforce.com.

How to Use This Book

This book is divided into parts and then chapters based loosely on three widely accepted pillars of customer relationship management: sales, marketing, and customer service. I've organized the sections based on your function in the company and what you might want to know about salesforce.com based on your role.

You can choose to read this book from front to back (although I don't work up to a surprise ending in the last chapter). If you're like me, you'll use this book as a reference, similar to other *For Dummies* books. You can go to any topic in this book and know what to do without having to leaf to other sections.

You can get the most out of this book if you're using it while you're logged in to salesforce.com (and sitting on your favorite chair). The best way to know what to do, in my experience, is by doing it, and for that you need the salesforce.com Web site open, revved, and raring to go.

In this book, I provide you the easiest or best way to perform a task in salesforce.com. Like other easy-to-use applications, the method I show you might not be the only way, and sometimes you might find another method that works better for you. That's okay, and it doesn't hurt my feelings.

Foolish Assumptions

Please forgive me, but I make one or two foolish assumptions about you, the reader. I assume these things:

✔ You have access to an Internet connection and you've used a browser before. If I've made this assumption in error, you have much more pressing problems than understanding the effective use of salesforce.com.

✔ You have a salesforce.com account and some interest in knowing how to use it beyond the mere curiosity of reading my riveting prose.

✔ You have some business experience — at least enough to understand that winning deals is good and losing deals is bad.

✔ You have at least a vague idea of what a database is, including basic concepts such as fields, records, files, and folders.

Icons Used in This Book

To help you get the most out of this book, I place icons here and there that highlight important points. Here's what the icons mean:

Next to the Tip icon, you can find shortcuts, tricks, and best practices to use salesforce.com more effectively or productively.

Pay extra attention where you see a Warning icon. It means that you might be about to do something that you'll regret later.

When I explain a juicy little fact that bears remembering, I mark it with a Remember icon. When you see this icon, prick up your ears. You can pick up something that could be of wide or frequent use as you work with sales force.com.

When I'm forced to describe high-tech stuff, a Technical Stuff icon appears in the margin. You don't have to read what's beside this icon if you don't want to, although some readers might find the technical detail helpful.

Part I
Salesforce.com Basics

The 5th Wave   By Rich Tennant

Why can't I close this guy?

GOALS   TEAMWORK   STAY THE COURSE   LEAD DON'T FOLLOW

In this part . . .

Salesforce.com is a customer relationship management (CRM) system, but it's different from just about any other software solution you've ever used. Maybe that's because unlike traditional software, salesforce.com is an Internet-based service that requires no software installation on your part; you simply log in as you would any other secure Web site, and you and your company can begin managing your customers.

But that's an oversimplification. The real reasons that make salesforce.com different from most other CRM tools boil down to three elements. First, by placing the technology burden on itself, salesforce.com allows you to concentrate directly on your business challenges. Second, its navigation is so simple that you'll actually enjoy using it. And third, salesforce.com focuses squarely on you, the user, so you can personalize your CRM system to suit your individual habits and preferences.

In this part, you find details and tips on each of these critical promises. I discuss high-level features of salesforce.com and how those features can be applied to typical business challenges. You discover just how easily you can navigate salesforce.com and how to personalize salesforce.com to manage your business.

Chapter 1

Looking Over Salesforce.com

. . . .

. . . .

*Y*ou might not realize it yet, but every time you log in to salesforce.com you're accessing an extremely powerful lever of change for you, your group, and your company.

Sounds like a tall order but consider this: What value do you put on your customer relationships? If you're a sales rep, it's your livelihood. And if you're in management, you have fewer assets more valuable than your existing customer base. What if you had a tool that could truly help you manage your customers?

Salesforce.com isn't the first customer relationship management (CRM) system to hit the market, but it's dramatically different. Unlike traditional CRM software, salesforce.com is an Internet service. You sign up, log in through a browser, and it's immediately available. (Salesforce.com and other companies call this new computing model an *on demand* model.) Salesforce.com customers typically say that it's different for three major reasons:

- ✔ **Fast:** When you sign on the dotted line, you want your CRM system up yesterday. Traditional CRM software could take more than a year to deploy; compare that to months or even weeks with salesforce.com.

- ✔ **Easy:** End user adoption is critical to any application, and salesforce.com wins the ease-of-use category hands down. You can spend more time putting it to use and less time figuring it out.

- ✔ **Effective:** Because it's easy to use and can be customized quickly to meet business needs, customers have proven that it has improved their bottom lines.

With salesforce.com, you now have a full suite of services to manage the life-cycle of your customer. This includes tools to pursue leads, manage accounts, track opportunities, resolve cases, and more. Depending on your team's objectives, you might use all salesforce.com tools from day one or just the functionality to address the priorities at hand.

The more you and your team adopt salesforce.com into your work, the more information you'll have at your fingertips to deepen customer relationships and improve your overall business.

In this chapter, I let you in on the many the great things that you can do with salesforce.com. Then, I describe how you can extend salesforce.com to work with many of the common applications that you already use. Finally, I help you decide which salesforce.com edition is right for you just in case you're still evaluating your options.

Using Salesforce.com to Solve Critical Business Challenges

I could write another book telling you all the great things you can do with salesforce.com, but you can get the big picture from this chapter. So instead, I focus this section on the most common business challenges that I hear from sales and marketing executives — and how salesforce.com can overcome them.

Understanding your customer

How can you sell and retain a customer if you don't understand their needs, people, and what account activities and transactions have taken place? With salesforce.com, you can track all your important customer data in one place so that you and your teams can develop solutions that deliver real value to your customers.

Centralizing contacts under one roof

How much time have you ever wasted tracking down a customer contact, an organizational chart, or even an address that you know exists within the walls of your company? With salesforce.com, you can quickly centralize and organize your accounts and contacts so that you can capitalize on that information when you need to.

Expanding the funnel

Inputs and outputs, right? The more leads you generate and pursue, the greater the chance that your revenue will grow. So the big question is, "How do I make the machine work?" With salesforce.com, you can plan, manage, measure, and improve lead generation, qualification, and conversion. You can see how much business is generated, sources, and who internally is making it happen.

Consolidating your pipeline

Pipeline reports are reports that give companies insight into future sales, and forecast reports let them confidently predict what accounts will close in a period. Yet I've worked with companies where generating the weekly pipeline or forecast could take a day of guess work. Reps waste time updating spreadsheets. Managers waste time chasing reps and scrubbing data. Bosses waste time tearing their hair out. With salesforce.com, you can shorten or eliminate that wasted exercise. As long as reps manage opportunities in salesforce.com, managers can generate updated pipeline and forecast reports with the click of a button.

Working as a team

How many times have you thought that your own co-workers got in the way of selling? Nine out of ten times, the challenge isn't people, but standardizing processes and clarifying roles and responsibilities. With salesforce.com, you can define teams and processes for sales, marketing, and customer service, so the left hand knows what the right hand is doing. Although salesforce.com doesn't solve corporate alignment issues, you now have the tool that can drive and manage better team collaboration.

Collaborating with your partners

In many industries, selling directly is a thing of the past. To gain leverage and cover more territory, many companies work through partners. With salesforce.com, your channel reps can track and associate partners and end customers at the same time. With a tool that allows you to target and manage your partner relationships, you can build more mindshare and grow the channel business.

Beating the competition

How much money have you lost to competitors? How many times did you lose a deal only to discover, after the fact, that it went to a competitor? If you know who you're up against, you can probably better position yourself to win the opportunity. With salesforce.com, you and your teams can track competition on deals, collect competitive intelligence, and develop action plans to wear down your foes.

Improving customer service

As a sales person, have you ever walked into a customer's office expecting a renewal only to be hit with a landmine because of an unresolved customer issue? And if you work in customer support, how much time do you waste on an inquiry trying to identify the customer and their entitlements? With salesforce.com, you can efficiently capture, manage, and resolve customer issues. By managing cases in salesforce.com, sales reps get visibility into the health of their accounts, and service is better informed of sales and account activity.

Accessing anytime, anywhere

Companies are more mobile than ever before. People work from home or on the road. Offices are spread out. You expect to get access to information from multiple devices, easily and reliably. With salesforce.com, you can access and manage your critical customer information, at 3 p.m. or 3 a.m., online or offline, in multiple languages, and from multiple devices.

Measuring the business

How can you improve what you can't measure? Simple, huh, and yet how many companies have you worked for that couldn't accurately or reliably measuring the business? If you and your teams use salesforce.com correctly and regularly to manage customers, you have data to make informed decisions. That benefits everyone. If you're a rep, you know what you need to do to get the rewards you want. If you're a manager, you can pinpoint where to get involved to drive your numbers. And with salesforce.com's reporting and dashboards, you have easy-to-use tools to measure and analyze your business.

Extending the Value Chain

Salesforce.com understands that most companies already rely on existing tools for parts of their businesses. Such tools might include your e-mail, Office tools, your public Web site, and your intranet. Salesforce.com isn't naïve enough to think people will stop using common productivity tools. In fact, you can readily integrate salesforce.com with many of the tools you use today to interact with your customers.

Synchronizing with Outlook

If you work for a company, you probably use Microsoft Outlook every day for common tasks, such as maintaining your address book, managing your calendar, and jotting down your to do list. With Intellisync for salesforce.com, you can synchronize that information bi-directionally at your discretion. So you can continue to work with your familiar tools, and even if you're not online, you can still get access to important contact information.

Working with Outlook e-mail

E-mail is a standard way in which businesses communicate today. Not every e-mail you send or receive needs to be in salesforce.com, but you might want to retain the important customer e-mail threads. By doing this, you and your team can stay up to date on e-mail discussions. With Outlook Edition for salesforce.com, you can still continue to send and receive e-mail with Outlook, but you can easily capture those e-mails on your records in salesforce.com. You can also create a case directly from an e-mail. In fact, with Outlook Edition, you never have to leave Outlook to access salesforce.com.

Working with Word and Excel

If you're like me, you can't live without Microsoft Word or Excel. With Office Edition for salesforce.com, you can log in to salesforce.com from both Word and Excel. What that means to you, productivity-wise, is potentially dramatic. With Word, you can use salesforce.com to automatically generate personalized quote forms, proposals, and agreements. With Excel, you can construct a complex report and update it with data from salesforce.com with the click of a button.

Integrating with your Web site

For many companies, the public Web site is a primary way to communicate information to their customers. You might use your Web site as a channel for visitors to request information or log customer service issues. With salesforce.com, you can capture leads and cases directly from your Web site and route them directly into salesforce.com and assign them to the right reps. And with salesforce.com's assignment rules, you can make sure that incoming leads or cases get to the right reps in a timely manner. With minimal effort, you can even offer self-service options in the form of a public knowledge base or a private portal, enabling customers to help themselves.

Connecting to other Web sites

As part of your job, you might regularly use public or private Web sites for tasks like researching potential customers, driving directions, and getting the inside scoop on your competition. With the help of your system administrator and creativity, your company can build Web integration links in salesforce.com that can connect you directly with the relevant pages of important sites. Accessing your intranet; populating a Web form to provision a demo; creating and propagating a salesforce.com record — all these are within reach. And all this means time saved for you.

Integrating with other applications

Your company might have other applications with critical customer data — financial and enterprise resource planning (ERP) applications are just a few examples. Many applications provide unique and indispensable value to your organization. Your company isn't going to retire them just because you're using salesforce.com. But based on company objectives, those applications might need to integrate with salesforce.com. With salesforce.com's open architecture, your company can make this happen with the right technical assistance.

Building your own tabs

When you log in to salesforce.com, you see several tabs. Salesforce.com prioritized the development of each of those tabs based on core sales, marketing, and customer service functions. But depending on your business needs, you might require other tabs with different functionality. Order entry, expenses, and benefits are just a few examples. With salesforce.com's CustomForce (its customization toolkit), sforce (its development platform), and your existing development tools, your company can easily build custom tabs with unique hosted applications to fit your specific business needs.

Deciding Which Edition Is Best for You

If you already use salesforce.com, this topic might be a moot point. At the very least, you'll know which version of salesforce.com you have.

Salesforce.com has five versions of its award-winning Internet service. All versions have the same consistent look and feel, but each varies by feature, functionality, and pricing. (If you're considering using salesforce.com for your CRM needs, you should consult with an account executive for more details.)

- ✔ **Personal Edition:** Basic account, contact, and opportunity management for one person.
- ✔ **Team Edition:** Account, contact, and opportunity management for teams of five users or less.
- ✔ **Professional Edition:** Full-powered CRM without complexity for any size organization.
- ✔ **Enterprise Edition:** Flexible CRM for even the most complex organizations.

Most companies tend to make a decision between Professional and Enterprise Edition. Budget might be an issue, but the decision usually boils down to core business needs. Consider these questions:

Does your company . . .

- ✔ Have different groups with distinct sales processes, customers, and products?
- ✔ Sell multiple products as part of opportunities and needs visibility into products?
- ✔ Need scheduling on opportunities to track shipments or estimate revenue recognition?
- ✔ Plan to integrate salesforce.com with other applications?
- ✔ Require complex data migration into salesforce.com?
- ✔ Need greater control over profiles and their permissions?
- ✔ Sell in defined teams with specific roles?
- ✔ Require workflow to further automate processes?

If the answer to any of these questions is a definitive *Yes,* your company should probably use Enterprise Edition.

Whichever edition you choose, the good news is that every edition of salesforce.com is feature-rich with tools that can help companies of every size address their business challenges. And when salesforce.com rolls out new releases of its service (which it does three times a year), those enhancements are available to the different editions wherever relevant. So you don't have to purchase one version and constantly install new upgrades every four months.

Chapter 2

Navigating Salesforce.com

*I*f an application isn't easy to use, you won't use it. Period. Salesforce.com succeeds not only because it offers a universe of integrated tools, but because users can pick it up within minutes. You navigate it much the same way you use other popular Web sites: by pointing and clicking over text links and buttons.

Still, you have so many ways to navigate salesforce.com that it makes sense to lay down the obvious (and not-so-obvious) best practices for getting around the application.

Even if you're familiar with salesforce.com, you might want to breeze through this chapter because I cover certain terms used repeatedly throughout this book.

In this chapter, you find out how to log in to the site and use the home page to manage your activities, create records, and jump to other tabs. I briefly go over the major tabs and show you how to use the interior home pages, list pages, detail pages, and related lists. Finally, I show you where you can go for help.

Getting Familiar with Basic Terms

Before I delve into the mechanics of navigating salesforce.com, be sure to familiarize yourself with certain basic terms:

- ✔ **Salesforce.com:** When I use the term salesforce.com, I mean the secure Web site that your users log in to that contains your customer information. Salesforce.com, Inc., has thousands of clients who use its service, but each company's secure Web site is separate from the other Web sites and might look different to suit their unique needs.

- ✔ **Home page:** When I refer to the home page, I mean the main home page that appears when you log in to salesforce.com or click the Home tab.

- ✔ **Tabs:** Clickable tabs appear at the top of any salesforce.com page. Each tab represents a major module within the application that companies use to organize and manage information about customers. By clicking a tab, you go to a tab-specific home page. For example, if you click the Accounts tab, the Accounts home page appears.

- ✔ **Tab home pages:** Where you go to find, organize, and manage specific information related to that tab. For example, if you wanted to see and access your opportunity records, you could go to the Opportunities home page.

- ✔ **A record:** A collection of fields related to a specific item. For example, a contact record typically contains fields pertinent to a person, including name, title, phone, and e-mail address. A record is displayed on a detail page.

- ✔ **A detail page:** A Web page that shows both the saved record and a set of related lists pertinent to the record. I often use the terms *record* and *detail page* interchangeably. From a detail page, you can perform and track a variety of tasks related to the specific record. For example, if you had and were looking at an Account detail page for Cisco, you would see fields about the company and lists of other records related to Cisco.

- ✔ **Related lists:** Lists of other records linked to the record that you're looking at. For example, the Account detail page for Cisco might display related lists of contacts, opportunities, activities, and so on associated with that company.

- ✔ **Taskbar:** The bar just below the tabs that enables you to create many types of common records.

- ✔ **Sidebar:** The left margin of a salesforce.com page. The sidebar displays a search tool and recent items.

Accessing Salesforce.com

You need to log in to your account because every company's salesforce.com Web site is different and salesforce.com goes to great lengths to protect your information.

Setting up a password

The first time you log in to the salesforce.com service, you receive an e-mail entitled "salesforce.com login confirmation." To log in the first time and reset your password, follow these steps:

1. **Open the e-mail and click the first link, which contains both your user name and temporary password.**

   A page appears, prompting you to set a new password and select and answer a question that can verify your identity if you forget your password (see Figure 2-1).

2. **Complete the fields.**

   Use this password from now on unless your administrator resets the passwords.

3. **When you're done, click Save.**

   The home page of salesforce.com appears.

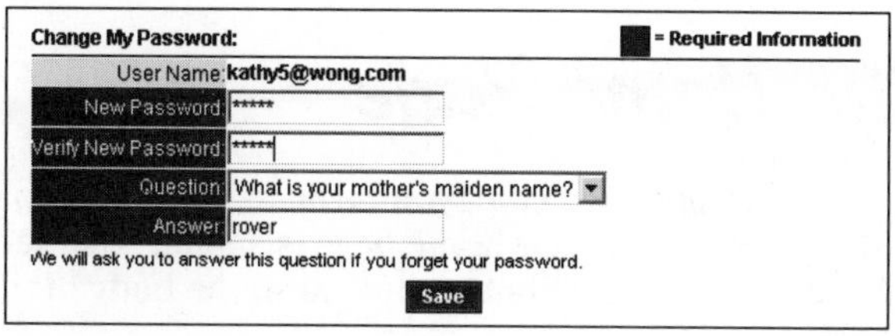

Figure 2-1:
Resetting
your
password
upon initial
entry.

Change My Password:	■ = Required Information
User Name: kathy5@wong.com	
New Password: *****	
Verify New Password: *****	
Question: What is your mother's maiden name? ▼	
Answer: rover	
We will ask you to answer this question if you forget your password.	
Save	

Logging in

You log in to salesforce.com just as you would any other secure Web site.

To log in, open a browser and follow these steps:

1. **In your browser's address bar, type** www.salesforce.com **and press Enter.**

   The salesforce.com public Web site appears.

2. **Click the Customer Login tab highlighted in black.**

   The login page appears.

3. **Enter your user name and password and click the Login button, as shown in Figure 2-2.**

   Your user name is typically your corporate e-mail address. Select the Remember User Name check box if you want your computer to remember it. After you click the Login button, your main home page appears.

Figure 2-2:
Logging
in.

:: Login

User Name:
tester@testcorp.com
Password:
*****
☑ Remember User Name
▶ Login
Unauthorized access is
prohibited

To save yourself steps when logging in, use your browser tools to bookmark the login page.

Navigating the Home Page

Every time you log in to salesforce.com, you begin at your home page. The look and feel of the elements on your home page is similar to other users' home pages, but the tasks and events that appear in the body of the page are specific to you.

Use the home page to manage your calendar and tasks, jump to other areas by clicking tabs, or search and access specific information with the sidebar. If your company is using the new, customizable home page feature, you might also see key charts or graphs from your company's dashboards. (*Dashboards* are visual snapshots of key performance metrics based on your custom report data.)

Managing your calendar

The calendar section of the home page defaults to a calendar of the current month and your scheduled events for the next seven days. Like other calendar tools, the calendar allows you to drill down. Your scheduled events are based on events that you or other users have assigned to you.

From this calendar section (shown in Figure 2-3), you can do the following:

Figure 2-3:
Looking
over your
calendar
options.

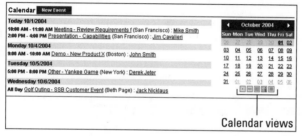

Calendar views

✔ Click the New Event button if you want to schedule a new activity. A New Event page appears in Edit mode.

✔ If you see a listed event, click the link to view the event record. A page appears with details on the activity.

✔ Click the calendar's directional arrows to move to another month. The calendar changes, but everything else on the home page remains the same.

✔ Click a date link on the calendar to drill into your schedule for a specific day. The Day View page appears.

✔ Click one of the five calendar icons (as shown under the calendar in Figure 2-3) to manage your calendar by Day, Week, Month, Multi User, or List View.

✔ If you want to schedule a group activity, click the Multi User View icon (which kind of looks like two little people). A page appears for the selected day that displays the availability of multiple users.

To view other user or public calendars, click the Day, Week, or Month View calendar icon, and then click the Change link in brackets at the top of the view. In the pop-up window that appears, you can choose from the options to see another calendar.

Tracking your tasks

On the home page, you see a section entitled My Tasks, which displays tasks that you've created for yourself or that have been assigned to you. The My Tasks section also appears on the Day View and Week View of the calendar.

A *task* is an activity that needs to be done and can have a due date but — unlike an event — doesn't have a specific date and time. For example, if you want to remind yourself to send a proposal, you typically create a task rather than scheduling an event. (See Chapter 7 if you want additional tips on managing tasks.)

From the My Tasks section (as shown in Figure 2-4) you can do the following:

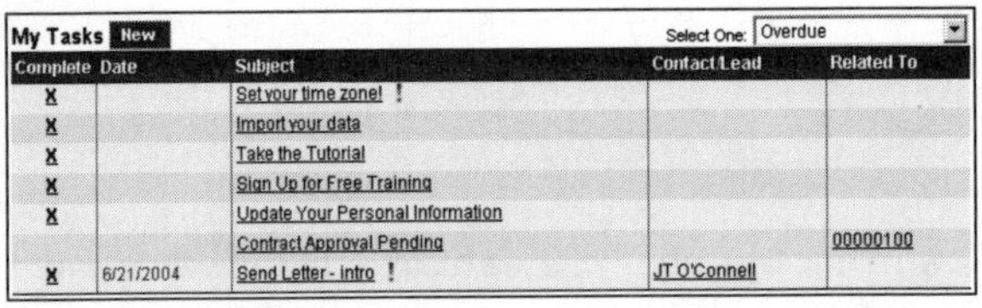

Figure 2-4:
Reviewing
the My
Tasks
section
from the
home page.

My Tasks New				
Complete	Date	Subject	Contact/Lead	Related To
X		Set your time zone!		
X		Import your data		
X		Take the Tutorial		
X		Sign Up for Free Training		
X		Update Your Personal Information		
		Contract Approval Pending		00000100
X	6/21/2004	Send Letter - intro !	JT O'Connell	

Select One: Overdue

- ✔ Click the New button if you want to add a new task. A New Task page appears in Edit mode.

- ✔ Use the Select One drop-down list at the top of the My Tasks section to select from common lists of task views. For example, select Overdue if you want to see your open tasks that are past their respective due dates.

- ✔ Click a link in the Subject column to review a task. A task record appears with details.

- ✔ Click links in the Contact/Lead or Related To columns to go to associated records.

- ✔ Click an X link in the Complete column to complete the task and enter any details before saving. (You can also use this link to update a task, but if the task isn't completed, remember to adjust the Status field before you save it.)

- ✔ Click the View More link at the bottom of the My Tasks section on the home page to see more tasks on the list. The Day View appears and the My Tasks section displays in the right column.

Using dashboard snapshots from the home page

If your company has customized your home page, you might also see and select up to three key charts and tables from your dashboards. *Dashboards* display important information from reports in salesforce.com that can provide key performance indicators on the health of your business. Each dashboard chart or table is called a *component.* See Chapter 16 for details on building dashboards to measure and analyze your business.

If you see a chart or table on your home page, you can also perform these actions from the Dashboard section:

✔ Click a chart or table to drill into the detail. A report page appears with the data that supports the graphic.

✔ Click the Customize Page button at the top of the section to choose a different dashboard. The Customize your Home Page page appears, and here you can select from available dashboards. Your home page displays a snapshot of only the three components along the top of any dashboard.

✔ Click the Refresh button in the top-right corner of the section to refresh the dashboard snapshot.

Accessing information with the sidebar

The sidebar is the column on the left that appears on just about every page of salesforce.com except dashboards and reports. On the home page, use the sidebar to search for records, quickly go back to pages you recently clicked, and stay informed of important company messages or Web sites.

Finding items with Search

You can find a majority of the information you want by using Search. Depending on your company's sharing rules, your results might vary. See Chapter 19 for additional tips on setting up sharing.

To search for information, follow these steps:

1. **From the sidebar, enter keywords into the Search field and click the Search button.**

   A Search results page appears, as shown in Figure 2-5. Salesforce.com organizes the search results in lists according to the major types of records, including accounts, contacts, opportunities, and leads.

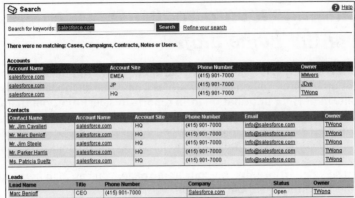

Figure 2-5:
Looking at
a search
results
page.

2. **Scroll down the page and, if you find a record that you want to look at, click a link in the** *Whatever* **Name column.**

The detail page appears, allowing you to review the record and its related lists.

3. **If you don't find what you want, click the Refine Your Search link.**

The Advanced Search page appears.

If you're focusing on a page (such as a list of search results or a report) but need to jump to a record, instead of clicking the Refine Your Search link, right-click it and choose Open in New Window. This can save you a lot of time.

Utilizing Advanced Search

Sometimes you might have to dig deeper to find what you want. Advanced Search filters through more records than Search, including notes, descriptions, and comments. You can also further restrict your search so that you don't have to wade through so many results. And salesforce.com lets you use many of the little tricks you already utilize with other search tools. For example, you can use quotation marks, asterisks, and operators such as AND and OR to refine your search.

To use Advanced Search, follow these steps:

1. **Click the Advanced Search link below the Search field.**

The Advanced Search page appears.

2. **Complete the fields, as shown in Figure 2-6.**

Salesforce.com provides plenty of tools on this page to refine your search.

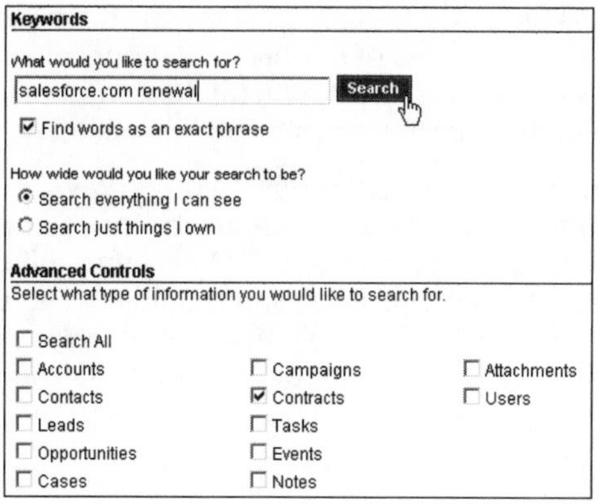

Keywords

What would you like to search for?

| salesforce.com renewal | Search |

☑ Find words as an exact phrase

How wide would you like your search to be?

⦿ Search everything I can see
◯ Search just things I own

Advanced Controls

Select what type of information you would like to search for.

☐ Search All

☐ Accounts	☐ Campaigns	☐ Attachments
☐ Contacts	☑ Contracts	☐ Users
☐ Leads	☐ Tasks	
☐ Opportunities	☐ Events	
☐ Cases	☐ Notes	

Figure 2-6: Research-ing with Advanced Search.

3. When you're done, click the Search button.

The Search results page appears.

Revisiting recent items

The Recent Items section displays up to the last ten records that you most recently clicked. You can leverage the list to quickly get back to records you've been working on even if you logged out and logged back in. The recent items show an icon and the name or number of the record. They include mostly the records that are organized under a tab heading like accounts, contacts, and so on.

To visit a recent item, simply click a listed link. The detail page for that item appears.

Getting more out of your home page sidebar

With the help of your administrator, you can offer other tools and informa-tion from the sidebar on the home page to improve productivity and drive overall adoption. Review the following tips, see Chapter 18 on customizing salesforce.com, and consult with your administrator if some of these features could help your organization:

✔ **Add new search tools.** The Search and Advanced Search tools can't find product, document, and solution records in salesforce.com. Your com-pany can customize home page layouts with any or all of these specific search tools. Depending on your profile, some or all of these tools might help you do your job better. For example, if you're in customer service, you might need a search tool on your home page to help you quickly search for solutions to common inquiries.

✔ **Update company messages.** Your administrator can add messages to the home page to keep users informed of important announcements. For example, if you're in sales management, you might want to use the home page to alert reps on end-of-quarter goals or bonus incentives.

✔ **Emphasize important Web links.** If you rely on other Web sites or Web based applications to do your jobs, your administrator can help you post them for all your users or just ones that fit certain profiles. For example, if you have a company intranet, your company could add useful links to the home page sidebar so you could quickly access information outside of salesforce.com without ever leaving salesforce.com.

Navigating the Tabs

If the tabs in salesforce.com look strangely familiar, they should. When the founders of salesforce.com designed it, they patterned the site after popular Web sites such as Amazon, where you click a tab to jump to an area.

In this section, I describe the major tabs in salesforce.com and how to use the tab home pages to quickly access, manage, or organize information.

Finding out about the tabs

Each of the tabs within salesforce.com represents a major module or data element in an interconnected database. That's as technical as I get.

In the following list, I provide a brief description of each of the standard tabs (as shown in Figure 2-7). I devote a chapter to each of the tabs that I mention here.

Figure 2-7: Navigating the tabs.

✔ **Leads** are suspects (that is, people and companies you want to do business with), but don't start grilling your lead about where she was the morning of June 23 because the only clue you'll gather is the sound of a dial tone.

- ✔ **Accounts** are companies that you do business with. You can track all types of accounts, including customers, prospects, partners, and competitors.

- ✔ **Contacts** are individuals associated with your accounts.

- ✔ **Opportunities** are the deals that you pursue to drive revenue for your company. Your open opportunities constitute your pipeline and opportunities can contribute to your forecast.

- ✔ **Cases** are customer inquiries that your support teams work to manage and resolve.

- ✔ **Solutions** are answers to cases and other frequently asked questions.

- ✔ **Documents** are the sales and marketing collateral and documents that you use as part of your selling or service processes.

- ✔ **Reports** are data analyses for you and your entire organization. Salesforce.com provides a variety of best practices reports, and you can build custom reports on the fly to better measure your business.

- ✔ **Dashboards** are graphs, charts, and tables based on your custom reports. You can use dashboards to visually measure and analyze key elements of your business.

- ✔ **Products** are your company's products and services, associated with the prices for which you offer them. You can link products and their prices to your opportunities.

- ✔ **Forecasts** are your best estimates of how much revenue you can close in a quarter or month, depending on the way you forecast.

- ✔ **Campaigns** are specific marketing activities that you manage to drive leads, build a brand, or stimulate demand.

- ✔ **Contracts** are the agreements involved in your selling process. You can use contracts in salesforce.com to manage your approval process and keep important documents in one place.

Discovering a tab home page

When you click a tab, the tab's interior home page appears. For example, if you click the Accounts tab, the Accounts home page appears. The tab's home page is where you can view, organize, track, and maintain all the records within that tab.

Do this right now: Click every tab visible to you.

Notice how the look and feel of the interior home pages never changes regardless of which tab you click (except for the Home, Reports, and Dashboards tabs). On the left, you have the sidebar with Search, Recent Items, and — depending on your company and the tab — a Quick Create tool. In the body of the page, you have a Views menu, a Key *Items* section, and sections for popular Reports and Tools (see Figure 2-8).

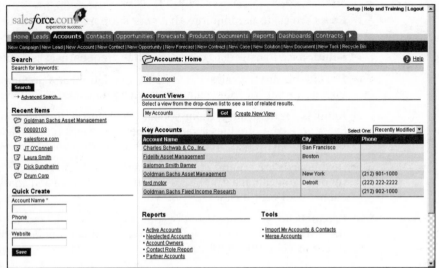

Figure 2-8: Deconstructing the tab home page.

If you're clicking some of the tabs for the first time, an introductory page might appear with an overview of the tab. In the bottom-right corner, click the Continue button or the Don't Show Me This Page Again link to go to the tab's home page.

Using the Views menu

Strategy and execution are all about focus. With views, you can see and use lists to better focus on your business. A *view* is a segment of the tab's records based upon defined criteria. When you select a view, a list of records appears based on your criteria.

On each tab, salesforce.com provides a selection of popular default views to get you started. To try a view (using Accounts as the example), follow these steps which apply to all tabs:

1. Click the Accounts tab.

The Accounts home page appears.

2. **Use the Account Views drop-down list to select the My Accounts option.**

   A list page appears with a set of columns representing certain standard account fields and a list of your account records. If no account records appear, you currently don't own any records in salesforce.com.

3. **From the list page, you can perform a variety of functions:**

   - Click a column header if you want to re-sort the list, as shown in Figure 2-9. For example, if you click the Account Name header, the list sorts alphabetically.

   - Click a letter link above the list to view records beginning with that letter.

   - If you have a long list, at the bottom of the page, click the up or down buttons to show fewer or more records on the page, or click the Next Page link to see the next set of records.

   - To view a specific record, click the link for that record in the Account Name column. The Account detail page appears with the record and its related lists.

   - To update a specific record, click the Edit link at the beginning of its row. The account record appears in Edit mode.

   - To delete a record, click the Del link near the beginning its row. A pop-up window appears, prompting you to click OK to accept the deletion. If you click OK, the list page reappears minus the account that you just wiped out. Don't worry: Later in this chapter, in the section "Resurrecting from the Recycling Bin," I show you how to restore deleted records.

Figure 2-9:
Re-sorting a
list.

Building a custom view

If you need a particular view for the way you like to look at records, you can build a custom view. If you have the right permissions, you can share these views with other groups or your entire organization. (Or maybe you should just keep your views to yourself.)

To create a custom view (using Contacts as the example), follow these steps, which apply to all tabs:

1. **Click the Contacts tab.**

   The Contacts home page appears.

2. **Next to the Views menu, click the Create New View link.**

   A Create New View page appears.

3. **Name the view by typing a title in the Name field.**

   For example, if you want to create a list of your contacts that are senior executives, use a title like "My Senior Execs." (Just don't make a typo and title it "My Senile Execs.")

4. **Select whether you want to search All Contacts or just My Contacts by clicking one of the two check boxes.**

   In this example, select the My Contacts check box.

5. **Under the Search Criteria step, enter search criteria, as shown in Figure 2-10.**

   A basic criteria query is made up of three elements:

   • **Field:** The leftmost box is a drop-down list of all the fields on the contact record. In this example, you would choose Title.

   • **Operator:** The middle box is a drop-down list of operators for your search. That sounds complicated but it's easier than you think. For my example, you would select the contains option.

   • **Value:** In the rightmost box, you type the value that you want in the search. In this example, you might type **vp, vice, president, ceo, cio, cto.**

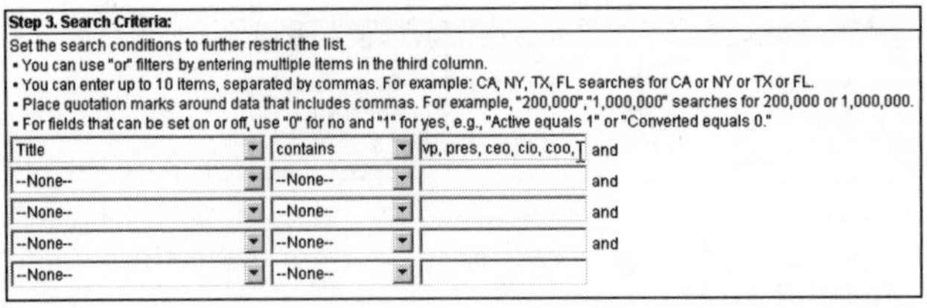

Figure 2-10:
Entering
criteria to
create a
custom
view.

Step 3. Search Criteria:		
Set the search conditions to further restrict the list.		
• You can use "or" filters by entering multiple items in the third column.		
• You can enter up to 10 items, separated by commas. For example: CA, NY, TX, FL searches for CA or NY or TX or FL.		
• Place quotation marks around data that includes commas. For example, "200,000","1,000,000" searches for 200,000 or 1,000,000.		
• For fields that can be set on or off, use "0" for no and "1" for yes, e.g., "Active equals 1" or "Converted equals 0."		
Title ▼	contains ▼	vp, pres, ceo, cio, coo, ▼ and
--None-- ▼	--None-- ▼	and
--None-- ▼	--None-- ▼	and
--None-- ▼	--None-- ▼	and
--None-- ▼	--None-- ▼	

6. **Select the columns that you want displayed by clicking a drop-down list and selecting a value in some or all of the fields provided.**

Although salesforce.com's preset views take common fields like Phone and Email, you can select any of up to 11 fields to display on your custom list page.

7. **Decide whether you want others to see your custom view.**

   Administrators and certain users have this permission. Your decision is made simple if the step doesn't appear. Otherwise, select one of the three options. (Basically, the three radio buttons translate to all, none, or selective.) If you chose the third option, use the drop-down list to first select a group and then click the arrows to move group into the Shared To column.

8. **When you're done, click Save.**

   A new view appears based on your custom view criteria. If you don't get all the results that you would anticipate, you might want to double-check and refine the search criteria. For example, if your list should include directors but doesn't, click the Edit link and update the view.

Keying in on the Key Items section

On a tab's home page, just below the views you see a Key *Items* section. This section comes with three or four relevant columns that can't be modified. You can see as few as ten items and as many as 25 items at a time by clicking the link at the bottom of the table.

To test the Key *Items* section (by using Leads as the example), go to the leads home page and follow these steps, which can be applied to all tabs:

1. **Under the Key Leads section, select an option from the Select One drop-down list at the top-right corner of the table.**

   The table reappears based on what you selected.

2. **Click a link in the table to go to a record.**

   The detail page appears with the record and related lists.

Reviewing common reports

In the bottom-left corner of a tab's home page, salesforce.com displays a small selection of commonly used reports associated with that tab. You can click a link to go directly to the report or click the Go to Reports link, which takes you to the Reports home page.

Tooling through the Tools section

In the bottom-right corner of a tab's home page, salesforce.com provides a set of unique tools associated with a particular tab. Depending on which tab you're viewing, use these tools to help you manage and maintain records within that tab. For example, on the Accounts home page under the Tools section, you can click the Merge Accounts link to merge duplicate accounts. See the related chapters later in this book for details on using specific tools.

Using the Taskbar

The taskbar is located directly beneath the tabs on every page within salesforce.com. Most of the time you use the taskbar to solve many of the headaches commonly experienced from creating (and sometimes deleting) records. The exception to this is when and only when you're viewing a task or event: In that case, you utilize the taskbar to jump to different calendar views.

Creating records

By using the taskbar, you can easily add new records into salesforce.com.

To create a record (by using Contacts as the example), follow these steps, which can be applied to all New *Item* links on the taskbar:

1. **From the home page, click the New Contact link on the taskbar, as shown in Figure 2-11.**

   A New Contact page appears in Edit mode.

Figure 2-11:
Creating records from the taskbar.

2. **Complete the fields as necessary.**

   Notice that while you're in an Edit mode, the taskbar doesn't display.

3. **When you're done, click Save.**

   The Contact detail page appears, and here you can begin tracking information.

If you ever forget to save a record but you haven't logged out, try using your browser's Back button. Often you can get right back to the edit page and rescue all your hard work.

Resurrecting from the Recycle Bin

Occasionally, you delete a record and regret it. Don't panic, with sales-force.com's Recycle Bin, you've got 30 days to restore the record, any associated records (such as activities deleted in the process), and your credibility.

To restore a deleted record, follow these steps:

1. **Create a test record (see the preceding section) and click Save.**

   The detail page appears.

2. **Delete the record by clicking the Delete button at the top of the detail page.**

   A pop-up window appears to verify the deletion.

3. **Click OK.**

   The tab home page corresponding to the record appears.

4. **On your taskbar, click the Recycle Bin link.**

   The Recycle Bin page appears. If you're an administrator, you can view and restore records deleted within the last thirty days by other users.

5. **Navigate the list as you would a normal list page until you find the desired record or records.**

6. **Select the check boxes in the Action column corresponding to records you want to restore.**

   You can click the Select All link to select all the records on the page.

7. **When you're done, click the Undelete button, as shown in Figure 2-12.**

   The Recycle Bin page reappears, and a link to your restored record appears in the sidebar under Recent Items.

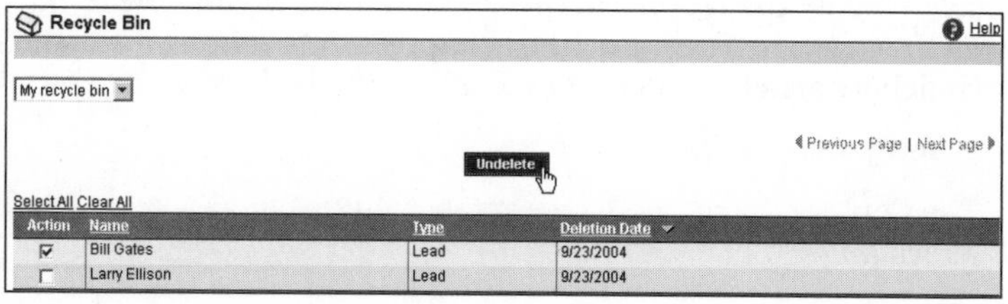

Figure 2-12:
Recycling a
deleted
record.

Action	Name	Type	Deletion Date
☑	Bill Gates	Lead	9/23/2004
☐	Larry Ellison	Lead	9/23/2004

Recycle Bin

My recycle bin

Undelete

◀ Previous Page | Next Page ▶

Select All Clear All

Help

Accepting the exception to the rule

Just when you think there aren't any exceptions to the rule, you find one. For task and event records, the taskbar displays different functions. And you know what? The change in the taskbar makes sense because you're basically managing your schedule.

When viewing a task or event, use the taskbar to jump to different calendar views. To try this out, follow these steps:

1. **Click your Home tab.**

   The home page appears.

2. **Under My Tasks, locate and go to a task by clicking a link in the Subject column.**

   The task page appears with a taskbar.

3. **Click the Jump to This Week link, as shown in Figure 2-13.**

   The week view appears for the current week. Notice that the taskbar reverts back to the one you commonly use.

Figure 2-13:
Jumping to
the week
view on an
activity
taskbar.

Detailing the Record

After you create a record, the record appears on its own detail page (see Figure 2-14). You can use the detail page to update the record fields or manage and track activities and common operations on the related lists displayed below the record. In this section, I show you how to navigate the detail page. Then see the other chapters in this book for specific details on managing particular related lists.

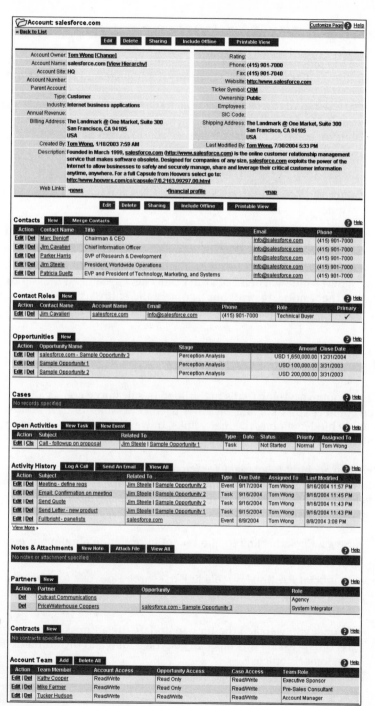

Figure 2-14:
Looking
over the
detail page.

Using links and buttons on the detail page

At the top of any record's detail page, you can use several links and buttons to perform different actions. Go to any detail page and try these out:

- ✔ At the top of the page below the folder icon, click the Back to List link. If you've been working from a list, the list page appears. Click the Back button on your browser to return to the detail page.

- ✔ Click the Edit button to edit the record. The record appears in Edit mode. Click the Back button.

- ✔ Click the Delete button to delete it. Click the Cancel button in the pop-up window.

- ✔ Click the Sharing button to share the record with other users. (This button doesn't appear on all records.) Click the Back button.

- ✔ Click the Printable View button to view a printable version of the page in a new window. Then click the Print This Page link in the top-right corner of the window to print out a copy of the entire page. Many users like to print hard copies to review while traveling. Close the window.

Leveraging Web links

Just about everything that's underlined in salesforce.com is a hyperlink that can connect you to details on other useful customer or user information. Slightly hidden among the many links, however, is the Web Links section of a detail page located at the bottom of the record fields.

Open an account detail page for a major customer. Direct your attention to the Web Links section. Depending on your company's customization, you might use some of the following and, maybe, many more hyperlinks added by your administrator:

- ✔ **News:** Click this link to find recent information about your customer from AltaVista's search engine.

- ✔ **Financial Profile:** Use this link to search Hoover's for financial and other data on your customer. Hoover's is a well-known research site for corporate information.

- ✔ **Map:** If you've taken the time to update the address fields for your record, pressing this link can get you a map and then directions to your customer's offices.

Companies are leveraging these and other Web links not only to connect with useful public sites but also to connect their users with Web applications that are critical to selling and servicing their customers. See Chapter 18 for tips on Web integration links and consult with your administrator if you have ideas.

Capitalizing on related lists

Related lists. Say it three times so you don't forget the term. By designing the page with related lists, salesforce.com enables you to gain 360 degree customer visibility and ensure that more detailed information is but a click away. For example, if you open an account detail page for a one of your major customers and scroll down below the record fields, you should be able to see multiple contacts, activities, opportunities, cases, notes, attachments, and so on listed as links from organized related lists. And if you don't, you've got work to do.

See the specific chapters in this book for details on using related lists.

Getting Help and Setting Up

In the top-right corner of any salesforce.com page are three links that can help you get more out of salesforce.com. You can

- ✔ **Click Setup** to modify your personal setup, or if you're an administrator, to administer and customize salesforce.com for your company. A page opens with the Personal Setup menu.

- ✔ **Click Help and Training** to access the help guide, sign up for free training, or get additional support. A window opens with the help menu and additional tabs for training and support.

- ✔ **Click Logout** to log out of salesforce.com. The Login page of the salesforce.com public Web site appears. Alternatively, you can just close your browser to log out of your session.

Chapter 3

Personalizing Your System

Salesforce.com was built by salespeople for salespeople. The tool had to be simple to use, relevant to the business of selling, and personally customizable so that you could use it to do your job more effectively.

From the Personal Setup page, you can personalize your application to better suit the way you look at and manage your business. And if you capitalize on the tools available to you in salesforce.com, you can give yourself an edge against the competition and your peers.

In this chapter, I describe how to modify your settings by using Personal Setup, change your display, and access salesforce.com anytime, anywhere from popular devices and programs.

Using the Personal Setup Menu

Personal Setup, accessible from the Setup link when you log in to salesforce.com, is a set of tools and options that you can use to set up and customize salesforce.com according to your individual preferences. You can decide to only show certain tabs, synchronize your salesforce.com data with Outlook, and connect with salesforce.com wirelessly.

Salesforce.com makes it easy for you to better personalize your system by providing all your setup tools in one area.

To locate and navigate your Personal Setup area, follow these steps:

1. Click the Setup link in the top-right corner of any page.

The Personal Setup page appears with an expandable sidebar, as shown on the left in Figure 3-1. The body of the page and the sidebar work hand in hand, but I like to use the sidebar so I don't get lost.

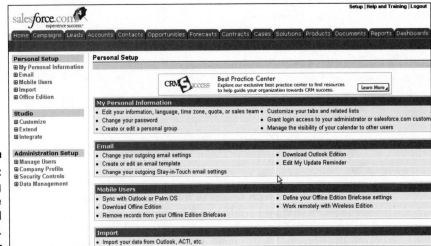

Figure 3-1:
Looking over the Personal Setup page.

2. Click all the small + icons under the Personal Setup heading on the sidebar so you can see the full range of options (shown in Figure 3-2).

Menus appear. Notice that the body of the page doesn't change if you simply expand the heading within the sidebar.

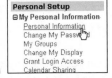

Figure 3-2:
Expanding the menu.

3. Click any heading.

The page for that heading appears.

4. Click the Back button on your browser or click another heading.

You've now mastered the basic way to navigate the Personal Setup menu.

Modifying Your Personal Information

With your personal information folder, you can keep your user record current, expand sharing privileges to other users and groups, and customize your personal display to suit your tastes.

Updating your user information

In salesforce.com, you have a user record that corresponds to you. You can use that record to keep other users up to date on your contact information. You can also update your user record to associate quotas, share information, and more.

To find out how to navigate to the Personal Setup area, see the preceding section.

To modify your user record, follow these steps:

1. **Click the My Personal Information link on the sidebar (refer to Figure 3-1).**

   Your User page appears.

2. **Click Edit.**

   The page appears in Edit mode. Review the accuracy and update your information.

   Especially if you travel frequently, make sure that you update your time zone both in salesforce.com and on your laptop, reflecting your current location. This is particularly important if you're managing your schedule and synchronizing with offline tools such as Outlook.

3. **When you're done, click Save.**

   The home page of salesforce.com appears.

Creating personal groups

Groups are sets of users. By using groups, you can more efficiently share data (like accounts) or calendars with specific sets of users. Only administrators can establish public groups, but all users can create personal groups. So if you're accustomed to working in teams and you find your company's sharing model too restrictive, you can still create personal groups and provide wider access to your information.

To set up a group, follow these steps:

1. **Click the My Groups link on the sidebar (refer to Figure 3-2).**

   The My Personal Groups page appears.

2. **Click the New Group button.**

   The New Group page appears.

3. **Name the group and select members from the list of users, roles, or groups, as shown in Figure 3-3.**

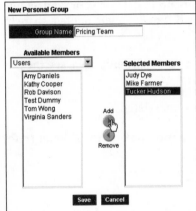

Figure 3-3:
Creating a
personal
group.

4. **When you're done, click Save.**

   The My Personal Groups page reappears.

Changing Your Display

If you log in and feel as if you only really need a fraction of the tabs or a select number of related lists, you can customize your personal display. Note that your administrator can still override your personal setup if necessary. For example, if you sell but you don't want to see or use the opportunities tab, something would have to change (probably your job). (Refer to the "Using the Personal Setup Menu" section to find out how to get to the Personal Setup area.)

Modifying your tabs

Salesforce.com already provides many standard tabs. Companies can now create their own tabs. For some users, you just don't need to see it all.

To customize your tabs, follow these steps:

1. **Click the Change My Display link on the sidebar (refer to Figure 3-2).**

   The Change My Display page appears.

2. **Click the Customize My Tabs link if you want to add, remove, or change the order of your Tabs.**

   The Customize My Tabs page appears.

3. **Use the two list boxes to highlight a tab and either remove or add it from your display, as shown in Figure 3-4.**

   For example, if you're in sales and you never get involved with marketing or customer service, you might decide to remove the Cases, Solutions, and Campaigns tabs.

Figure 3-4:
Modifying
your tabs.

4. **Use the Up and Down arrows to change the order of the tabs.**

5. **When you're done, click Save.**

   The Change My Display page reappears, and your tabs reflect your changes.

Customizing pages

You can also personalize your display by changing the layout on a record page. Doing so enables you to see the most relevant sections first. For example, if you work in a call center, you may want to see cases at the top of your related lists on an account page.

To customize the display of a page, follow these steps:

1. **Click the Change My Display link on the sidebar (refer to Figure 3-2).**

   The Change My Display page appears.

2. **Select a link to the page of a specific tab that you want to modify (the Accounts tab, for instance), and click the Click Here to Customize link.**

   The Customize My Page page appears.

3. **Use the two list boxes to select lists and then add or remove them from your page, as shown in Figure 3-5.**

   For example, if you sell directly to customers, you might want to remove the Partners related list from the Account detail page.

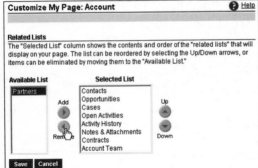

Figure 3-5:
Customizing
your
personal
page layout.

4. **Use the Up and Down arrows to change the order of the lists on your page layout.**

5. **When you're done, click Save.**

   The Change My Display page reappears.

Granting login access

When you need help from your administrator or salesforce.com customer support, you can grant either or both temporary login access to your account. By doing this, the person who is helping you can provide better assistance because she can view your pages.

To grant login access, follow these steps:

1. **Click the Grant Login Access link on the sidebar (refer to Figure 3-2).**

   The Grant Login Access page appears.

2. **Grant *support* and/or *administrator* access by clicking the relevant calendar icon to select an expiration date, and then click the Save button, as shown in Figure 3-6.**

   The My Personal Information page appears.

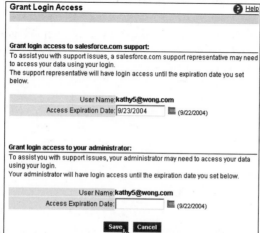

Figure 3-6: Granting access to your account.

If you're an administrator and have been granted access by a user, you can log in to the user's account as follows: Under the Manage Users heading on the sidebar, click the Users link and then select the Active Users list. On the list, click the Login link next to the user's name.

Optimizing Your E-Mail

Sending and receiving e-mail is a standard way in which most businesses communicate today. Recognizing this fact, salesforce.com provides you a variety of tools to send e-mail, use templates, send automated reminders, and work with Microsoft Outlook. If you want to make use of those tools, you need to set up your e-mail in salesforce.com. (See Chapter 8 for all the details on configuring your e-mail settings, creating templates, and installing and running Outlook Edition.) In this section, I cover the setup for only two types of e-mail reminders: Stay-in-Touch and Opportunity Update reminders.

Setting up Stay-in-Touch

Stay-in-Touch e-mail is a feature that enables you to keep your contact database up to date. You can send a templated e-mail to contacts with the contact information you have. If they reply with changes, you can easily apply those updates into salesforce.com. (See Chapter 6 for details on using Stay-in-Touch e-mails.)

If you want to set up your Stay-in-Touch settings, follow these steps:

1. **Click the My Stay-in-Touch Settings link under the Email heading on the sidebar.**

   The My Stay-in-Touch Settings page appears, as shown in Figure 3-7.

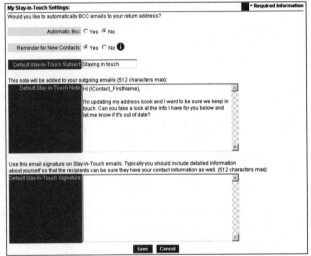

Figure 3-7:
Reviewing your Stay-in-Touch settings.

2. **Modify and complete the fields as needed.**

3. **When you're done, click Save.**

   The Email page appears.

Constructing opportunity updates

You can set up salesforce.com to send you and your direct reports a weekly or monthly snapshot of key sales metrics. You can also send a copy of that snapshot to other e-mail addresses. By using automated opportunity updates, you can keep the pressure on and use the snapshots to focus your meetings if you periodically get together with your sales reps.

To modify your update reminder settings, follow these steps:

1. **Click the My Update Reminder link under the Email heading on the sidebar.**

   The My Update Reminder page appears.

2. **Select or deselect the Active check box to activate or deactivate reminders.**

3. **Modify the recipients and message.**

4. **Define the frequency by using the Recurrence drop-down lists.**

   If you want the update reminders weekly, you would select Every from the first drop-down list. Choose one of the other five options if you want to send updates monthly. Then use the second drop-down list to select which day.

5. **When filtering on the close date, first select or deselect the check box if you want to include all open opportunities that have a close date within the last 90 days. Then use the related drop-down list to choose the close date.**

6. **Select the fields to be included in the report, as shown in Figure 3-8.**

   Salesforce.com currently makes available eight predefined fields.

7. **When you're done, click Save.**

   The Email page appears.

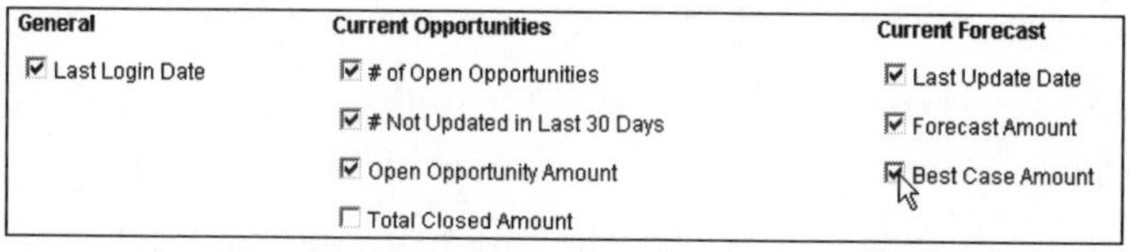

Figure 3-8:
Selecting
the fields for
the update
reminder.

General	Current Opportunities	Current Forecast
☑ Last Login Date	☑ # of Open Opportunities	☑ Last Update Date
	☑ # Not Updated in Last 30 Days	☑ Forecast Amount
	☑ Open Opportunity Amount	☑ Best Case Amount
	☐ Total Closed Amount	

Working with Salesforce.com on the Road

If travel is a part of your job, you might not always be connected to the Internet, let alone to your laptop. In spite of this, you still have many options for accessing your customer information from salesforce.com, including: synchronizing with Outlook and Palm, working with Offline Edition, and connecting through wireless devices.

Synchronizing with Outlook and Palm

Intellisync for salesforce.com is a plug-in that allows you to synchronize contacts, events, and tasks bi-directionally with Microsoft Outlook or Palm. (See Chapter 7 for details on running the synchronization.) In this section, I show you how to install and configure Intellisync and then back up your data prior to your first synchronization.

If you're the administrator responsible for maintaining accurate data in salesforce.com, encourage your company to adopt salesforce.com as the system of record or "the single source of truth." For example, tell users to make updates to accounts and contacts in salesforce.com instead of in Outlook or Palm. Then have them configure Intellisync to allow salesforce.com to win if a conflict resolution occurs between salesforce.com and Outlook or Palm. By doing this, you can reduce common synchronization issues and influence greater salesforce.com adoption.

Installing Intellisync

In most cases, installing Intellisync is a simple process. If you connect to the Internet via a proxy server or your company has a firewall, you might want to consult with your IT department.

To download and install Intellisync, follow these steps:

1. **Click the Sync to Outlook/Palm link under the Mobile Users heading on the sidebar.**

   The Sync to Outlook/Palm Overview page appears.

2. **Click the Download Intellisync Now link.**

   A Download and Install page appears with instructions.

3. **Review the page, then click the link to download Intellisync for salesforce.com.**

   A dialog box appears to open or save the file.

4. **Click Save and then on the Save As dialog box, click Save to save the file to your desktop.**

5. **Double-click the file** `sync installer.exe` **on your desktop to run the installation.**

   A introduction dialog box appears, as shown in Figure 3-9.

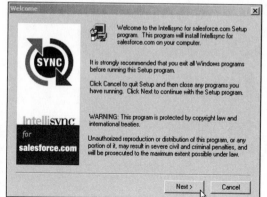

Figure 3-9:
Installing
Intellisync.

6. **Follow the dialog boxes through the wizard and at the completion of the installation, click Finish.**

Configuring Intellisync

If you're running Intellisync for the first time, I highly recommend that you run a test on a limited data set first just to get your feet wet. For example, you could decide to synchronize only open or pending tasks.

To configure Intellisync prior to synchronizing, follow these steps:

1. **On your desktop, choose Start➪Programs➪Intellisync for salesforce.com.**

   The login screen appears.

2. **Enter your salesforce.com user name and password, and then click the Configure button, as shown in Figure 3-10.**

   The Configure screen appears.

3. **Click the check boxes to select the type of records to sync.**

   In this example, you might select only the Tasks check box.

4. **Click the Choose Application button, select Palm Organizer or MS Outlook, and click OK.**

   The Configure screen reappears.

5. **Click the Advanced Settings button.**

   The Advanced Settings screen appears.

6. **Click the tabs and select options for conflict resolution, confirmation, and filters.**

Figure 3-10:
Logging
in to
Intellisync.

7. **When you're done, click OK.**

   The Configure screen reappears.

8. **When you're satisfied with your settings, click Done.**

   Now you're ready to run the synchronization.

If your company plans to synchronize your calendars with Outlook, make a habit of synchronizing daily to keep your activities up to date.

Setting up sync profiles

Synch Profiles is a feature within salesforce.com that enables you to synchronize other users' contacts, so long as you have read/write access to those contacts. Synch Profiles use personal or public groups of users that you or your administrator set up. This is particularly helpful if you and your co-workers need shared contact information in individual Outlook or Palm devices.

To do this, follow these steps:

1. **Click the Sync to Outlook/Palm link under the Mobile Users heading on the sidebar.**

   The Sync Outlook/Palm page appears.

2. **At the bottom of the page, click the Set Your Sync Profile link.**

   The Sync Profile page appears.

3. **Select the group whose data you want to add to your synchronization and click Save.**

   The Sync to Outlook/Palm page reappears.

4. **Alternatively, first click the New Personal Group button and follow the steps in the earlier section "Creating personal groups." Then set the Sync Profile.**

When setting up Sync Profiles, you need to first create a group consisting of the users whose contact data you want to synchronize.

Backing up your data

Synchronizing is a tricky thing, especially if you're in a large organization with potentially complex sharing rules. I always recommend backing up the data from your offline tool before your initial synchronization.

Use the menu bar in Outlook to back up your data prior to synchronizing for the first time.

To back up your data, follow these steps:

1. **Open Microsoft Outlook.**

2. **Choose File⇨Import and Export.**

   The Import and Export Wizard opens in a dialog box.

3. **Select the Export to a File option in the list box and click Next.**

4. **Select the Personal File Folder (.pst) option in the list box and click Next.**

5. **Select a folder to export (Calendar, Contacts, or Tasks) and click Next.**

6. **In the Save the File As field, use the default or enter a new location in which to save the file, and then click Finish.**

7. **Repeat Steps 2 through 6 for each folder (Calendar, Contacts, and Tasks).**

If you plan to synchronize salesforce.com directly with your Palm device, you'll also want to back up your data just in case. To back up your Palm data, follow these steps:

1. **Open your Palm Desktop.**

2. **Click an area to export: Date Book, Address List, or To Do.**

3. **Choose File⇨ Export.**

   A dialog box appears, as shown in Figure 3-11.

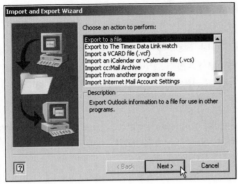

Figure 3-11:
Backing up
your Palm
data with
the Import
and Export
Wizard.

4. **In the box provided, click a folder to choose a location and in the File Name field, enter a name.**

5. **Select the Archive type in the Export As list and select All for the Range.**

   By doing this, you are simply saving all of your data in a format that your Palm Desktop software can read in the event you need to restore your data.

6. **Click Export, and then click OK.**

7. **Repeat Steps 1 through 6 for each area (Date Book, Address List, and To Do).**

If you discover that you accidentally deleted records in salesforce.com while synchronizing, you can go to your Recycle Bin and restore those records within 30 days from the date you deleted the records.

Working with Offline Edition

In today's world of hotspots and Wi-Fi, it's hard to imagine ever being untethered from the Internet. Still, on those occasions when you can't get connected, you can use Offline Edition and hardly notice the difference. Offline Edition (which salesforce.com commonly refers to as the offline Briefcase) is a downloadable application that you access through a browser and has the same look and feel as its online big brother. Like a briefcase, this application carries a set of your salesforce.com information consisting of accounts, contacts, opportunities, and activities. Before you can run the offline Briefcase, you need to install the application, configure the Briefcase, and then update it when you run it the first time.

Installing Offline Edition

You'll know if you have Offline Edition by looking at the entitlements checked off at the top of your user page. (See the "Updating your user information" section to find out how to access your User page.) Installing the application is simple and fast.

To install Offline Edition, follow these steps:

1. **Click the Offline Edition link under the Mobile Users heading on the sidebar.**

   The Offline Edition page appears.

2. **Click the Install Now button and follow the directions for installing the application.**

3. **Click Yes when prompted to install and run the wizard.**

4. **Follow the prompts in the wizard to complete the installation process.**

Setting up the Briefcase

Your offline Briefcase is basically composed of two categories of records:

✔ **Your planner,** which consists of your contacts plus "recent" tasks and events as defined by salesforce.com. Click the Help and Training link in salesforce.com for the specific parameters around the activities included in your planner.

✔ **Your set of accounts,** which you can choose to select manually or grouped by opportunities, activities, or all your accounts. When you choose your set of accounts, your Briefcase will include the accounts' associated opportunities, contacts, and activities.

To set up your Briefcase, follow these steps:

1. **Click the Offline Edition link under the Mobile Users heading on the sidebar.**

   The Offline Edition page appears.

2. **Click the Briefcase Setup button.**

   The Briefcase Settings page appears.

3. **Click the Edit button on the Briefcase Settings list.**

   The Offline Briefcase Edit page appears (shown Figure 3-12).

4. **Select the setting that you want to use to dictate the accounts and related records that will be loaded into your Briefcase, and then click Save.**

   The Briefcase Settings page reappears.

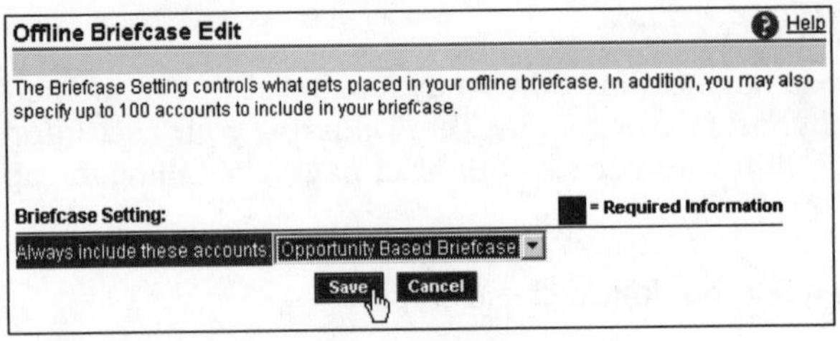

Figure 3-12:
Selecting
your
briefcase
settings.

> **Offline Briefcase Edit** ⑦ Help
>
> The Briefcase Setting controls what gets placed in your offline briefcase. In addition, you may also specify up to 100 accounts to include in your briefcase.
>
> **Briefcase Setting:**   * = Required Information
>
> Always include these accounts [Opportunity Based Briefcase ▼]
>
> [Save] [Cancel]

Running Offline Edition

After you install and establish your settings, you're ready to run Offline Edition.

To run Offline Edition, follow these steps:

1. **On your desktop, choose Start⇨Programs⇨ salesforce.com⇨ salesforce.com Offline Edition.**

   A browser opens with a login screen.

2. **Enter your salesforce.com user name and password and click the Login button.**

   A pop-up window appears notifying you that you must update your Briefcase prior to running Offline Edition.

3. **Click OK to close the window.**

   The home page of your Offline Edition appears.

4. **Click the Update button on the sidebar or the Update Briefcase link in the top-right corner of the page. (The result is the same.)**

   A dialog box opens, showing you the progress of your synchronization (see Figure 3-13).

If you work offline, remember to click the Update Briefcase link in Offline Edition to synchronize your data with salesforce.com the next time you're online. By doing this, you'll never worry which version has the most updated information. Also, you might want to consider regularly emptying your Briefcase after you update salesforce.com as a best practice to avoid confusion.

Going wireless

If you're a gadget guy or gal who relies on the latest wireless handhelds, you can access salesforce.com in real time via your wireless device. Wireless Edition from salesforce.com is not only available from handhelds that provide wireless Web but also devices that use wireless e-mail. You can tell if you're enabled for Wireless Edition by checking your entitlements on your user record in salesforce.com.

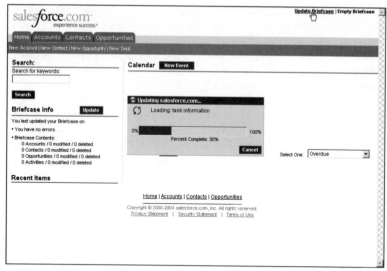

Accessing through wireless Web

Wireless Edition is available without any setup through a browser on your wireless device. To access salesforce.com through wireless Web, follow these steps:

1. **In a Web browser, enter** http://wireless.salesforce.com **in the address bar and press Enter.**

   A login page appears.

2. **Enter your salesforce.com user name and password and click the Login button.**

   Your wireless home page appears. From this page, you can do the following:

   - Click an icon to access tab lists. For example, if you click the Accounts icon, you see links to popular views in salesforce.com.

   - Enter keywords in the Your Request field and click Go. For example, if you want to look for events, you could enter **meeting** and click Go. A list returns with records that match your search.

   - Click the Help icon or link for hints on entering queries to access information quickly.

3. **When you're done, click the Logout link.**

Accessing through wireless e-mail

If you're a wireless e-mail user, you can also access salesforce.com through wireless handhelds such as Blackberries. To do so, you have to know a little bit about natural language queries. A natural language query with Wireless

Edition typically begins with a simple command (view, edit, create) followed by a record type that Wireless Edition can access. Currently, you can access the following record types with Wireless Edition: accounts, contacts, opportunities, tasks, events. (For more tips on natural language queries, click the Help and Training link in the top-right corner of salesforce.com and search for natural language queries.)

To use your salesforce.com account for wireless e-mail, follow these steps:

1. **Click the Wireless Edition link under the Mobile Users heading on the sidebar.**

   The Wireless Edition page appears.

2. **At the bottom of the page, type your Wireless Edition e-mail address and click Save.**

   You'll typically use the e-mail address associated with your handheld device.

3. **From your wireless e-mail, type a natural language query request in the Subject line and send it to** access@wireless.salesforce.com.

   For example, to check this week's calendar, you could type **list my events this week**. With Wireless Edition, you can view, edit, and create records.

4. **Wait for an e-mail reply with the information you requested.**

If you use a Pocket PC or Palm OS handheld device, you can also work offline with Offline Edition for PDA. It provides similar features as Offline Edition and the service is available for an additional fee. Click the Help and Training link in the upper-right corner of any salesforce.com page for additional information.

Importing Your Contacts

One of the keys to making salesforce.com productive for you from day one is to get your contacts into the system. If your contacts exist primarily in Microsoft Outlook, you might be better off synchronizing your data (see the earlier sections of this chapter). Otherwise, salesforce.com provides easy-to-use wizards to import contacts and accounts. See Chapter 5 for the details on importing and see your administrator if your data goes beyond the limits of the import wizard. (For example, if you have historical activity linked to contacts, you can't import those records with standard wizards.)

Working with Office Edition

You can use Office Edition to access salesforce.com in popular productivity tools such as Microsoft Word and Excel. By installing and using Office Edition, you can dramatically boost productivity and simplify tasks that involve manipulating data in salesforce.com. Such tasks include

- ✔ Generating mail merge documents such as quote forms, contracts, and proposals by combining document templates with data from salesforce.com (see Chapter 12 for details on mail merge).

- ✔ Pulling sales data from salesforce.com into your favorite existing opportunity report — especially if the report is in a unique format.

- ✔ Building hybrid reports that combine up-to-the moment data from salesforce.com with the various Excel tools. For example, you could build and save a report with a pivot table and refresh the report periodically with updated data from salesforce.com.

Installing Office Edition

To use Office Edition, you need to first install a small plug-in to add salesforce.com menus to your Microsoft Word and Excel programs. To install Office Edition, log in to salesforce.com and follow these steps:

1. **Click the Setup link in the upper-right corner.**

   The Personal Setup page appears.

2. **Click the Install Office Edition link under the Office Edition heading on the sidebar.**

   The Office Edition page appears.

3. **Shut down any Office applications currently running on your computer, and then click the Install Now button.**

   A dialog box with installation instructions appears.

4. **Click Yes when prompted to install Office Edition.**

5. **When the installation is complete, close the dialog box.**

Running Office Edition in Word or Excel

Because Excel and Word are different tools, you use Office Edition differently in the two programs. With Word, you can get access to standard and custom merge fields in salesforce.com. See Chapter 12 for all the details on using Office Edition to build mail merge templates. With Excel, you can get access to your data from reports saved in salesforce.com.

To run and test Office Edition for Excel or Word, follow these steps:

1. **Open Excel or Word.**

   Office Edition adds a new menu labeled salesforce.com to the menu bar.

2. **Choose salesforce.com⇨Login.**

   A dialog box opens, prompting you for your salesforce.com user name and password.

3. **Enter your user name and password in the fields and the click Login button.**

   When the dialog box disappears, you have successfully logged in.

4. **In Excel, choose salesforce.com⇨Import a Report. For Word, see Chapter 12 for the details on using Office Edition to generate mail merge templates.**

   A dialog box appears with a list of custom and standard reports from salesforce.com available to you.

5. **Select a report from the Report list box and choose the destination worksheet.**

   The Destination worksheet field defaults to Sheet 1 but you can overwrite it.

6. **Click a radio button to select the format and when you're ready, click OK.**

   The worksheet you chose is populated from the report you selected.

Part II
Driving Sales

In this part . . .

Sales is the lifeblood of any organization. When sales are growing, life is good. Employees are energized, groups are happy to work together, and the company has money to innovate and stay ahead of the competition. When sales are down, life gets rough. Everyone feels more pressure to perform, and the company tightens its belt. So how can you and your sales teams consistently perform so that you have enough leads at the top of the funnel to ensure a consistent flow of sales at the bottom of the funnel?

Salesforce.com, a tool built by sales people for sales people, is designed to do just that. With the core sales tabs in salesforce.com, you can effectively manage your leads, accounts, contacts, and opportunities.

In this part, I explain each of those tabs and their records, how they connect to each other, and most importantly, how to use them so that you can sell more, faster. I show you how you can use salesforce.com to manage your sales activities, including calendared events and tasks. You discover the ins and outs of e-mail and how by sending e-mail from salesforce.com you can connect with more leads and contacts than you thought possible. I also show you how to create and update forecasts so that you can easily communicate your sales numbers up the company ladder without having to waste precious time passing around redundant spreadsheets.

Chapter 4

Prospecting Leads

*O*ften I hear frustrated sales people say, "We could hit our numbers if we just had enough leads to fill our pipeline." Leads are the building blocks by which many companies drive their sales.

Loosely defined, a *lead* is a person or a company that might be interested in your services. Some organizations refer to them as *suspects* because that person might not even be aware of you. Others call them *prospects* because a lead has to be someone who has expressed interest in your service. Whatever your favorite terminology is, you can use leads to efficiently follow up on sales inquiries, aggressively attack new markets, and vastly improve your sales pipeline.

In this chapter, you discover all the basic tricks you need to convert leads into revenue. You need to get your existing leads into salesforce.com, organize them in a logical fashion, and update them as you follow up with them. Also, I discuss how to convert that lead into an actual opportunity that can be linked to an account and a contact. And finally, if you're a lead manager or administrator, I devote an entire section to you on managing and maintaining your lead database.

Introducing the Lead Record

A lead record consists of a number of fields that you use to capture information about a potential lead. A lead record has only two modes: an Edit mode where you can modify the fields, and a Saved mode where you can view the fields and related lists.

The standard record comes predefined with approximately 25 fields. Most of the terms are immediately clear, but if you want specific definitions, click the Help and Training link in the top-right corner of salesforce.com. In the following list, I describe the most important standard fields:

- ✓ **Lead Owner:** The person or queue who owns the lead. A lead can be owned by a person or be placed in a queue. You can then assign a group of users who can take leads from a queue.

- ✓ **Lead Status:** One of three required fields on a lead record. Lead Status is a drop-down list of values and is critical if you want to follow a standard lead process.

- ✓ **Lead Source:** A standard but not required field on a lead record. If you use it, you can define and track the sources of your leads with this field.

When you first get a lead, you will likely want to qualify that lead to make sure there really is a sales opportunity for you. For example, perhaps you want to be certain that they have the budget and have real interest, and is not just a person kicking the tires. A qualified lead is a lead that meets your qualification requirements.

You will have your own definition of what qualifies a lead, so jot it down, and then seek out someone to customize your lead record. (See Chapter 18 for the how-to details on building fields, rearranging your layouts, and other design tricks.) You'll have greater success with leads if you collect the right information.

Building an effective lead process

The key to a successful lead program that contributes to sales is a well-constructed lead process built into your Lead Status drop-down list. Salesforce.com provides a default list of four statuses: Open, Contacted, Qualified, and Unqualified. These statuses appear straightforward, but they require definition. And those four choices might not mirror your process or your terminology. The good news is that after you define the statuses, your administrator can quickly modify or replace the values. The process starts with the Lead Status field, but it doesn't end there. Here are some additional suggestions as you construct your lean mean lead-generating machine:

- ✓ Build fields to capture qualification criteria.

- ✓ Make it clear at what point in the process a lead should be converted to an opportunity.

- ✓ Decide who will manage the lead program and what that entails. Make sure that he or she has sufficient permissions to administer the lead database.

- ✓ Figure out at what point in the process a lead should be deleted or archived.

- ✓ Set up queues, if it makes sense, to manage the workload and drive the competitive spirit

- ✓ When you figure out your process, train your users so that everyone knows what's expected of them.

Setting Up Your Leads

Before you can begin working your leads, you need to add the lead records into salesforce.com. In this section, I show you three quick approaches for lead creation. Then if you want to capture leads from your Web site, see Chapter 13 for details on generating Web-to-Lead forms.

Adding new leads

The best way to create a lead is to use the taskbar just below the Leads tab. To create a lead using this method, follow these simple directions:

1. **Click the New Lead link on the taskbar, as shown in Figure 4-1.**

   A New Lead page appears in Edit mode. Notice that the only field pre-filled in is the Lead Status field.

2. **Fill in the fields as much as you can.**

   Remember that at a minimum you must complete the Last Name and Company fields. (See Figure 4-2 for an example of a record in Edit mode.)

   You can add a list of target companies as leads even if you don't yet know the names of the right people. In certain cases, you might have only the name of a company because you know you want to target them but you don't yet know who to call. This is alright; I recommend in these cases that you type **?** or **unknown** in the Last Name field so that you know this information is missing.

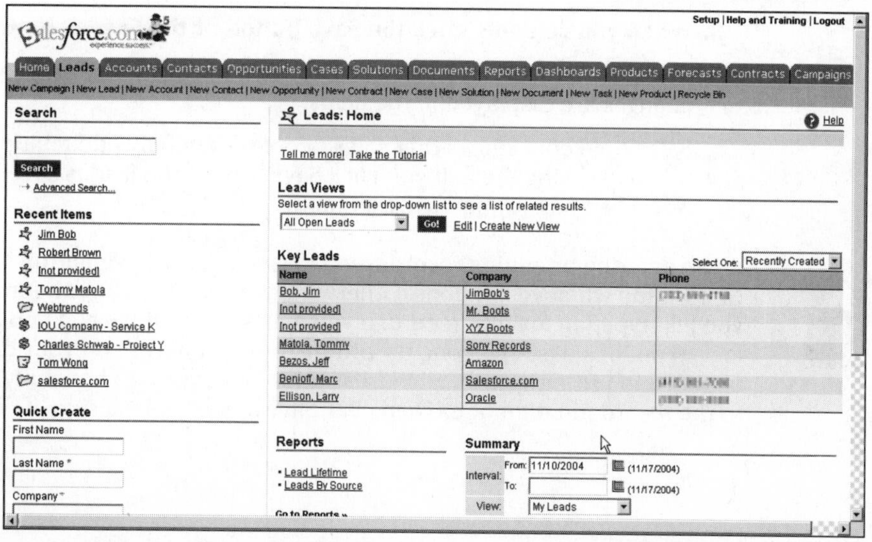

Figure 4-1:
Creating a
lead from
the taskbar.

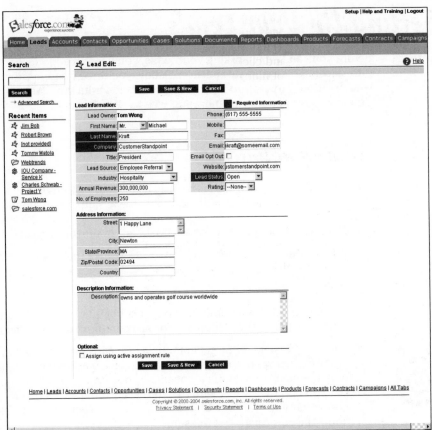

Figure 4-2:
Filling out a
lead record.

3. When you're done, click the Save button or the Save & New button.

If you click Save, the lead record appears in Saved mode, and your changes are displayed in the fields.

Salesforce.com knows that sales people commonly add multiple leads before working them. If you click Save & New, the lead is saved and a New Lead page appears in Edit mode.

When entering or editing records, you must click the Save button or Save & New button when you're done. Otherwise, you won't save the information that you just typed in for that record. If you make this mistake and you haven't yet logged out of salesforce.com, try hitting the Back button on your browser (as opposed to hitting your head in frustration) and you can hopefully get back to the record in Edit mode. Then click Save and breathe a sigh of relief.

If you're really in a rush, you can use the Quick Create tool located in the sidebar of the Leads home page to create lead records. Simply complete the fields displayed (First Name, Last Name, Company, Phone, Email, and optionally Campaign) and click Save. While you might save a couple seconds, you run the risk of not filling out other lead fields that may be important to (or even required by) your company. If you don't see the tool, your company has probably chosen wisely to hide it.

Cloning an existing lead

If you're working a particular company and you want to enter multiple leads for that company, you can save time by cloning leads. For example, you already created a lead record for Bill Gates at Microsoft Corporation. When you talk to his assistant, he or she courteously refers you to Steve Balmer. In this case, cloning can save you many extra steps.

To clone a lead record from an existing lead, follow these instructions:

1. **Click the Clone button at the top of the lead record.**

   A new lead record appears in Edit mode. Notice that all the information is identical to the previous lead record.

2. **Edit the information on the new lead where appropriate.**

   Pay attention to what is prefilled because you want to avoid inaccurate information on the new lead record.

3. **Click Save when you're done.**

   The newly created lead reappears in Saved mode. To verify this, simply click the link to the older lead, which you can find in the Recent Items section on the sidebar.

Importing your leads

If you already have a file of leads, you usually need a faster way to get them into salesforce.com than entering them manually. You must be an administrator to import leads, so if you're not, find your administrator, tell her what you're trying to do, and have her read this section. To import lead files, use these steps:

1. **On the Leads home page, click the Import Leads link at the bottom of the page under the Tools heading.**

   The Lead Import Wizard page appears, providing you with a four-step process to import your records, plus helpful hints.

2. **In your existing lead file or system, compare your fields against the lead fields in salesforce.com.**

   If you can map all the necessary fields, move to the next step. If not, add fields to the lead record by customizing salesforce.com. (See Chapter 18 for simple instructions on adding fields.)

   Mapping is a technical term for matching one field to another field, typically in different databases, in order to properly move data. For example, in Microsoft Outlook you type a corporation's name into the Company field. In salesforce.com, you typically use the field Account Name. These are just two different labels with same meaning. Mapping is the process by which you decide that data from the Company field in Outlook should correspond to the Account Name field in salesforce.com.

3. **Export your file.**

   You might have leads in an existing database such as ACT, Goldmine, or Microsoft Access. Most systems like these have simple tools for exporting data into various formats. Select the records and the fields that you want. Then export the file and save it in a .csv format. If your leads are already in spreadsheet format (such as Excel), just resave the file in .csv format.

4. **Review your lead data.**

   You've probably heard the old adage "garbage in, garbage out." Clean up your information before you bring it in to salesforce.com and you'll save yourself the effort after.

   If you're importing large files, keep in mind that you can import only 1,000 lead records at a time. So if you have a file with 1,200 leads, divide it into two files and run the wizard twice.

5. **When you're done with the preparation, click the Start the Import Wizard link.**

   A pop-up window labeled Step 1 of 3 Upload the File appears.

6. **Complete the fields in Step 1 of the wizard, as shown in Figure 4-3.**

   Assuming that you've already prepared your file, this is usually a matter of

   a. **Loading the file by clicking the Browse button and selecting the correct file on your computer.**

   b. **Selecting a default Lead Source if relevant.**

   c. **Applying an Assignment Rule if you want leads to route directly to assigned Reps.** If you don't use an Assignment Rule, all the leads that you import will be assigned to you unless you otherwise specify a Lead Owner in the file. (See the later section "Creating assignment rules for automatic routing.")

d. **Select the check box if you want to use assignment rule settings to send e-mail notifications to the record owners.**

e. **Verifying the character coding.** Salesforce.com prefills this based on your Company Profile, and you rarely have to change it.

f. **Select the check box if you want to trigger workflow rules to new and updated records.** (See Chapter 20 for tips on improving workflow.)

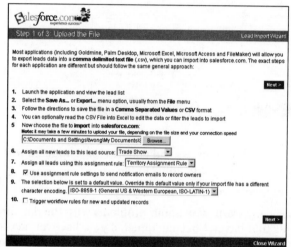

Figure 4-3:
Uploading
the lead file.

When you're beginning to import data into salesforce.com, I recommend that you test an import with five or so leads first just to make sure you know what you're doing. When the test data is imported, review your new lead records to make sure they contain all the information you want brought in. Delete the test records, refine your import file, and then run through the final import.

7. **When you're done with Step 1 of the wizard, click Next.**

The field mapping page appears.

8. **Map the fields between your file and salesforce.com, and then click Next.**

The Field Mapping Page displays all the salesforce.com lead fields as labels with drop-down lists that correspond to the fields in your file. Simply go down through the list of fields and select the field from the corresponding file that you're importing that maps to the Salesforce.com field, as shown in Figure 4-4.

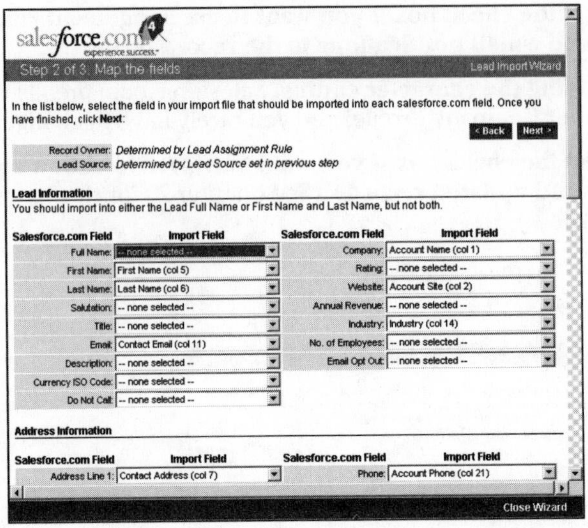

Figure 4-4:
Mapping
the lead
fields.

After you click Next, the review and confirm page appears with a list or warnings, if any, on your impending import.

9. **Review the messages for possible errors.**

   This step basically warns you about problems with the data or lets you know of fields that haven't been mapped. If you discover an error, you can either click the Back button and refine your mapping or even close the wizard so you can improve your import file. You might have to start over, but at least you avoid importing bad or incomplete data.

10. **When you're completely satisfied with your mapping, click the Import Now button.**

    An Importing page appears to let you know the import is in progress and with an estimate of how long it will take.

11. **Click the Finish button.**

    The pop-up window closes.

12. **Check the lead records you've imported.**

    Salesforce.com sends you an e-mail after your file has been successfully imported. To check your handiwork, click the Leads tab to go to your Leads home page. Under the Views drop-down list, select Today's Leads to see a list of the leads that were created today. Click the link for a lead that you just imported and review the information for accuracy.

Importing leads is one of the fastest ways for you to set up your leads in salesforce.com so that you can begin working them.

Breaking into unchartered waters

A leading Internet performance monitoring company wanted to sell their services to a variety of new, untested markets. This salesforce.com customer had a stronghold in financial services but wanted to extend their client base to other Fortune 500 companies. Due to the specific nature of their business, the actual names of the decision makers they wanted to target was publicly unavailable. So marketing simply imported the Fortune 500 list and set the Last Name field as Unknown. Then the company used salesforce.com with a pool of cost-efficient telemarketers to generate leads and set up appointments between actual buyers and the company's outside field reps. In just six months, this use of salesforce.com helped dramatically improve qualified lead generation and increased the pipeline and new bookings while breaking ground in new markets.

Organizing Your Leads

When you have some leads in salesforce.com, you want to organize them to make them productive. When I work with companies, I often hear this request from sales people: "I just want to see my data, and it needs to be the way that I want to look at it."

In this section, I show you how you can use views from the Leads home page to provide greater focus for you and your sales teams. Then for even more robust organization of your lead information, see Chapter 15 for specifics on how to build custom lead reports.

Using lead views

When you select a view, you're basically specifying criteria to limit the results that you get back. For example, if you're one of many sales reps, you might not want to waste your time sifting through all your company's leads but just the ones that you own. With salesforce.com, you can do that in one click. On the Leads home page, salesforce.com comes with four predefined views:

- ✔ **All Open Leads** provides a list of all the lead records where the Lead Status is still Open.
- ✔ **My Unread Leads** gives you a list of your leads that you haven't yet viewed.
- ✔ **Today's Leads** shows you only leads that were created today.
- ✔ **Recently Viewed Leads** lets you look at a list of leads that you've recently viewed.

To try out a preset view, go the Leads home page and do the following:

1. **Click the down arrow on the Views drop-down list.**

   You see the four options in the preceding bullet list and maybe some other choices that have been created for you.

2. **Select one of the views.**

   For example, if you select the My Unread Leads view, a list page appears with any of your unread leads. From this list page, you can perform a variety of standard operations including editing, deleting, and viewing a record. See Chapter 2 for details on using list pages.

Creating custom lead views

For many users, the preset views are a good start. But if you want special lists for the way that you follow up on your leads, you should build custom views. For example, if you only call on companies in the Manufacturing industry located in the State of Florida with revenue over a billion dollars, take a minute and build a custom view.

To create a view from scratch, follow these simple steps:

1. **On the Leads home page next to the Views drop-down list, click the Create New View link.**

   A New View page appears with a wizard to help create your view.

2. **Enter a name for the view.**

   For example, you might call the view Big Florida Manufacturers.

3. **Decide whether this view is searching the entire leads database, your leads, or a queue.**

4. **Under the Search Criteria step, select the criteria for your search, as displayed in Figure 4-5.**

   A basic criteria query is made up of three elements:

   - **Field:** The first box is a drop-down list of all the fields on the lead record. An example would be the Industry field.

   - **Operator:** The second box is a drop-down list of operators for your search. That sounds complicated, but it's easier than you think. Taking the example from the preceding bullet, you would select Equals from the drop-down list.

   - **Value:** In the third box you type the value that you want in the search. For this example, you would type **manufacturing**.

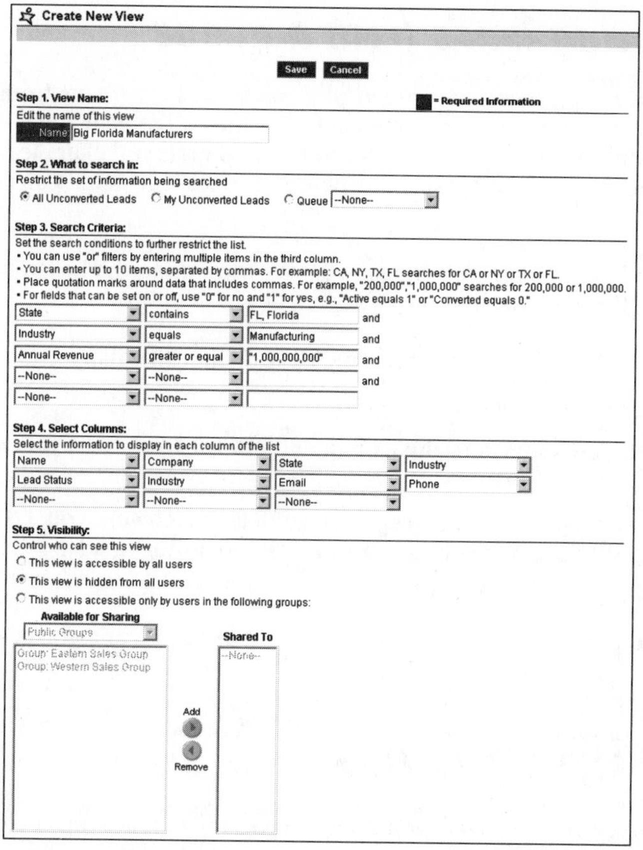

Figure 4-5:
Building a
custom lead
view.

5. **Select the columns that you want displayed on your list page.**

   Although salesforce.com's preset views display common fields such as Email and State, you can select any of up to 11 lead fields to display on your list page.

6. **Under the Visibility step, decide whether you want others to see your custom view and select the appropriate radio button.**

   Your decision is made simple if the Visibility step doesn't appear. Otherwise, think about whether other users would benefit from this view and complete this last step.

7. **When you're done, click Save.**

   You're taken to a new list page completely customized based on the search criteria that you chose.

Accepting leads from a queue

If you are a rep assigned to a queue, you can access the queue from the View drop-down list on the Leads home page. The queue list page looks and feels just like a regular list page, but you can use it to grab and claim leads. (See the later section called "Making use of lead queues" for details on setting up queues.)

To pull leads from a queue and make it your own, go to the Leads home page and follow these steps:

1. **Select the queue name from the View drop-down list.**

   The queue list page appears.

2. **Select check boxes in the Action column for leads that you want to claim.**

   Your manager might have specific guidelines. If I were you, I'd probably click into some records and try to pick the hottest leads.

3. **Click the Accept button.**

   The queue list page reappears minus the lead or leads you selected.

Following Up on Leads

After you receive a new lead, you want a quick way to follow up and determine what you caught: a big one, a warm one, or just another student looking for a freebie. Your company might already have a standard lead qualification process, but here are some of the ways you can use salesforce.com to pursue leads.

Finding and merging duplicate lead records

Before following up on a new lead, use the Find Duplicates button to see whether a record already exists. With leads, you probably know that duplicates frequently occur. For example, if you capture leads from your Web site, the same visitor might fill in your Web form multiple times, even with the best of intentions. Rather than wasting your time or upsetting the existing lead, check first for duplicates.

By doing this, you might up your chances of a qualified lead. When you merge duplicate records, the remaining record inherits not only the information you select, but also linked records on related lists.

To find duplicates, review these steps:

1. **Go to a lead record that you suspect or know has duplicates.**

2. **Click the fiery red Find Duplicates button at the top of the lead record.**

   A Search Results page appears, giving you two options: Convert the lead by following the standard conversion steps or merge duplicates.

3. **Review the duplicate lead records and select a maximum of three records to be merged.**

   In salesforce.com, you can merge only three records at a time.

4. **Click the Merge Leads button on the Matching Leads related list.**

   A Merge Leads page appears, displaying side by side the selected records and any fields that have been completed.

5. **Compare the information and click the radio buttons to select the values that you want to retain, as shown in Figure 4-6.**

   At the top of each column, you can also choose to keep all the values from one record by clicking the Select All link.

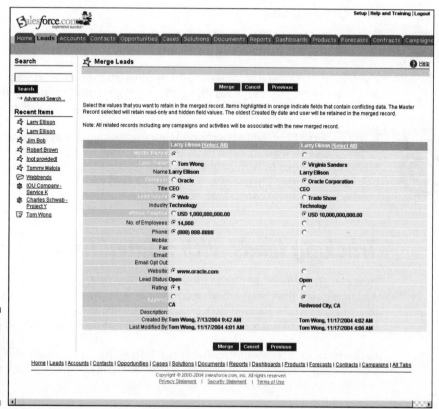

Figure 4-6:
Merging
duplicate
lead
records.

6. **When you finish reviewing, click the Merge button.**

   A pop-up window appears, prompting you to validate that you want to perform the merge. After clicking OK, the merged lead reappears. Any records from related lists are kept.

Researching by using Web Links

Before you call back or respond to your lead, you might want to do some homework first so that you appear smarter when you call. Salesforce.com provides three standard links under the Useful Links section of a Lead detail page that might help you collect valuable information.

- ✔ **Financial Profile:** This link takes you to Hoover's, a popular business research site with lots of valuable information about well-known public and private companies. If the name in the lead's Company field matches a company in Hoover's, you're taken directly to that information.

- ✔ **Map:** If the address information is filled out on your lead record, you can get quick directions to the corporate address when you click this link. If you travel to prospects and customers, you'll find this link to Yahoo! Maps invaluable.

- ✔ **News:** You can get current news and press releases from Alta Vista based on the name in the Company field of your lead record.

If you depend on specific Web sites for pertinent information on your prospects and customers, you can build other custom Web Links for your lead records. (See Chapter 18 for detailed instructions on building Web integration links.)

If you're part of the lead generation team for your company, take advantage of Web Links on lead records to boost your productivity. I've seen sales teams create links to Web pages with scripts, qualifying questions, common objections, sample customers, and more. Armed with this information, you can be faster, highly consistent, and more productive.

Tracking leads with related lists

How can you remember all the interactions that took place with a lead? I have a hard enough time remembering what I did yesterday let alone three months ago with 200 leads. Related lists on a lead record can help you capture all that information so that it's at your fingertips the next time you call a lead.

In Chapter 7, I discuss all the wonderful things that you can do with related lists to keep track of activities with people and the companies they work for.

But if you're looking for typical ways that sales people use lead related lists, read the following list, look at Figure 4-7 for an example, and then refer to Chapter 7 for the details:

- ✔ **Log A Call:** The next time you respond to a lead and want to record what you said to the lead's assistant, click the Log A Call button and type in the details.

- ✔ **New Task:** You plan to call the lead back next Friday when you know the assistant is on vacation. Click New Task and set a tickler for yourself for Friday.

- ✔ **Send An Email:** You get through to the lead and he asks you to send him an introductory e-mail about your company. Click the Send An Email button to send and track the e-mail directly from salesforce.com.

- ✔ **New Event:** The lead agrees to a demo. Click New Event and schedule a meeting so that you don't forget.

- ✔ **Mail Merge:** Before you demo your new product, you require the lead to sign your standard non-disclosure agreement (NDA). Click the Mail Merge button and quickly create the NDA with the lead's information prefilled.

- ✔ **Add Campaign:** You decide to invite the lead to the annual customer golf outing, a campaign tracked in salesforce.com. Add the lead to the campaign so that your marketing team remembers to send the lead an invitation.

Updating lead fields

In the course of your lead qualification, you'll inevitably collect pertinent information that you'll want to save directly on the lead record. Every time you capture important data on your lead, update your lead record by doing the following:

1. **Click the Edit button on the lead record to modify the fields.**

2. **Complete the fields as necessary to determine whether the lead is qualified.**

3. **Update the Lead Status field as you make progress.**

   Even if you discover that the lead is a waste of your time, that would be progress.

4. **Click Save when you're done making changes.**

At some point, you might decide that a lead won't at this time become a qualified opportunity. In that case, you can archive the lead by changing its status. This allows you to get a sense of how many leads are still being worked.

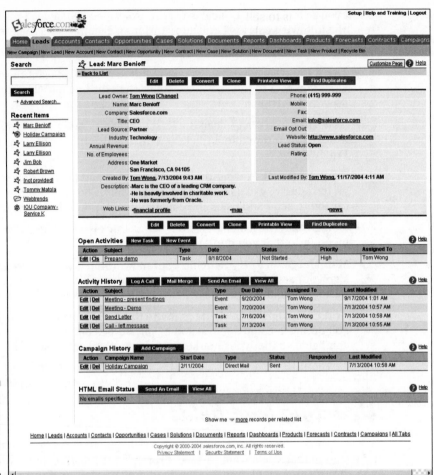

Converting qualified leads

When you decide that a lead is actually a qualified opportunity, you can start using salesforce.com's full opportunity tracking system. To do so, you must convert the lead to an opportunity. This conversion gives you two benefits.

✔ Converting a lead to an opportunity allows you to track multiple contacts within an account, which is easier than tracking a single individual lead. In other words, if you have ten leads from Microsoft, none of them are linked with each other in salesforce.com. But if by converting a lead, you create an account called Microsoft, all the co-workers can be linked as contacts for the same account.

✔ Your goal is to sell, so the sooner you can start managing opportunities and not just leads the healthier your pipeline and wallet. For a qualified lead, your sales process begins where your lead process ends.

When deciding whether to add names of companies or business people as leads or as accounts with contacts, remember that the leads module of sales-force.com is non-relational from lead to lead. If you're serious about going after a particular company and the inter-relationships of business contacts will be important, I recommend that you add the target as an account instead of as a lead (in which case Chapter 5 can help you out).

To convert a lead to an opportunity, follow these steps:

1. **Click the Convert button on a lead record that you want to convert.**

   The Convert button is located at the top and bottom of the lead record. A Convert Lead page appears.

2. **Complete the required fields.**

   Required fields are highlighted in red. The following is a summary (see the example in Figure 4-8):

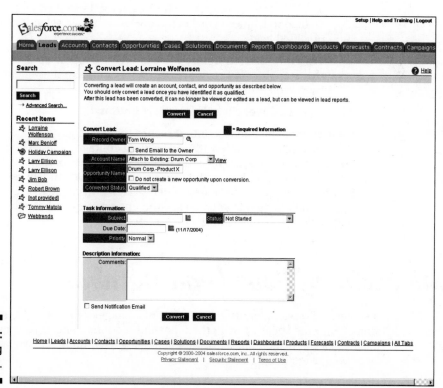

Figure 4-8: Converting a lead.

- **Record Owner:** If the Lead Owner remains the Record Owner, don't change the selection. If the owner changes, click the Lookup icon and choose from the list of users. Select the Send Email to the Owner check box if needed.

- **Account Name:** If salesforce.com doesn't find an account that closely matches the Company field from your lead, it creates a new account record. In the event that it does find a match, select an option from the drop-down list if you want to create a new account or associate the lead to the existing account.

- **Opportunity Name:** If you want to create an opportunity, complete this field by giving the opportunity a name. (I typically recommend that the name of an opportunity be the Account Name followed by a hyphen and then a summary of the product interest. For example: Amazon – New Hardware.) You don't have to create an opportunity record upon conversion. Sometimes the lead that you're converting is associated to an existing opportunity. In these situations, select the check box to avoid creating a new opportunity. Then see Chapter 9 for details on linking contacts to existing opportunities.

- **Converted Status:** Salesforce.com prefills this field with the default value that your company has chosen for a qualified lead. Don't change this unless your company has multiple selections for a qualified lead.

- **Task Information fields:** You can create a follow-up task right in this step, but you're not required to. Complete these fields only if it saves you a step.

3. **When you're done, click the Convert button.**

   If salesforce.com finds a contact record that matches your lead, you can then decide to associate with the existing contact record. Otherwise, a contact record appears for your former lead. That contact is linked to an account corresponding to the lead's Company field, and all associated records from related lists are carried over. If you chose to create an opportunity in Step 2, you can see the opportunity on both the account and contact record's Opportunity related lists.

Maintaining Your Lead Database

If you are a system administrator or a lead manager with the right permissions (I specific specify this in the following sections), one of your greatest challenges will be administering and managing what hopefully will become a large pool of leads.

Lead databases can become unwieldy over time, so you need to keep them clean. For example, if you work for a company that regularly collects leads from industry conferences, after a year, your leads database might have many duplicates and plenty of garbage. Salesforce.com provides a number of simple tools to make short work of this and other tasks.

The biggest problems I see with leads surround assigning, de-duping, transferring, archiving, and deleting. I know: You hate to get rid of anything. However, sometimes it's necessary and relatively painless.

Making use of lead queues

If you have a sales team made up of multiple reps responsible for attacking leads collectively, you might want to set up lead queues. For example, some companies hire telemarketers to handle leads on a first-come, first-serve basis. You might just find that your reps will work harder if they all have an equal chance to go after a fresh pool of leads.

If you're an administrator or user with permission to customize salesforce.com, you can set up lead queues. Follow these steps:

1. **Click the Setup link in the top-right corner of salesforce.com.**

   This takes you to the main Personal Setup page.

2. **On the sidebar, click the Customize heading under the Studio heading.**

   This provides the menu for the different salesforce.com modules.

3. **Click the Leads heading under the Customize heading.**

   This expands the menu of options under the Leads heading.

4. **Click the Queues link.**

   In the body of the page, you see simple instructions for lead queues.

5. **Click the New button.**

   A New Lead Queue page appears.

6. **Name the queue and specify the people in your company who will be part of the queue.**

   For my example, you might label the queue Telemarketers and then choose users who make up the telemarketing team. (See Figure 4-9 for an example of creating a queue.)

7. **When you're done, just click Save.**

   You can now use this queue when organizing and reassigning lead records.

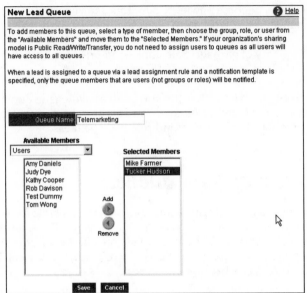

New Lead Queue   ? Help

To add members to this queue, select a type of member, then choose the group, role, or user from
the "Available Members" and move them to the "Selected Members." If your organization's sharing
model is Public Read/Write/Transfer, you do not need to assign users to queues as all users will
have access to all queues.

When a lead is assigned to a queue via a lead assignment rule and a notification template is
specified, only the queue members that are users (not groups or roles) will be notified.

Queue Name Telemarketing

Available Members
Users

Amy Daniels		Selected Members
Judy Dye		Mike Farmer
Kathy Cooper		Tucker Hudson
Rob Davison		
Test Dummy	Add	
Tom Wong	▶	
	◀	
	Remove	

Save   Cancel

Figure 4-9:
Creating a
lead queue.

Creating assignment rules for automatic routing

If your company generates lots of leads, assignment rules can help distribute
the workload and get leads to the right users. This gives you a better chance
that leads won't become stagnant. A lead assignment rule is a feature that
lets the administrator define who should receive a lead and under what conditions. For example if your reps have sales territories defined by ZIP Codes,
you could those ZIP Codes to dictate who should get what.

To create a lead assignment rule, follow these steps:

1. **Click the Setup link on any salesforce.com page.**

   The Personal Setup page appears.

2. **Click the Leads heading under the Customize heading on the sidebar.**

   The Leads heading expands with a menu of setup options.

3. **Click the Assignment Rules link.**

   The Lead Assignment Rules page appears.

4. **Click the New button.**

   The New Lead Assignment Rule page appears in Edit mode.

5. **Enter a title in the Rule Name field, select the check box if you want to make it the active assignment rule, and click the Save button.**

   The New Lead Assignment Rule page appears in Saved mode. You can have only one active rule at any time, but the rule can have multiple entries.

6. **Click New on the Rule Entries related list.**

   A Rule Entry Edit page appears.

7. **Complete the steps as follows:**

   a. **Enter a number in the Order field to set the order.**

   b. **Select criteria to define the rule.** See the section "Creating custom lead views" for details on selecting criteria. In this case, you might put ZIP Code Equals 02474.

   c. **Use the drop-down list and Lookup icon to select the user or queue.**

   d. **Use the Lookup icon to choose a Notification Template.** The assignment rules can be set to send e-mail alerts to recipients of new leads.

8. **When done, click the Save button or the Save & New button.**

   If you click the Save button, the New Lead Assignment Rule reappears.

   If you click the Save & New button, a new Rule Entry Edit page appears, and you can repeat Steps 7 and 8 until you finish.

Reassigning lead ownership

You might need to reassign leads for a variety of reasons. For instance, after you set up your lead records in salesforce.com, you need to give them to the right people. Or maybe some reps just weren't following up, so you took their leads away after swatting their noses with a rolled-up newspaper.

To re-assign multiple leads at a time, you must be an administrator or a user with Manage Leads and Transfer Leads permissions. If you want to reassign many leads at the same time, take these steps:

1. **From the Leads home page, select a view from which you can see some leads that you want to reassign.**

   The list page appears.

2. **In the Action column of the lead list, select the check boxes for the lead records that you want to assign to someone else.**

3. **Click the Change Owner button at the top of the page.**

   The Change Lead Owner page appears.

4. **Select the user or queue that you intend to reassign leads to, and then click Save.**

   The lead list reappears, and you can see that the lead owners have been changed.

If you're an administrator, you can use the Mass Transfer Leads tool in Setup to accomplish the same goals of reassigning *en masse*. See Chapter 19 for details on mass-transferring leads.

If you're reassigning one lead at a time, you can transfer ownership directly from a lead record. Follow these steps:

1. **On the lead record, next to the Lead Owner field, click the Change link.**

   The link is in square brackets. The Change Lead Owner page appears.

2. **Select the user or queue that you're assigning the lead to.**

   Note that this is the same page that you use when you're assigning multiple leads, but here you can choose to notify the recipient with an e-mail.

3. **When you're done, click Save.**

   The lead record reappears with your ownership change. The new owner instantly receives an e-mail if you selected the Send Notification check box.

Changing the status of multiple records

An administrator or a user with Manage Leads and Transfer Leads permissions can also change the status of multiple records at a time. This feature comes in handy if during a process a lead manager reviewed leads prior to assigning to reps.

To change the status of multiple leads at the same time, follow these steps:

1. **From the Leads home page, select a view.**

   The list page appears.

2. **In the Action column of the lead list, select the check boxes for the lead records that require a status change.**

For example, if you were eyeballing a list of leads from a tradeshow, you might select obvious bogus leads.

3. **Click the Change Status button at the top of the page.**

   The Change Status page appears.

4. **Select a status from the New Status drop-down list and click Save.**

   The lead list reappears.

If you require industrial strength de-duplication tools, a number of proven technology partners handle de-duplication with salesforce.com, plus a variety of other data management tasks. One such partner, DemandTools, has a downloadable toolset that has received rave reviews. I've seen it in action de-duplicating records from salesforce.com and it's worth a look if you have problems with clean data. You can check out their Web site at www.demandtools.com.

Mass deleting lead records

Periodically, be sure to delete records that are unqualified or of no value to your company. You must be an administrator to mass delete records.

Some companies add a To Be Deleted value to their Lead Status field to denote garbage. Then periodically, the system administrator deletes those records.

If you want to delete multiple records at a time, check out these steps:

1. **On the Leads home page, click the Mass Delete Leads link under the Tools heading.**

   A Mass Delete Leads page appears with a three-step deletion wizard.

2. **Review the steps, and then type the search criteria for the leads that you want to delete.**

   For example, if you want to delete unqualified leads, enter a filter where Lead Status Equals Unqualified, as shown in Figure 4-10.

3. **Click the Search button.**

   The page reappears with your results at the bottom of the page.

4. **Select all records or just the records that you want to delete by clicking the check boxes.**

   To select all the search results for deletion, click the Select All link at the top of the list.

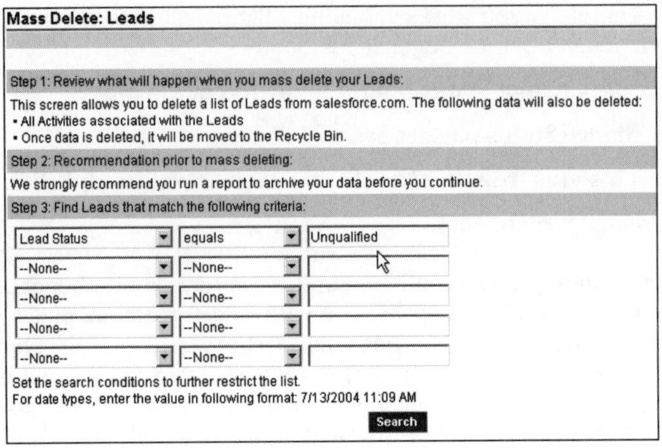

Mass Delete: Leads

Step 1: Review what will happen when you mass delete your Leads:

This screen allows you to delete a list of Leads from salesforce.com. The following data will also be deleted:
- All Activities associated with the Leads
- Once data is deleted, it will be moved to the Recycle Bin.

Step 2: Recommendation prior to mass deleting:

We strongly recommend you run a report to archive your data before you continue.

Step 3: Find Leads that match the following criteria:

Lead Status ▾	equals ▾	Unqualified
--None-- ▾	--None-- ▾	
--None-- ▾	--None-- ▾	
--None-- ▾	--None-- ▾	
--None-- ▾	--None-- ▾	

Set the search conditions to further restrict the list.
For date types, enter the value in following format: 7/1 3/2004 11:09 AM

[Search]

Figure 4-10:
Setting
criteria to
mass delete
leads.

When deleting records, always be cautious but don't overly stress out. When you delete records, that information is placed in your Recycle Bin and is accessible for 30 days. To undelete a record, click the Recycle Bin link on your taskbar, find the record, and undelete it. Then count your blessings and breathe into a paper bag until the panic attack subsides.

Chapter 5

Managing Accounts

In This Chapter

▶ Understanding the account record

▶ Entering accounts

▶ Organizing account lists

▶ Using the account related lists

▶ Keeping your accounts up to date

*W*ho are your customers? What do you know about them? What are their top compelling business problems? If you had trouble answering any of these questions, pay close attention to this chapter. In this chapter, I discuss how to use salesforce.com to manage your accounts.

In salesforce.com, an *account* is basically a company that you do business with. Accounts can include all types of companies — customers, prospects, partners, and even competitors. Among the top reasons why companies implement any customer relationship management (CRM) tool is that they need a centralized place where they can store account data, and they find themselves searching all over the place for critical customer information. With salesforce.com, you can keep all your important account information in one place so that you and your team can apply that knowledge to sell more and keep customers happy. For example, if you work for a pharmaceutical company, you can use the accounts area to manage your territory of hospitals, clinics, and top offices and capture everything from call reports to business plans.

In this chapter, I describe all the ways you can use accounts to manage and track companies. First, you need to get your important company lists into salesforce.com and organize them according to the way that you work. Then, you find how out to make the best use of the account record to profile your companies. Finally, you discover how to capitalize on the account related lists to gain a 360 degree view of your customer and ensure that no one drops any balls.

Getting Familiar with the Account Record

The account record lets you collect all the critical information about the companies you interact with. That account record is supported by other records (contacts, opportunities, cases, activities, and so on) that collectively give you a complete view of your customer. From this vantage point, you can quickly take in the view from the top, and if you need to, you can easily drill into the details.

Here is a short list of valuable things you can do with accounts:

✔ Import and consolidate your lists of target accounts in one place.

✔ Enter new accounts quickly and maintain naming consistency.

✔ Create parent/child relationships that describe how a companies divisions or subsidiaries relate to each other.

✔ Realign sales territories.

✔ Segment your markets with ease.

✔ Eliminate paper-based business planning.

✔ Assign account teams to better serve your customers.

✔ Track your top customers and de-emphasize bottom-feeders.

✔ Define the movers and shakers within an account.

✔ Devise schemes to beat your competitors.

✔ Manage your channel partners.

Understanding standard fields

The account record is the collection of fields that make up the information on a company that you're tracking. The record has only two modes: an Edit mode where you can modify fields and a Saved mode where you can view the fields and the account's *related lists* (which are located below the record fields).

An account record comes preconfigured with approximately 22 fields commonly used for account management.

Most of the standard fields are self-explanatory, but in the following list, I highlight certain terms that warrant greater definition:

- **Account Owner:** The person in your organization who owns the account. An account record has only one owner, but many users can still collaborate on an account.

- **Account Name:** This required field represents the name of the company you want to track.

- **Account Site:** The Account Site field goes hand in hand with the Account Name field when you're distinguishing different physical locations or divisions of a company. This field, although not required, is very important if your company sells to different locations of a customer with decentralized buying patterns. For example, if you sell mattresses to Hilton Hotels but each Hilton Hotel buys independently, this field is useful for classifying different sites.

- **Type:** One of the fields on an account record that classifies the relationship of an account to your company. The Type field consists of a dropdown list of values and is critical if you want to differentiate types of companies. For example, if you work for a software company that uses value-added resellers (VARs) to sell and service your products, you might want to select Reseller as one of your drop-down list values.

- **Rating:** Use this drop-down list to define your internal rating system for companies you are tracking. Salesforce.com provides default values of Hot, Warm, and Cold, but you can replace these with numbers, letters, or other terms based on how you want to segment companies.

Customizing account fields

Use standard fields and you'll have a simple way to collect basic profiles on companies. But to get the most out of your account record, you should think about how you and your company define a target customer. For example, if I were selling corporate healthcare plans, I might want to know certain information about each of my target companies: number of employees, number of people insured, existing healthcare plan, level of satisfaction, and so on.

If fields on your account record can answer these four questions, you have a solid foundation for your account record:

- What attributes describe your target customer?

- What are the important components of your account plan?

- Is a company's infrastructure important to what you sell?

- What information, if you had it, would help you sell to a company?

If you find your account record lacking relevance to your business, write down fields that you want and then seek out your system administrator to customize your account record. (See Chapter 18 for the how-to details on building fields, rearranging your layouts, and other design tricks.) You will have greater success with accounts if you're focusing on your customer.

Creating and Updating Your Accounts

Before you can begin using salesforce.com to manage accounts, you must get the account records into salesforce.com. In this section, I show you how to get started and how to update saved records.

Adding new accounts

The best way to enter a new account is to use the New Account link located on the taskbar. By doing this, you get a clear picture of the account fields that are most important to your company. To create accounts with this method, follow these simple steps:

1. **Enter the name of the account you want to create in the Search tool on the sidebar, and then click the Search button.**

   A Search results page appears with a list of records that match your query. If you see records that match particularly account or lead records, don't throw in the towel yet. Click into links listed in the Name columns to drill into the details and see whether the account is being worked. Consult with your sales manager if you have questions.

2. **If you don't get any results, click the New Account link on the taskbar, as shown in Figure 5-1.**

   The Edit mode of a new account appears.

Figure 5-1:
Creating a new account from the taskbar.

Before adding an account (or any other record for that matter), always search for it first. You might not be the only person to have worked with a particular company. By searching first, you avoid creating duplicate entries, you potentially profit from prior history on an existing account, and you don't waste time possibly chasing accounts that don't belong to you. (Although I know this *never* happens.)

3. **Fill in the fields as much as you can or as required.**

Remember that at a minimum, the Account Name field must be completed. Try to provide as much detail as possible to make it valuable for your selling objectives. This data could be as simple as basic phone and address information and as detailed as account segmentation data such as type, industry, annual revenue, and so on. (See Figure 5-2 for an example of a record in Edit mode.)

TIP

When creating account records, strive for accurate and consistent spelling of the corporate name. Your customer database is only as good as the data being entered into the system. As a best practice, look up and use the name of the company from a reliable source (examples could include Dun & Bradstreet, Hoover's, or the company name as displayed on its corporate Web site).

4. **When you're done, click one of the following buttons:**

- **Save:** After you click the Save button, the Account detail page appears, where you can click the Edit button at any time if you need to modify information on the record.

Figure 5-2:
Completing
account
fields.

Account Edit: salesforce.com

| Save | Save & New | Cancel |

Account Information:　　　　　　　　　　　　　　　　　■ = Required Information

Account Owner:	Tom Wong		Rating:	--None-- ▾
Account Name:	salesforce.com		Phone:	
Account Site:	HQ		Fax:	
Account Number:			Website:	http://www.salesforce.c
Parent Account:		🔍	Ticker Symbol:	CRM
Type:	Customer ▾		Ownership:	Public ▾
Industry:	Internet business applications ▾		Employees:	
Annual Revenue:			SIC Code:	

Address Information:　　　　　　　　　　　　　　　　　Copy Billing to Shipping

Billing Street:	The Landmark @ One Market, Suite 300		Shipping Street:	The Landmark @ One Market, Suite 300
Billing City:	San Francisco		Shipping City:	San Francisco
Billing State:	CA		Shipping State:	CA
Billing Zip/Postal Code:	94105		Shipping Zip/Postal Code:	94105
Billing Country:	USA		Shipping Country:	USA

Description Information:

Description: Founded in March 1999, salesforce.com (http://www.salesforce.com) is the online customer relationship management service that makes software obsolete. Designed for companies of any size, salesforce.com exploits the power of the Internet to allow businesses to safely and securely manage, share and leverage their critical customer information anytime, anywhere.

| Save | Save & New | Cancel |

- **Save & New:** Clicking this button saves the current account record and automatically opens a new, blank account record in Edit mode.

If you need to enter accounts fast, you might be able to use the Quick Create tool located on the Accounts home page. Click the Accounts tab and look on the sidebar for the Quick Create header. You can use the Quick Create tool to create an account record just by typing in the account name and clicking Save. (However, a word to the wise: Get in the habit of adding accounts the conventional way because quick isn't always better.)

If you have an existing spreadsheet of companies that you want to import into salesforce.com, you can use an import wizard tool and avoid the manual entry. See Chapter 6 for how-to details on importing accounts and contacts.

Updating account fields

In the course of working with your accounts, you will inevitably collect pertinent information that you'll want to save directly in the account record. Every time you capture important data on your account, remember to update your record by doing the following:

1. **Enter the name of your account in the Search tool on the sidebar and click the Search button.**

   A Search results page appears.

2. **Click the desired link in the Account Name column to go to your account.**

   The Account detail page appears.

3. **Click the Edit button on the account record.**

4. **Update the fields as necessary, and then click Save.**

   The account reappears in Saved mode, and the fields you edited have been changed.

Sharing accounts with others

One of the advantages (and risks) of centralizing all your account data in one place is that you and your co-workers have access to information so you can work more effectively when selling or servicing your accounts. Salesforce.com provides your company with the ability to define an overall data access policy, called a *sharing model,* to make sure that the right people in your company have access to information to perform their jobs. The sharing model can range from highly restrictive (private) to very open (public). See Chapter 17 if you want the nitty-gritty details on sharing models.

If you're a sales rep, you might not be able to dictate that sharing model, but you can still grant sharing privileges to data you own on an account by account basis. (It's good to be the king.) As long as you're using Professional, Enterprise, or Developer Edition, you can do this in seconds with the Sharing button on an Account detail page.

To share an account with other users, go to the account record and follow these steps:

1. **Click the Sharing button at the top of the account record.**

   The Sharing Detail page for the account appears. On that page, you see simple instructions and a related list to share the account with users or groups.

2. **Click the Add button on the User and Group Sharing related list.**

   A New Sharing page appears, as shown in Figure 5-3.

3. **Use the Currently Not Shared drop-down list and select the user, role, or groups that you want to share your account with.**

4. **Select a user, role, or group in the Currently Not Shared list box and click the Add button to move the person or group to the New Sharing list box.**

5. **Modify the access rights by using the Account Access, Opportunity Access, and Case Access drop-down lists.**

   You use these drop-down lists to provide your colleagues viewing privileges (Read Only) or viewing and editing rights (Read/Write) to the account and its associated opportunity and case records.

6. **When the task is completed, click Save.**

   The Sharing Detail page reappears with your changes. Repeat these steps as often as you need if you want different users or groups to have different access.

Figure 5-3:
Sharing an
account.

Action	Type	Name	Account Access	Opportunity Access	Case Access	Reason
	User	Tom Wong	All	Read Only	Read/Write	Owner

Organizing Your Accounts

When you have all or a portion of your accounts entered in salesforce.com, you can begin to organize them to suit the way that you sell.

In this section, I show you how you can use views and other tools from the Accounts home page to provide greater focus for you and your sales teams. I also show you an important feature of the account record that lets you create parent/child relationships between accounts. Then for even more robust organization of your account information, check out Chapter 15 for specifics on how to use standard and custom account reports.

Using account views

An *account view* is a list of accounts that match certain criteria. When you select a view, you're basically specifying criteria to limit the results that you get back. The advantage of a view versus searching is that you can use this view over and over again. For example, if you are one of many sales reps, you probably want to see only your accounts. On the Accounts home page, sales-force.com comes preset with six defined views:

- ✓ **All Accounts** provides a list of all the account records entered into sales-force.com. Depending on the way your company has set up your security model, you might not see this or its results.

- ✓ **My Accounts** gives you a list of just the accounts that you own in sales-force.com.

- ✓ **My Active Accounts** shows you a list of your accounts that have been modified in the last month. You might find this view helpful to gauge if you're regularly keeping in contact with all your customers.

- ✓ **New This Week** generates a list of accounts that have been created since the beginning of the week.

- ✓ **New Last Week** shows you just the account records created last week.

- ✓ **Recently Viewed Accounts** lets you look at a list of accounts that you've recently viewed.

To try out a predefined view, do the following:

1. **On the Accounts home page, click the down arrow on the Views drop-down list.**

   You see the six options that I mention in the preceding bullet list and maybe some other choices that have been created for you.

2. **Select the My Accounts view.**

   If you've already entered or imported account records, a list page appears, showing accounts that are currently owned by you. Notice that salesforce.com lays out the list with six standard columns that correspond to commonly used account fields plus an Action column so you can quickly modify a record.

3. **Click a column header to re-sort the list page.**

   For example, if you click the Billing State header, the list page re-sorts by state in alphabetical order, as shown in Figure 5-4.

4. **Click into any account by pointing and clicking a link in the Account Name column.**

   The Account detail page appears.

5. **Click the Back button on your browser and instead click the Edit button on the same row as the account you just clicked.**

   The account record appears in Edit mode, allowing you to make changes to the data.

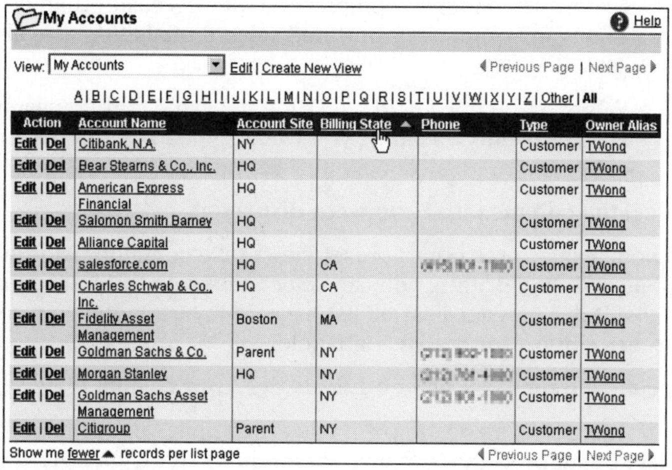

Action	Account Name	Account Site	Billing State ▲	Phone	Type	Owner Alias
Edit | Del	Citibank, N.A.	NY			Customer	TWong
Edit | Del	Bear Stearns & Co., Inc.	HQ			Customer	TWong
Edit | Del	American Express Financial	HQ			Customer	TWong
Edit | Del	Salomon Smith Barney	HQ			Customer	TWong
Edit | Del	Alliance Capital	HQ			Customer	TWong
Edit | Del	salesforce.com	HQ	CA	(415) 901-7080	Customer	TWong
Edit | Del	Charles Schwab & Co., Inc.	HQ	CA		Customer	TWong
Edit | Del	Fidelity Asset Management	Boston	MA		Customer	TWong
Edit | Del	Goldman Sachs & Co.	Parent	NY	(212) 902-1000	Customer	TWong
Edit | Del	Morgan Stanley	HQ	NY	(212) 761-4000	Customer	TWong
Edit | Del	Goldman Sachs Asset Management		NY	(212) 901-1000	Customer	TWong
Edit | Del	Citigroup	Parent	NY		Customer	TWong

Figure 5-4: Re-sorting a standard account view.

Creating custom account views

If you want special lists for the way that you manage your accounts, you should build custom views. For example, if you're a new business sales rep who focuses solely on California telecom companies and always researches the prospect's Web site before calling, creating a custom view will help you to be more effective because you can build your list of target accounts, define columns, and use it over and over again.

To build a view from scratch, follow these simple steps:

1. **On the Accounts home page next to the Views drop-down list, click the Create New View link.**

   The Create a View page appears.

2. **Name the view by entering text in the Name field.**

   For my fictitious California telecom example, you might call the view "California Telco Prospects."

3. **Select the appropriate radio button if you want to search All Accounts or just My Accounts.**

4. **Under the Search Criteria step, select your search criteria, as shown in Figure 5-5.**

   A basic criteria query is made up of three elements:

   - **Field:** The first drop-down list offers of all the fields on the account record. One example is be the Type field.

   - **Operator:** The second drop-down list offers operators for your search. That sounds complicated, but it's easier than you think. Taking my example, you would select Equals from the drop-down list.

   - **Value:** In the third field, you type the value that you want in the search. For my example, you would type **Prospect** because for this example you go after only new business.

5. **Select the columns that you want displayed.**

   Although salesforce.com's preset views take common fields such as Phone and Billing State, you can select any of up to 11 account fields to be displayed on your custom list page. In my example, you would add another column for the Web site field.

6. **Decide whether you want others to see your custom view.**

   Your decision is made simple if you aren't given an option. Otherwise, select the appropriate option if you want to share your view with others. If you choose limited accessibility, use the two list boxes to select which users will see the view.

7. **When you're done, click Save.**

   A new view appears based on your custom view criteria. If you don't get all the results you would anticipate, you might want to recheck and refine the search criteria. For example, if your company has a habit of using initials or full spelling for the State field (NY or New York, respectively), this impacts results.

Figure 5-5:
Setting criteria for a custom view.

Step 3. Search Criteria:			
Set the search conditions to further restrict the list.			
• You can use "or" filters by entering multiple items in the third column.			
• You can enter up to 10 items, separated by commas. For example: CA, NY, TX, FL searches for CA or NY or TX or FL.			
• Place quotation marks around data that includes commas. For example, "200,000","1,000,000" searches for 200,000 or 1,000,000.			
• For fields that can be set on or off, use "0" for no and "1" for yes, e.g., "Active equals 1" or "Converted equals 0."			
Billing State	contains	California, CA	and
Industry	contains	telecom	and
Type	equals	Prospect	and
--None--	--None--		and
--None--	--None--		

Making use of the Key Accounts section

When you go to the Accounts home page, just below the Views drop-down list you also see a Key Accounts section. This table comes with three columns: Account Name, City, and Phone. These columns cannot be modified. You can see as few as 10 items and as many as 25 items at a time by clicking the link at the bottom of the table.

Use the drop-down list in the top-right corner of the table to quickly get to account records based on the following:

- **Recently Created** are the last 10 to 25 accounts you created.
- **Recently Modified** are the last 10 to 25 accounts you modified.
- **Recently Viewed** are the last 10 to 25 accounts you looked at.

Reassigning account ownership

You might find that after you set up your accounts in salesforce.com, you need to give them to the right people. Part of organizing your accounts is getting them into the right hands. You might even want to reassign accounts to yourself because an account wasn't properly given to you.

If you want to reassign multiple accounts at the same time, see the section "Transferring accounts" later in this chapter. If you're just reassigning an account on a case-by-case basis, you can transfer ownership directly from an account record. Go to the detail page of an account that you want to reassign and follow these steps:

1. **Next to the Account Owner field, click the Change link (which appears in square brackets).**

   The Change Account Owner page appears.

2. **Select the user you're assigning the account to.**

   By clicking the Send Notification Email check box on the page, you can choose to notify the recipient with an e-mail.

3. **Select the check boxes to determine whether and how associated records change ownership.**

   See Figure 5-6 for an example.

4. **When you're done, click Save.**

   The account record reappears. Notice that the Account Owner field has changed to the assigned user.

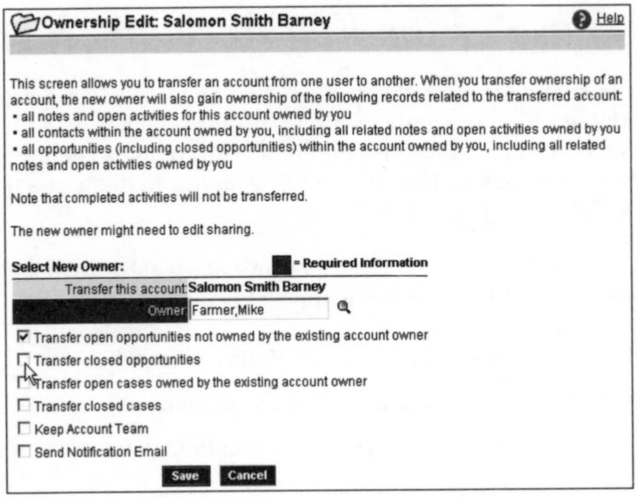

Figure 5-6:
Reassigning
an account.

Building parent/child relationships

If you sell into different locations or divisions of a company and you're currently challenged by how to keep this information organized, use account hierarchies to solve your problem. In salesforce.com, you can link multiple offices of a company together by using the Parent Account field on an account record. And you can create multiple tiers to the hierarchy if your customer is organized that way.

To establish parent/child relationships, perform the following:

1. **Create accounts for the parent and subsidiary companies (see the section "Adding new accounts" earlier this chapter).**

   (You can skip this step if the accounts are already created.) You might want to type a term such as **Headquarters** or **HQ** in the Account Site field to signify which account is the parent.

2. **Click the subsidiary account (also called a child account) that you want to link and click Edit.**

   The record appears in Edit mode.

3. **By the Parent Account field, click the Lookup icon.**

   A pop-up window appears with a Search field and a list of recently viewed accounts.

4. **Search for the parent account by typing the name of the account in the Search field, and then click Go.**

   If you see the parent account in the list provided, skip this step.

5. **From the list of results, click the name of the company to select the parent account (as shown in Figure 5-7).**

   The pop-up window closes, and your selection appears in the Parent Account field.

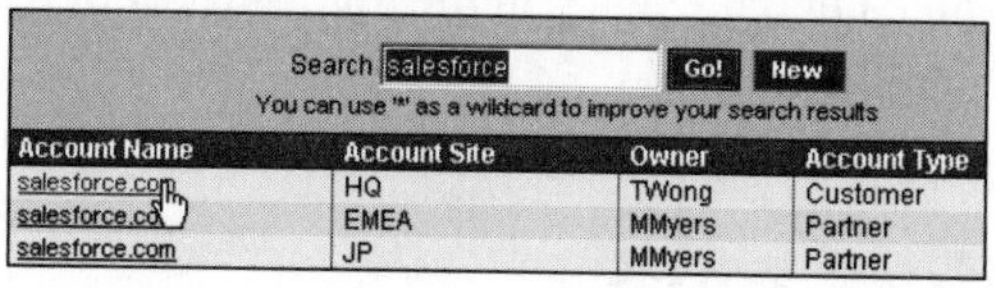

Figure 5-7:
Selecting a
sample
parent
account.

Account Name	Account Site	Owner	Account Type
salesforce.com	HQ	TWong	Customer
salesforce.com	EMEA	MMyers	Partner
salesforce.com	JP	MMyers	Partner

Search salesforce Go! New
You can use '*' as a wildcard to improve your search results

6. **If you want to further denote the child account, use the Account Site field.**

   Some companies use city, state, country, division, and so on depending on how they organize their accounts. For example, if Staples, Inc., has locations in Dallas and Atlanta, you might want to type the city into the Account Site field for each of the child accounts so that you can tell which is which.

7. **When you're done, click Save.**

   The Account detail page appears.

8. **To view the account hierarchy, click the View Hierarchy link to the right of the Account Name field on the record.**

   An Account Hierarchy list page appears (as shown in Figure 5-8) and like other lists, you can click an item to go a specific account.

Figure 5-8:
Viewing a
sample
account
hierarchy.

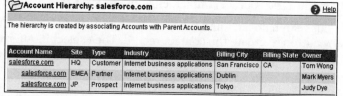

Account Hierarchy: salesforce.com   Help

The hierarchy is created by associating Accounts with Parent Accounts.

Account Name	Site	Type	Industry	Billing City	Billing State	Owner
salesforce.com	HQ	Customer	Internet business applications	San Francisco	CA	Tom Wong
salesforce.com	EMEA	Partner	Internet business applications	Dublin		Mark Myers
salesforce.com	JP	Prospect	Internet business applications	Tokyo		Judy Dye

Performing Actions with Account Related Lists

Fields on an account record are useful for storing important data specific to a company. But where do you go to capture all the critical interactions and relationships when you're working an account? To keep track of this detail, use the related lists located on the Account detail page.

Many of the actions on account related lists are common to other modules. For example, major modules such as Accounts, Contacts, and Opportunities all have related lists for Open Activities, Activity History, and Notes & Attachments. Rather than being redundant, see Chapter 7 for details on using related lists for tracking tasks and calendar events. In the following sections, I describe certain related lists that are unique to the account record.

Defining contact roles

Many sales reps do a great job of collecting business cards for contacts within an account, but this action alone does not get them closer to a sale. Contacts and their titles often don't tell the whole story about decision makers and chain of command within an account.

To better define the buying influences on an account, go to an account record and follow these steps:

1. **Review your records under the Contacts related list.**

   If important contacts are missing, add them first, which I describe how to do in Chapter 6.

2. **Click the New button on the Contact Roles related list.**

   The Account Contact Role page appears.

3. **Type the name of a contact in the Contact field and click the Lookup icon.**

   A pop-up window with your search results appears.

4. **If you find the correct contact, click the link for that contact's name.**

   If your search doesn't find the contact, refine your search or click the New button to create the contact record. Then select it. After you select the contact, the pop up disappears and the Contact field is filled in.

5. **Select correct role from the Role drop-down list.**

   If the right role for your contact doesn't appear, advise your system administrator to edit the roles.

6. **Select the check box if the contact is your Primary Contact, and to finish click the Save button or the Save & New button.**

   If you click Save, the Account detail page reappears, and your contact displays on the Contact Roles related list. If you click the Save & New button, a new Account Contact Role page appears, and you can associate another contact to a role immediately.

Establishing account teams

Many companies organize themselves in predefined account teams because their selling model requires team collaboration. For example, if in your company an account manager acts as a quarterback and manages the overall customer relationship, you might have other employees who assist the account manager for proposals, customer service, and so on. Some companies find that they can manage more relationships and be more productive with set account teams where the members understand their roles and responsibilities.

 If you decide to build account teams, make sure that you have clear team role descriptions and guidelines for rules of engagement (so that everybody plays nice). Some companies actually publish those sales policies in salesforce.com by using Web links or documents. (See Chapter 10 for details on how to store documents.) Account teams are more productive and trusting of sharing information when everyone knows what's fair and expected.

If you want to set up an account team for an account, go to the account record and follow these steps:

1. **Scroll down the detail page to the Account Team related list, and then click the Add button.**

   A New Account Team Members page appears with five rows to associate five team members.

2. **Type the name of a user in the Team Member field and click the Lookup icon.**

   A pop-up window appears with your search results.

3. **If you find the correct member of your team, select it by clicking the link for the user name.**

   If your search doesn't find the user, refine your search until you find your colleague, and then select the user. After you select the user, the pop up disappears and the Team Member field is filled in.

4. **Review the three Access fields to verify the access level that you want to grant to the team member.**

   Depending on your sharing model, you can use the drop-down lists to grant read/write or read-only privileges to the team member for the account and its related contacts and cases.

5. **Select the correct role from the Team Role drop-down list (which you see on the right in Figure 5-9).**

   If the right role for your contact doesn't appear, advise your system administrator to edit the roles.

6. **Repeat Steps 2 through 5 for each of the team members for your account and then click Save, as shown in Figure 5-9.**

The Account detail page reappears, and your team is displayed on the Account Team related list. If your account team requires more than five users, click the Save & More button and repeat the Steps 2 through 5 to add more users.

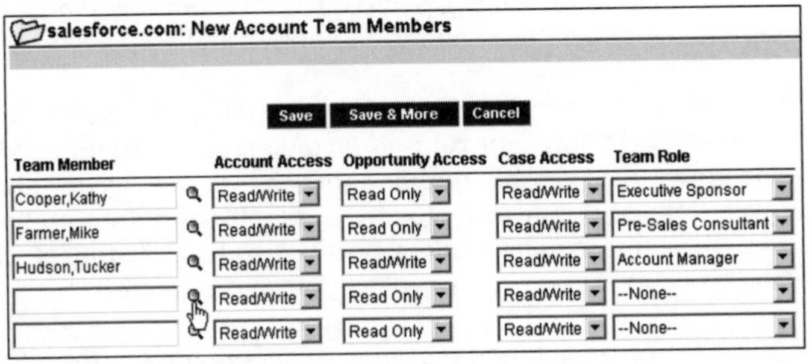

Figure 5-9:
Adding
account
team
members.

Team Member		Account Access	Opportunity Access	Case Access	Team Role
Cooper,Kathy	🔍	Read/Write ▼	Read Only ▼	Read/Write ▼	Executive Sponsor ▼
Farmer,Mike	🔍	Read/Write ▼	Read Only ▼	Read/Write ▼	Pre-Sales Consultant ▼
Hudson,Tucker	🔍	Read/Write ▼	Read/Write ▼	Read/Write ▼	Account Manager ▼
	🔍	Read/Write ▼	Read Only ▼	Read/Write ▼	--None-- ▼
		Read/Write ▼	Read Only ▼	Read/Write ▼	--None-- ▼

salesforce.com: New Account Team Members

[Save] [Save & More] [Cancel]

Displaying an account's opportunities

Over the course of managing an account, you will hopefully uncover specific opportunities to sell them your products or services. You can use the Opportunity related list to quickly perform the following tasks:

✔ Stay aware of all the open opportunities that you and your team are pursuing on an account.

✔ Add new opportunities and link them automatically to the account.

✔ Edit and delete opportunity records with a single click.

✔ Gauge the progress of an account by quickly seeing all open and closed opportunities at their various sales stages and amounts.

See Chapter 9 for the scoop on adding, editing, and managing opportunities.

Viewing cases

Account health is much more than measuring the growth of sales for a customer. After selling, sales reps want to stay informed of customer service issues so that they can continue to keep their customers satisfied, resolve issues early, and receive warnings about potential landmines. Use the Cases related list to view all the open and closed customer service cases that relate to an account.

Associating partners

If you work for a company that depends heavily on partners for the success of your marketing, sales, or service efforts, the Partners related list might be the answer to your problems. This feature is very useful in multi-tier selling models where you work with partners that could include resellers, distributors, and so on to drive your business. For example, if you team with consulting companies like Accenture in order to sell or deliver services to end customers, the Partners related list would help you track both Accenture and related end customers.

To link a partner account to a customer account, go to the customer account and follow these steps:

1. **Click New next to the Partners related list.**

   A Partners page appears.

2. **Type the name of the account for your partner in the first Partner field and click the Lookup icon.**

   A dialog box appears with your search results.

3. **If you find the correct account, select it by clicking the link with your partner's name.**

   If your search doesn't find the partner, refine your search or click New to create an account record for your partner (see the "Adding new accounts" section earlier this chapter). Then select it. After you select the partner, the pop up disappears, and the Partner field is filled in.

   The New button located next to the search tool on a Lookup dialog box appears only if your company has enabled Quick Create. When you click the New button, a pop-up window appears where you can create an account with minimal fields. If you don't have this feature, you have to create the partner account through the standard method first.

4. **Select the correct role from the Role drop-down list.**

   If the right role for your partner doesn't appear, advise your system administrator to edit the partner roles.

5. **Repeat Steps 2 through 4 to associate multiple partners to the account and click Save when done.**

   The Account detail page reappears, and your selections are displayed under the Partner related list. Notice that if you click the partner link to go to the partner account, the customer account now appears on its Partners related list.

Reviewing contracts

After your account has committed to buying from you, your job is probably just beginning. How do you manage the paperwork and approval process? Where can your sales team keep an eye on important contract details so that business doesn't fall through the cracks? By using the Contracts related list, you can stay up to speed on important dates and the statuses of critical paperwork for an account.

Maintaining Your Account Database

The more you use salesforce.com for account management, the more important it will be to maintain over time.

In the following sections, I show you simple tools for keeping your account database up to date.

Merging duplicate records

Try as you might, the best sales reps and teams still create duplicate account records. For example, you're a new business rep and you create and manage an account record for General Electric. Unbeknownst to you, an account manager in the cubicle right next to you has been tracking all his customer activity on an account called GE. Three months later, you both might have logged multiple activities, contacts, and other records. Do you throw up your hands in despair and continue working in with independent records, delete your friend's record, or fight it out? Salesforce.com's merge tool for accounts can help you avoid the loss of friendship and data.

To merge accounts, follow these steps:

1. **Click the Accounts Tab to go to the Accounts home page.**

2. **Under the Tools section, click the Merge Accounts link.**

   Step 1 of the Merge My Accounts tool appears.

3. **Type the names of the accounts that need to be merged and click the Find Accounts button.**

   A search results page appears with a list of records.

4. **Select the check boxes for a maximum of three records to be merged, and then click Next.**

   The Step 2 page of the tool appears with a side-by-side comparison of the selected account records.

5. **Compare the information and click the radio buttons to select the values that you want to retain, as shown in Figure 5-10.**

   At the top of each column, you can also choose to keep all the values from one record by clicking the Select All link.

6. **When you finish reviewing, click the Merge button.**

   You see a pop-up window prompting you to verify that you want to perform the merge. After clicking OK, the account record reappears. Any records from related lists are kept.

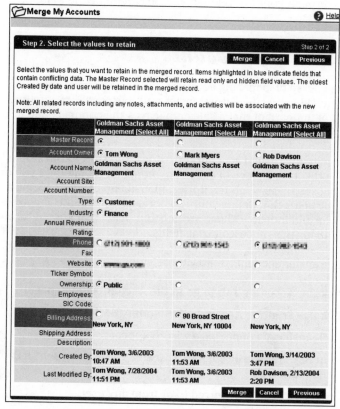

Figure 5-10:
Selecting
values while
merging
duplicate
accounts.

Deleting account records

If you find that you (or a subordinate) own accounts that need to be deleted, you can delete them one at a time by using the Delete button on the account records. The one caveat here is that some companies remove your permission to delete accounts altogether. If this is the case or you want to delete many accounts at one time, consult with your system administrator and see Chapter 19 for details on mass deletion. System administrators are the only users in your company who have the ability to mass delete records. (Kind of startling to realize that geeks have all the power, isn't it?)

When deleting records, remember that you're also deleting associated records. So if you're deleting an account, you could potentially be removing contacts, activities, opportunities, and other records that were linked to the account. You can rectify a mistakenly deleted record within 30 days of your deletion through your Recycle Bin, but be careful before deleting records.

Transferring accounts

Over the course of managing accounts and sales people, you will probably need to quickly and efficiently transfer multiple accounts at a time. For example, it's not unheard of that a sales rep leaves the company and accounts need to be moved immediately to someone else.

If you commonly realign account territories, salesforce.com's transfer tools can make this task a piece of cake. Depending on the method you or your company uses to carve up territories, plan ahead by customizing and then populating fields that define your territories. For example, if you segment by market cap and industry, those are account fields that should be filled in. See Chapter 18 for tips on customizing fields.

To mass transfer accounts, follow these steps:

1. **Click the Accounts Tab to go to the Accounts home page.**

2. **Click the Transfer Accounts link under the Tools section.**

   The Transfer Accounts page wizard appears.

3. **Fill in the Transfer From and Transfer To fields. (Use the Lookup icons as needed.)**

   Accounts can be transferred to or from any user.

4. **Specify the search criteria in the drop-down lists and fields.**

For example, if you want to transfer accounts located in California to a new rep, you could use Billing State contains California, CA as your search criteria (as shown in Figure 5-11).

5. **Click the Find button.**

   Figure 5-11 shows an example of using the transfer wizard. The search results appear at the bottom of the resulting page.

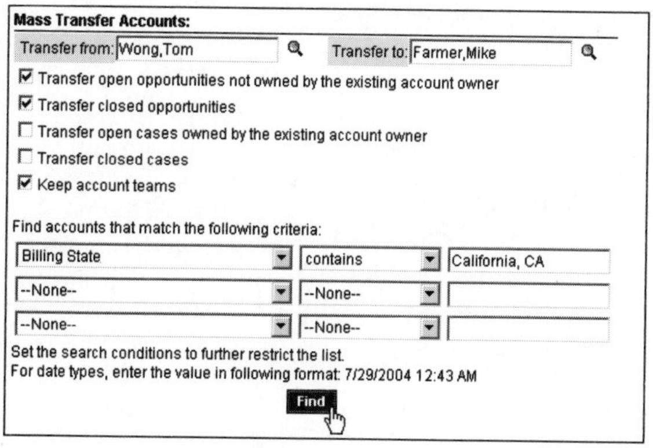

Mass Transfer Accounts:

Transfer from: Wong,Tom   🔍   Transfer to: Farmer,Mike   🔍

☑ Transfer open opportunities not owned by the existing account owner
☑ Transfer closed opportunities
☐ Transfer open cases owned by the existing account owner
☐ Transfer closed cases
☑ Keep account teams

Find accounts that match the following criteria:

Billing State ▾	contains ▾	California, CA
--None-- ▾	--None-- ▾	
--None-- ▾	--None-- ▾	

Set the search conditions to further restrict the list.
For date types, enter the value in following format: 7/29/2004 12:43 AM

[Find]

Figure 5-11:
Filling out
the transfer
wizard.

6. **Select check boxes in the Action column to select all or a portion of the accounts for transfer, and then click the Transfer button to complete the process.**

   The Mass Transfer Accounts page reappears minus the records that you transferred.

Chapter 6

Developing Contacts

- -

- -

*I*f you've been selling for more than a few years, I bet you've got a big ole Rolodex overflowing with business contacts, and it sits on the corner of your desk next to the phone. And if you're just starting out, I'm sure you wish you had one. Run your hands through the cards — feels pretty good, huh? But how much do you know about those contacts? Where do you keep track of the personal and business information that you've collected throughout the years? How many of those business cards are outdated because the contacts have moved, been promoted, or changed companies?

Salesforce.com enables you to plan, manage, and capture all the important interactions that you normally have with your prospects and customers. Just imagine the value that keeping this shared information in one place will have for you and your teams.

By using the Contacts section in salesforce.com, you can effectively keep all of your most important contacts together in one place, easily link them with the accounts they work for, gain insight into the relationships between contacts, and capture the critical personal drivers of each contact that is so key to your selling success.

In this chapter, I discuss how to use salesforce.com for your contact management needs. You also find out how to build your contact database by adding information directly or by importing your existing files. Later in the chapter, I describe how to organize your contacts lists so that you can quickly find the people you want to talk to. I also show you how to maintain the integrity of your contact data by editing contact records, merging duplicate records, and deleting old records. These tasks allow you to start putting your contacts to work for you.

Understanding the Contact Record

The *contact record* is the collection of fields that consists of the information on a person you do business with. Unlike a business card in your Rolodex or a lead record in salesforce.com, however, a contact is linked to an account. Like other records, the contact record has only two modes: an *Edit* mode where you can modify fields, and a *Saved* mode where you can view the fields and the contact's *related lists* (which are located below the fields).

A contact record comes preconfigured with approximately 22 fields commonly used for contact management. The exact number is not important because your company will probably add or subtract fields based on the way you want to track your contacts. Most of the standard fields are self-explanatory, but in the following list, I highlight a few fields that are less obvious:

- ✔ **Contact Owner:** The person in your organization who owns the contact. A contact has only one owner, although many users can still collaborate on a contact.

- ✔ **Reports To:** This lookup field on the contact record allows you to organize your contacts hierarchically.

- ✔ **Lead Source:** Use this drop-down list to define where you originated the contact.

- ✔ **Email Opt Out:** This check box reminds you whether a contact should or should not be e-mailed.

- ✔ **Do Not Call:** This check box reminds you whether a contact can or cannot be called.

- ✔ **Last Stay-in-Touch Request Date:** If you send out Stay-in-Touch e-mails, this field displays the last time a request was sent to the contact.

- ✔ **Last Stay-Touch Save Date:** This date field reflects the last time a request was returned and merged.

Privacy is a big issue with companies and the selling tactics they employ. Nothing damages a customer relationship more than a contact who is contacted when they have asked not to be. To protect your contacts' privacy, be diligent about Email Opt Out and Do Not Call fields. And users in your company should always check the contact record before calling or marketing to a contact.

Customizing Contact Information

If you complete the standard fields, you'll never have trouble knowing where to reach your contacts . . . whether they'll take your call is another question.

Think about all the personal or professional information that you commonly collect on your best contacts. For example, if Michael Jordan were my client, I might like to know that he loves golf, fine cigars, and has a wife and three kids. And he's always driven to be number one.

Ask yourself these questions as you customize your contact record:

- ✔ What professional information is important in your business (for example, prior employers or associations)?
- ✔ What personal information can help you build a better relationship?
- ✔ How do you evaluate the strength of your relationship with the contact?
- ✔ What probing questions do you commonly ask all contacts? (For example, what are their current initiatives and business pains?)

I always advise keeping it simple, but if any specific fields are missing, write them down and seek out your system administrator. (See Chapter 18 for the how-to details on building fields and other design tricks.) Because sales force.com can help you remember important details about your contacts, you can use that information to build better relationships.

Precision target marketing

A leading telecommunications provider wanted to improve the coordination between sales efforts and marketing programs. Over the course of a year, the provider's marketing department planned numerous campaigns that included direct marketing, tradeshows, customer case studies, client outings, and so on. In the past, marketing managers wasted substantial time trying to extract contact information form the sales teams. By customizing the contact record to collect important personal and business information and then training sales reps to update custom fields on contacts in salesforce.com, the company has realized substantial savings in time and better productivity in targeted marketing programs.

Entering and Updating Your Contacts

Your contact database is only as good as the information inside, so sales force.com has multiple ways for you to get your contacts into the system. You can either start from scratch and manually create new contact records, or if you already have contacts on a spreadsheet or in another tool, you can use salesforce.com's simple wizard to import your contacts within minutes. In this section, I discuss quick and simple ways to get started and how to update records.

Taking a shortcut: Quick Create

The Quick Create tool for contacts is located in the lower-left corner of the Contacts home page. The Quick Create tool is the easiest way to enter contacts manually because you bypass the majority of fields on the contact record. In fact, you have to complete only one required field to add a contact: Last Name.

To begin adding contacts with the Quick Create tool, click the Contacts tab, find the tool on the sidebar, and follow these steps:

1. **Click in a field and type the appropriate information.**

   Complete the five fields shown in Figure 6-1. Notice that the Last Name field is marked with an asterisk to signify that it's a required field.

2. **In the Account field, click the Lookup icon to find the account to which you want to link the contact.**

   A pop-up window with your search results appears.

3. **Select the correct account by clicking the name of the company listed.**

   The pop-up window disappears, and the Account field is filled in with your selection.

4. **When you're done, click Save.**

   The Contacts home page reappears. Below the Quick Create tool, you can click a link to go to the new contact record.

The Quick Create tool is the fastest way to manually enter a contact. Use it if you want to create records first and plan to build them out later. If you commonly track additional contact information from the start, check out the following section.

Quick Create

First Name

Marc

Last Name *

Benioff

Account

salesforce.com 🔍

Phone

[phone number]

Email

Save

Figure 6-1:
Adding a
contact with
the Quick
Create tool.

Entering new contacts

Because contacts belong to accounts, the best, most reliable way to create contact records is by starting from the relevant account detail page. From the account detail page, you can then add a contact using either the New Contact link on the taskbar or the New button on the Contacts related list. The result is the same in both situations, and you automatically pre-fill the Account lookup field. By doing this, you can always find your contact, and your contact's activities will be listed on the overall account detail page.

To create contacts by using the best practice, follow these steps:

1. **Search for the account and on the Search Results page, click the appropriate Account Name link.**

   The Account detail page appears.

   If you're really in a rush, you can use the Quick Create tool located in the sidebar of the Contacts home page to create contact records. Simply complete the five fields displayed (First Name, Last Name, Account, Phone, and Email) and click Save. Remember to click the Lookup icon on the Account field to link your contact to the right account. Although you might save a couple seconds, you run the risk of not filling out other contact fields that might be important to (or even required by) your company. If you don't see the tool, your company has probably chosen wisely to hide it.

2. **Click the New button on the Contacts related list, as shown in Figure 6-2.**

   The Edit mode of a new contact appears. (See Figure 6-3 for an example of a new record being created.)

3. **Fill in the fields as much as you can or as required.**

   Notice that the Account field is prefilled with the account you were working from.

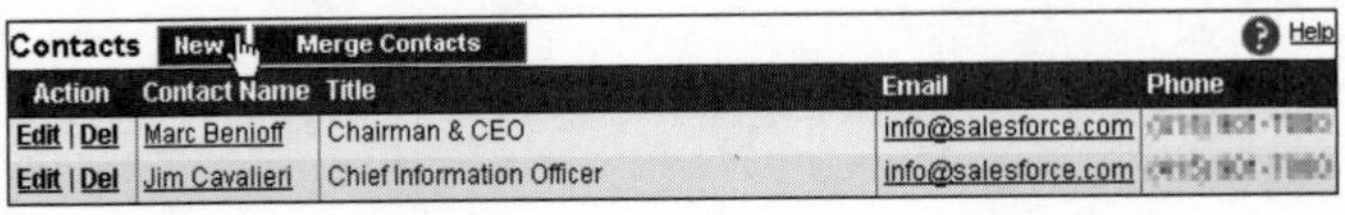

Figure 6-2:
The
Contacts
related list
on the
account
record
page.

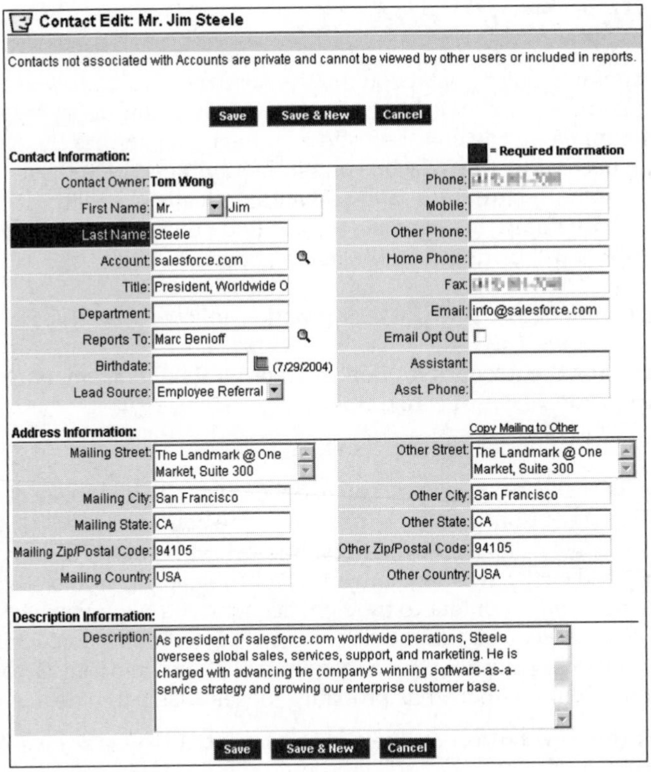

Figure 6-3:
Completing
fields on a
contact
record.

4. **When you're done, click one of the following buttons:**

   • **Save:** After you click the Save button, the Contact detail page appears, and from here you can click the Edit button whenever you need to modify information on the record.

   • **Save & New:** Clicking this button saves the current contact info and automatically opens a new, blank contact record in Edit mode.

If you're the type of person who wants all your contacts, both personal and professional, in one place, keep personal contacts Private by not linking them to an account. To do this, click the New Contact link on the taskbar from any page, and from there, just be sure to leave the Account field blank.

Importing your contacts and accounts

If you already have contact lists from another database (for example, Excel or ACT!), you can use the Import Wizards to create multiple contact records in salesforce.com, and you'll be done in no time. The Import Wizards are located in the Tools sections of either the Accounts or Contacts home page.

When you're importing accounts, you can choose to just import companies with their associated information, or you have the option of importing companies with related contacts in one action. Whichever route you take really depends on your existing data and what you want in salesforce.com.

To import your contacts and accounts automatically, follow these steps:

1. **On either the Accounts or Contacts home page, click the Import My Accounts and Contacts link at the bottom of the page under Tools.**

   The Import Wizard for My Contacts page appears, which includes four steps for importing records plus helpful hints.

   If you're a system administrator for salesforce.com, you can click the Import My Organizations Accounts and Contacts link, which allows you to import substantially more records at one time with different owners. If you're an administrator, that link also appears under the Tools sections of the Accounts or Contacts home pages. What's the big deal? Most users can import 500 records at a time, but if you're a system administrator, you can import 50,000 at a time and leap over tall buildings in a single bound.

2. **In your existing contact tool or file, compare your current fields with the fields in salesforce.com.**

   If you can map all the information to fields in salesforce.com, move to the next step. If not, add fields to the account or contact records by customizing salesforce.com. (See Chapter 18 for simple instructions on adding fields.)

3. **Export your file.**

   You might have contacts and accounts in an existing database, such as ACT, Goldmine, Microsoft Access, or Outlook. Most systems like these have simple tools for exporting data into various formats. Select the records and the fields that you want. Then export the file and save it in a .csv (comma separated value) format. If your accounts are already in spreadsheet format, such as Excel, just resave the file in .csv format.

4. Review and prepare your data.

Refine your accounts and contacts before bringing them into salesforce.com or clean them up after the import . . . it's up to you. Some sales reps prefer to make changes on a spreadsheet first because they're more accustomed to spreadsheets. See Figure 6-4 for a detailed example of a format that is ideal for the Import Wizard.

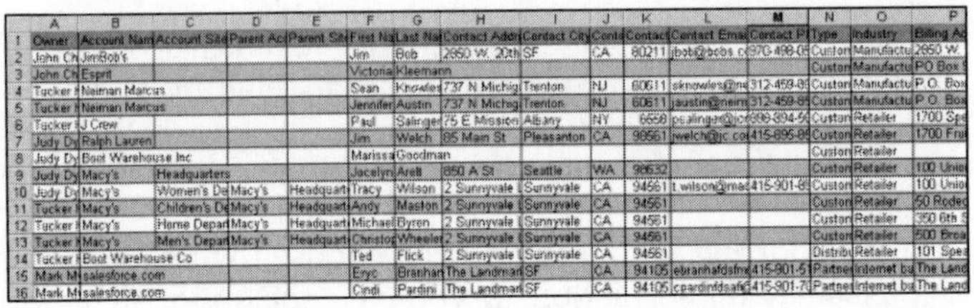

	A	B	C	D	E	F	G	H	I	J	K	L	M	N	O	P
1	Owner	Account Nam	Account Site	Parent Ac	Parent Site	First Na	Last Na	Contact Addr	Contact City	Conta	Contact	Contact Ema	Contact Ph	Type	Industry	Billing Ad
2	John Ch	JimBob's				Jim	Bob	2850 W. 20th	SF	CA	80211	jbob@bobs.c	970-498-05	Custom	Manufactu	2850 W.
3	John Ch	Esprit				Victoria	Kleemann							Custom	Manufactu	PO Box
4	Tucker	Neiman Marcus				Sean	Knowles	737 N Michig	Trenton	NJ	60611	sknowles@ne	312-459-85	Custom	Manufactu	P.O. Box
5	Tucker	Neiman Marcus				Jennifer	Austin	737 N Michig	Trenton	NJ	60611	jaustin@neim	312-459-85	Custom	Manufactu	P.O. Box
6	Tucker	J Crew				Paul	Salinger	75 E Mission	Albany	NY	6658	psalinger@jc	999-394-56	Custom	Retailer	1700 Spe
7	Judy Dy	Ralph Lauren				Jim	Welch	85 Main St	Pleasanton	CA	98561	jwelch@jc.co	415-895-85	Custom	Retailer	1700 Fru
8	Judy Dy	Boot Warehouse Inc				Marissa	Goodman							Custom	Retailer	
9	Judy Dy	Macy's	Headquarters			Jacelyn	Arell	850 A St	Seattle	WA	98632			Custom	Retailer	100 Unio
10	Judy Dy	Macy's	Women's De	Macy's	Headquart	Tracy	Wilson	2 Sunnyvale	Sunnyvale	CA	94561	t.wilson@mac	415-901-85	Custom	Retailer	100 Unio
11	Tucker	Macy's	Children's De	Macy's	Headquart	Andy	Maston	2 Sunnyvale	Sunnyvale	CA	94561			Custom	Retailer	50 Rodeo
12	Tucker	Macy's	Home Depar	Macy's	Headquart	Michael	Byren	2 Sunnyvale	Sunnyvale	CA	94561			Custom	Retailer	350 6th S
13	Tucker	Macy's	Men's Depar	Macy's	Headquart	Christop	Wheeler	2 Sunnyvale	Sunnyvale	CA	94561			Custom	Retailer	500 Broa
14	Tucker	Boot Warehouse Co				Ted	Flick	2 Sunnyvale	Sunnyvale	CA	94561			Distribu	Retailer	101 Spea
15	Mark M	salesforce.com				Eryc	Branham	The Landmar	SF	CA	94105	ebranhafdsfre	415-901-51	Partner	Internet bu	The Land
16	Mark M	salesforce.com				Cindi	Pardini	The Landmar	SF	CA	94105	cpardinfdsaf	415-901-70	Partner	Internet bu	The Land

Figure 6-4: Preparing your import file.

When preparing your import file, keep these points in mind:

- Enter your column headers in the first row. I recommend renaming column headers to be consistent with the field names in salesforce.com. For example, the Company field from Outlook could be renamed as Account Name.
- If you're importing data for your entire company, add a column for Record Owner to signify who should own the record in salesforce.com. Otherwise, as the person importing, you will own all the records from the file.
- If you sell to different locations of a company (for example Sony in Tokyo versus Sony in New York), you might want to add a column for Account Site and update the rows on your file to reflect the different sites.
- You can link accounts in the import file by adding columns for Parent Account and Parent Site and filling in fields as necessary to reflect the hierarchy.
- Make sure that a Type column exists and that fields are filled to correspond to the types of companies you'll be tracking (customers, partners, prospects, competitors, and so on.)
- If your file has more than 500 rows, divide the master file into smaller files to fit the Import Wizard's size limitation. You have to repeat the Import Wizard for each of the smaller files.
- If you're importing contacts and accounts at the same time, you might want to add a col0umn for the billing address fields if it's different from the contact's mailing address.

For more hints on importing, click the Help and Training link and check out the Training and Support information in salesforce.com by searching under the keyword *Importing.*

5. **After preparing the file, click the Start the Import Wizard link.**

   The Select the Source step appears in a new window.

6. **Use the radio buttons to select the source and click Next.**

   You can't go wrong if you select the Other Data Source option, but the other choices are helpful because salesforce.com knows how Outlook and ACT fields map to salesforce.com. When you click Next, the Upload the File step appears.

7. **Click the Browse button, shown in Figure 6-5, to locate and select your import file and click Next.**

   If you've already prepared your file, then you've done the heavy lifting on this page. Note that salesforce.com has prefilled the character coding of your file based on your Company Profile. If you have questions on this, ask your administrator. When you click Next, the Map Contact Fields step appears.

Figure 6-5:
Loading the
contact file.

5. Now choose the file to import into salesforce.com:
   Note: It may take a few minutes to upload your file, depending on the file size and your connection speed
   C:\Documents and Settings\twong\My Documents\S [Browse...]

When you're figuring out how to import data into salesforce.com, I recommend testing an import with five or so accounts first just to make sure that you know what you're doing. After importing the test data, review your new account records to make sure that they contain all the information you want brought in. Delete the test records, refine your import file if necessary, and then run through the final import.

8. **Map the contact fields between your file and salesforce.com and when you're done, click Next.**

   If you're importing only accounts, skip this step. Otherwise, all you have to do is go through the fields and use the drop-down lists to select the corresponding field from the file that you're importing that maps to the salesforce.com field, as shown in Figure 6-6. (The fields are repeatedly listed in each of the drop-down lists.) When you click Next, the Map Contact Phone and Address Fields step appears.

   Mapping fields is simply the process by which you associate a field from one database to a field in another database so your data appears in the right fields. For example, if you were importing your contacts from MS Outlook, you would want data from the field called Company in Outlook to map to the field called Account Name in salesforce.com.

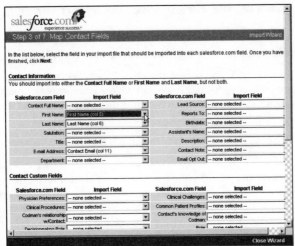

Figure 6-6:
Mapping
the contact
fields.

9. **Map the contact address and phone fields and click Next.**

   Again, you can skip this if you are just importing accounts. Map the relevant fields just as you did in the prior step. When you click Next, the Map the Account Fields step appears.

10. **Map the account fields and when you're done, click Next.**

    This is just like the previous steps with two exceptions: now you're mapping account data, and you can choose to update existing data. For example, if you already had an account record for Microsoft Corporation in salesforce.com, and you had entered no other information but the Account Name, you could update that existing account record with the Import Wizard and avoid creating a duplicate account record. So if you want to append existing records, select the check box at the top of this page. When you click Next, the Map Account Phone and Address Fields step appears.

11. **Map account phone and address fields and click Next.**

    No surprises here; by now, you should be a pro. When you click Next, the Map Extra Import Fields step appears.

12. **Map any extra import fields, and when you're satisfied, click the Import Now button.**

    This step basically warns you about problems with the data or lets you know of fields that haven't been mapped. If you discover an error, you can either click the Back button and refine your mapping or even close the wizard so you can improve your import file. You might have to start over, but at least you avoid importing bad or incomplete data. When you click Import Now, an Importing page appears to confirm that your import is in process.

13. **Click the Finish button and later check the records that you imported.**

    You're sent an e-mail from salesforce.com after your file has been successfully imported. To check your import, click the Accounts tab to go to your Accounts home page. Use the Key Accounts section drop-down list to select the Recently Created option, and you see a list of the accounts that were recently created. Click the link for an account that you just imported and double-check that the information is accurate.

If you're importing both accounts and contacts, scroll down on an applicable account to its Contacts related list and verify that all the right contacts are linked from your import file. Click into a specific contact record and check to see that the information matches your import file.

Updating contact fields

As you work with your contacts, you might need to modify their contact information. To update a contact, follow these steps:

1. **Type the name of your contact in the Search tool and click Search.**

   A Search results page appears.

2. **Click the desired Contact Name link.**

   The contact detail page appears.

3. **Click the Edit button at the top of the contact record.**

   The contact record appears in Edit mode.

4. **Update the fields as necessary and click Save.**

   The contact detail page reappears. Notice that the fields you edited have been changed.

Cloning an existing contact

If you want to add a contact that is similar to an existing record, cloning can save you key strokes and time. To clone a contact, go to the existing contact and follow these steps:

1. **Click the Clone button at the top or bottom of the contact record.**

   A new contact record in Edit mode appears. Notice that all the information is identical to the previous record.

2. **Edit the information on the new contact record where appropriate.**

   Pay attention to what is prefilled, because you want to avoid inaccurate information on the new contact record.

3. **When you're done, click Save.**

   Notice that you created a new contact without altering your existing contact. To verify this, simply click the link to the older contact, which you can find in the Recent Items section on the sidebar.

Organizing Your Contacts

When you have all or a portion of your contacts entered in salesforce.com, you can begin to organize them to suit the way you sell.

In this section, I show you how you can use views and other tools from the Contacts home page to provide greater focus for you and your sales teams. I also show you an important feature of the contact record that lets you build powerful organizational charts (also called *org* charts) for contacts of an account. Then for even more robust organization of your account information, flip to Chapter 18 for specifics on how to use standard and custom contact reports.

Leveraging contact views

A *contact view* is a list of contacts that match certain criteria. When you select a view, you're basically specifying criteria to limit the results that you get back. The advantage of using a view versus searching is that you can use the view over and over again. For example, if you like to send out a card on a contact's birthday, you could benefit from a preset view for this month's birthdays.

The Contacts home page comes with six predefined views:

- **All Contacts** provides you a list of all the contact records entered into salesforce.com. Depending on the way your company has set up your security model, you might not see this view or its results.

- **Birthdays This Month** does in fact generate a list of contacts whose birthdays land in the current month (assuming you collect that information).

- **My Active Contacts** shows you a list of your contacts that have been modified in the last month. You might find this view helpful to gauge whether you're staying in touch with contacts regularly.

- **New This Week** generates a list of contacts that have been created since the beginning of the week.

✔ **New Last Week** shows you contacts records created last week.

✔ **Recently Viewed Accounts** lets you look at a list of contacts that you have recently viewed.

To try out a predefined view, do the following:

1. On the Contacts home page, open the Contact Views drop-down list.

The six options that I discuss in the preceding list appear and maybe some other choices that have already been created for you.

2. Select the New This Week option.

The New This Week list opens, as shown in Figure 6-7.

If you have already entered or imported contact records, a list page appears of your contacts that have been modified in the last month. Notice that salesforce.com lays the list out with six standard columns that correspond to commonly used contact fields plus an Action column so you can quickly modify a record.

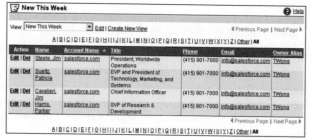

Figure 6-7:
Viewing a
preset
contact list.

3. Click a column header to re-sort the list page.

For example, if you click the Title column header, the list page re-sorts by title in alphabetical order.

4. Open the record for any contact by clicking a link in the Name column.

A Contact detail page appears.

5. Click the Back button on your browser, and then click the Edit button on the same row as the contact you just clicked.

The contact record appears in Edit mode, and you can make changes to the data.

Creating custom contact views

If you want special lists for the way that you track your contacts, I recommend building custom views. For example, if you sell medical equipment, and you like to call your contacts who are dentists once a month, you can create a view to simplify your work.

To build a view from scratch, follow these simple steps:

1. **On the Contacts home page next to the Contact Views drop-down list, click the Create New View link.**

   The Create a View page appears.

2. **Enter a name for the view in the Name field.**

   For example, you might call the view Dentist Call Plan.

3. **Under the What to Search In step, click the radio button to search All Contacts or just My Contacts.**

4. **Under the Search Criteria step, as shown in Figure 6-8, select your search criteria.**

   A basic criteria query is made up of three elements:

   • **Field:** The first box is a drop-down list of all the fields on the contact record. An example is the Title field.

   • **Operator:** The second box is a drop-down list of operators for your search. That sounds complicated, but it's easier than you think. Taking the dentist example, you should select Equals from the drop-down list.

   • **Value:** In the third field, you type the value that you want in the search. In my made-up example, you type **dentist** because you want a call list for dentists.

5. **Under the Select Columns step, use the drop-down lists to choose the information that you want displayed.**

   While salesforce.com's preset views display columns for common fields like Phone and Email, you can select any of up to 11 contact fields to be displayed on your custom list page.

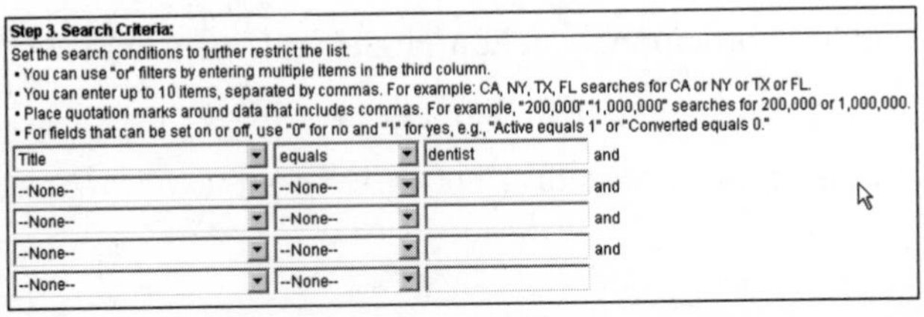

Figure 6-8:
Setting
criteria for
a custom
contact
view.

Step 3. Search Criteria:
Set the search conditions to further restrict the list.
• You can use "or" filters by entering multiple items in the third column.
• You can enter up to 10 items, separated by commas. For example: CA, NY, TX, FL searches for CA or NY or TX or FL.
• Place quotation marks around data that includes commas. For example, "200,000","1,000,000" searches for 200,000 or 1,000,000.
• For fields that can be set on or off, use "0" for no and "1" for yes, e.g., "Active equals 1" or "Converted equals 0."

Title	equals	dentist	and
--None--	--None--		and
--None--	--None--		and
--None--	--None--		and
--None--	--None--		

6. **Decide whether you want others to see your custom view.**

   Your decision is made simple if you aren't given an option. Otherwise, select the appropriate option if you want to share your view with others. If you choose limited accessibility, use the two list boxes to select which users will see the view.

7. **When you're done, click Save.**

   A new view appears based on your custom view criteria. If you don't get all the results you anticipated, you might want to double-check and refine the search criteria. For example, if your list should include oral hygienists, you would have to modify the criteria to include this group of doctors.

Using the Key Contacts Section

When you click to the Contacts home page, just below the views you also see a Key Contacts section. This section comes with three columns (Contact Name, Account Name, and Phone), and these columns can't be modified. You can see as few as 10 items and as many as 25 items at a time by clicking the Show . . . Items link at the bottom of the table.

Use the Select One drop-down list at the top-right corner of the table to quickly get to contact records based on the following:

- ✔ **Recently Created** are the last 10 or 25 contacts you created.
- ✔ **Recently Modified** are the last 10 or 25 contacts you modified.
- ✔ **Recently Viewed** are the last 10 or 25 contacts you looked at.

Reassigning contact ownership

You might find that after you create contacts in salesforce.com, you need to transfer them to the right people. Part of organizing your contacts is getting them into the right hands. You might even want to reassign contacts to your-self because a contact wasn't properly given to you. (I know this never, *ever* happens in your company.)

To reassign a contact, go to the contact record and follow these steps:

1. **Next to the Contact Owner field, click the Change link.**

   The link is in square brackets. The Change Contact Owner page appears.

2. Select the user you're assigning the contact to.

By clicking the check box on the page, you can choose to notify the recipient with an e-mail, as shown in Figure 6-9.

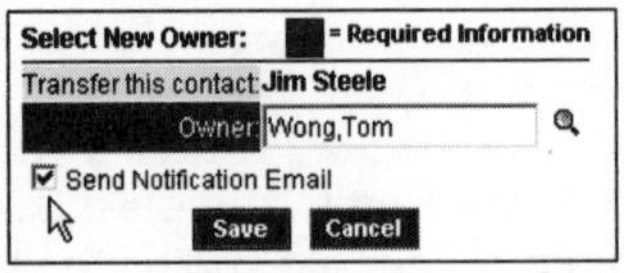

Figure 6-9:
Reassigning
a contact.

Select New Owner: ■ = Required Information	
Transfer this contact: **Jim Steele**	
Owner: Wong,Tom 🔍	
☑ Send Notification Email	
Save Cancel	

3. When you're done, click Save.

The contact record reappears. Notice that the Contact Owner field has changed to the assigned user.

Developing Organizational Charts

Having 20 contacts associated with an account is great, but you might not be any further along in understanding the pecking order. In practice, sales reps have been building organizational charts (or *org* charts) to strategize on accounts since someone thought up org charts, but often the charts resided on whiteboards and PowerPoint presentations. (And whiteboards are tough to lug around.) With the org chart feature in salesforce.com, you can quickly define the reporting structure for your contacts and use that to more easily identify your relationship with your customer.

To build an org chart, follow these steps:

1. Add all the contacts for an account.

See the earlier section on adding contacts in this chapter for details on adding records.

2. Go to a contact record for a person low in the totem pole and click the Edit button.

The record appears in Edit mode.

3. In the Reports To field, type the name of the contact's boss and click the Lookup icon.

A pop-up window with search results appears.

4. Select the correct contact or refine your search until you can select the right contact.

The pop-up window disappears, and the Reports To field is prefilled with the selected contact, as shown in Figure 6-10.

5. When you're done, click Save.

The Contact detail page appears.

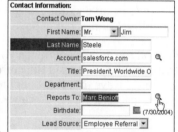

Figure 6-10:
Selecting
the boss.

6. To display the hierarchy, as shown in Figure 6-11, click the View Org Chart link to the right of the Reports To field on the contact record.

An Org Chart list page appears, and like other lists, you can click a link to go a specific contact.

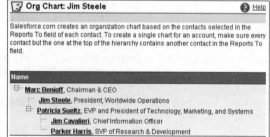

Figure 6-11:
Viewing the
org chart.

Some sales reps run into certain challenges based on the way they create the org charts in salesforce.com. One such challenge is gaps; you just might not know or even care about the entire reporting structure. By getting creative and building placeholder contacts, you can avoid pitfalls. For example, if you sell to both the business and the technology side of a customer, create a contact record called IT Organization and another called Business Organization, and then align your contacts accordingly. This technique also works well for *orphans,* where you know one contact in a department and don't want to leave the contact out of the org chart for the entire account.

Performing Actions with Contact Related Lists

Fields on a contact record are useful for capturing the essential contact information on a person. But where do you track and review all the interactions you've had with a contact? To add, edit, delete and generally keep track of this detail, use the related lists located on the Contact detail page.

Turn to Chapter 7 if you want to find out all the wonderful things you can do with related lists to keep track of activities with people and the companies they work for. But if you're looking for typical ways that sales people use contact related lists, go over the following list of features you can find in the contact related lists:

✔ If you want to track, edit, or close your pending activities for a contact, use the Open Activities related list. From there, you can click the New Task button to set up a to-do item or click the New Event button to schedule a calendared activity. See Chapter 7 for the how-to details on these activities.

✔ If you want to view what has happened with a contact to date, review the Activity History related list. Sales reps commonly use Log a Call to capture details for a call taking place or after the fact. Go to Chapter 8 for the ins and outs of sending e-mail and see the end of this chapter for details on requesting updates. Flip over to Chapter 12 for the wonderful world of using mail merge to generate sales documents.

✔ Ever wonder whether your contact is paying attention? If you send HTML e-mail from salesforce.com, you can use the HTML Email related list to see how your contact is responding to your e-mail. From this list you can send an e-mail, find out whether your contact is viewing your e-mail, and how soon he or she is viewing it.

✔ If you want to keep notes or store attachments that relate to a contact, use the Notes & Attachments related list. Click the New Note button and you can jot down your comments and even keep them private if you want. Click the Attach File button and you can store important documents like Confidentiality Agreements or contact resumes.

✔ If a contact brings you a new deal, you can click the New button on the Opportunities related list and automatically associate your contact to the opportunity record. See Chapter 9 for details on creating opportunities.

✔ To keep track of or edit your contact's participation in campaigns, use the Campaign History related list. And if you want a contact to be part of an active campaign, click the Add Campaign button. For example, if marketing is sending out invites to a customer event, using the Add Campaign feature could be an efficient way to add a contact to the list of recipients. See Chapter 13 for more tips on campaigns.

Maintaining Your Contact Database

Your once-tiny Rolodex is now a gigantic contact database because you're managing more contacts and covering more territory. However, don't let those large piles of data walk all over you. You've got to show that data who's boss. In the next section, I show you simple tools for keeping your contact database in line and up to date.

Merging duplicate records

Try as you might, sometimes you will come across duplicate contact records in the system. Rather than deleting one or several of the duplicate records and potentially losing valuable information that was captured on those records, salesforce.com makes merging contact records easy.

To merge contact records, you must be the Contact Owner of the records, the Contact Owner's manager (that is, the Contact Owner must be subordinate to you in the Role Hierarchy), or a system administrator.

To merge contacts, go to the account record that has a duplicate contact and follow these steps:

1. **On the Contact related list, click the Merge Contacts button, as shown in Figure 6-12.**

   Step 1 of the Merge My Contacts tool appears.

Figure 6-12: Merging duplicate contacts.

Contacts	New	Merge Contacts			❷ Help
Action	Contact Name	Title		Email	Phone
Edit | Del	Marc Benioff	Chairman & CEO		info@salesforce.com	(415) 901-7000
Edit | Del	Jim Cavalieri	Chief Information Officer		info@salesforce.com	(415) 901-7000
Edit | Del	Parker Harris	SVP of Research & Development		info@salesforce.com	(415) 901-7000
Edit | Del	Jim Steele	President, Worldwide Operations		info@salesforce.com	(415) 901-7000
Edit | Del	James Steele	President, Worldwide Operations		info@salesforce.com	(415) 901-7000
Edit | Del	Patricia Sueltz	EVP and President of Technology, Marketing, and Systems		info@salesforce.com	(415) 901-7000

2. **Type the name of contact that needs to be merged and click the Find Contacts button.**

   A search results page appears with a list of records.

3. **Select a maximum of three records to be merged and click Next.**

   In salesforce.com, you can merge only three records at a time. The Step 2 page of the tool appears with a side-by-side comparison of the selected contact records.

4. Compare the information and select the radio buttons for the values that you want to retain, as shown in Figure 6-13.

At the top of each column, you can also choose to keep all the values from one record by clicking the Select All link.

5. When you finish reviewing, click Merge.

You see a pop-up window prompting you to verify that you want to perform the merge. After clicking OK, the contact record reappears, and associated records from related lists are now linked on the single contact record.

Deleting contact records

To delete contacts, you can eliminate them one by one using the Delete button on a record. If you need to delete multiple contact records at a time, see your system administrator and see Chapter 19 for details on mass deleting records.

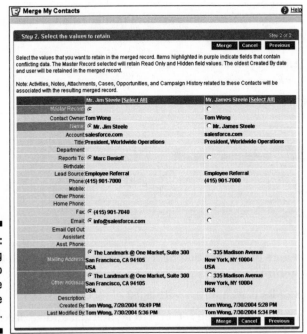

Figure 6-13: Selecting values to merge duplicate contacts.

Staying in Touch

If you're in an industry where contacts constantly move around, or if you simply struggle to keep your contact data accurate, send update reminders through salesforce.com. You can send request update e-mails one at a time or send a mass e-mail.

Your contact receives a personalized e-mail with a friendly request to review his contact information and reply to you with any changes. Many sales reps find this an easy and noninvasive way to stay in touch with their contacts.

Requesting a single update

If you want to send it to just one person at a time, you can use the Request Update button located on a contact record. To send a Stay-in-Touch request, go to a contact record and follow these steps:

1. **Click the Request Update button, which appears at the top of the contact record and by the Activity History related list.**

   A Send Stay-in-Touch Request page appears.

2. **Personalize the Subject, Note, and Signature fields as you would any e-mail, as shown in Figure 6-14.**

   If the default wording is fine, you don't need to make any changes.

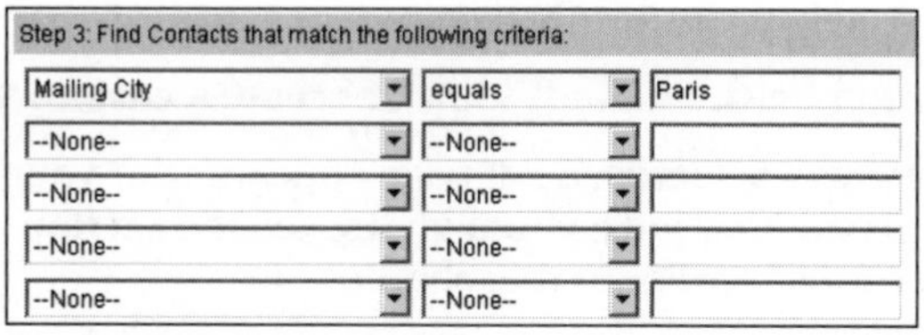

Figure 6-14:
You can personalize the Stay-in-Touch message.

Step 3: Find Contacts that match the following criteria:		
Mailing City	equals	Paris
--None--	--None--	
--None--	--None--	
--None--	--None--	
--None--	--None--	

3. **Review the contact information in the Current Information box.**

   This data comes directly from your contact record, but make sure that it doesn't contain any sensitive information. (For example, the Assistant field is included as part of the fields in the Current Information box. So sending the contact information like "Mary the gatekeeper" would be a Bad Idea.)

4. **Click the Check Spelling button if you're a bad speller. In fact, click it even if you're a good speller, just in case.**

   A pop-up window appears with a simple spelling tool.

5. **When you're satisfied, click the Send button.**

   Your contact soon receives an e-mail with the content you prepared.

 When sending Stay-in-Touch requests for the first time, I highly recommend sending a test to your own e-mail address first. Doing so is easy, as long as you create a contact with your e-mail address. By taking this extra step and walking through the process, you stand a better chance of keeping the customer happy.

Sending a mass Stay-in-Touch

You can send a Stay-in-Touch request to multiple contacts at the same time. You can save a lot of time if you have many contacts, but the tradeoff is that you're not given the option to highly personalize the Note field to each contact.

To send a mass Stay-in-Touch to a group of contacts, go the Contacts home page and follow these instructions:

1. **Click the Mass Stay-in-Touch link in the Tools section.**

   A Recipient Selection page appears with a View drop-down list. The drop-down list defaults to My Stale Contacts. The criteria for this is your contacts that haven't been created in the last 90 days nor received a update request e-mail in the last 90 days.

2. **Click the Go button on the default view or create a custom view.**

   Based on the view you selected, a list page appears with your search results. For details on creating custom views, see the section "Creating custom contact views," earlier in this chapter.

3. **Select the check boxes in the Action column to specify the contacts that you want to include in the mass e-mail, and then click Next.**

   A Review and Confirm page appears with the form e-mail that will be sent to the selected recipients.

4. **Review the e-mail and click Send.**

   A confirmation page appears with a summary of the number of e-mails sent.

Updating records based on replies

After you send out a Stay-in-Touch e-mail, sit back and wait for replies. If you receive a reply, follow these steps to update salesforce.com:

1. **Open the e-mail and review the information.**

2. **If the contact made changes, click the Update Now button.**

   A Stay-in-Touch window appears with a record that looks like a contact record in Edit mode.

3. **Review the contact's information, and then click the Accept Changes button or Reject Changes button as you see fit.**

   The contact record appears in Saved mode and the changes appear in the relevant fields.

Chapter 7

Managing Activities

*A*ctivities in salesforce.com are scheduled calendar events and tasks. In many ways, salesforce.com's events and tasks are just like the activities you use in Microsoft Outlook and Lotus Notes. You can schedule events on your calendar, invite people to meetings, book a conference room, and add tasks to your to-do lists so that you don't forget to get things done. (You can even synchronize salesforce.com with Outlook, so that you don't have to input activities twice; see the final section of this chapter.)

However, salesforce.com takes activities further: Events and tasks can easily be linked to other related records such as accounts, contacts, and so on. So you can view activities both in the context of a relevant item (for example, all activities that relate to an account) or as a standalone from your calendar and task lists in the comfort and convenience of your home page. And if you're a manager, salesforce.com allows you to stay up to speed on your users and how they're spending their time.

By managing activities in salesforce.com, you'll find you can better coordinate with your team, quickly assess what's going on in your accounts, and focus on the next steps to close deals or solve issues.

In this chapter, I first show you how to schedule events and create tasks. I cover how to find and view activities, both from your home page and from specific record pages like accounts and opportunities. You also discover how to synchronize activities with Microsoft Outlook.

Looking Over Activities

Activities are used in salesforce.com to track all the significant tasks and events involved in acquiring, selling, and servicing customers. Think about all the actions that you and your teams currently perform to accomplish your job — meetings, calls, e-mails, letters — and imagine the value of all that information in one place at your fingertips. You can do this in salesforce.com, and you can easily link those activities together in an organized fashion.

Salesforce.com features six types of activities that are accessible from the Open Activities and Activity History related lists displayed on many of the major records including accounts, contacts, leads, opportunities, and cases. In this chapter, I focus on events and tasks, but in the following list, I provide a brief explanation of the various activity records you can track in salesforce.com:

- **Task:** Essentially a to-do. It is an activity that needs to be completed but it doesn't have a specific time, date, or duration associated to it. For example, if you know you are supposed to follow up with a contact with a written letter, you would create a task such as Send Letter.

- **Event:** A calendared activity. An event has a scheduled time, date, and duration associated to it. Examples of common events are Meetings, Conference Calls, and Tradeshows.

- **Log a Call:** Essentially a task record of a completed call. Use Log a Call during or after a call to make sure that you capture important details. For example, use it when a contact calls you and you want to record comments or outcomes from the discussion.

- **Mail Merge:** Logs an activity for a document that you've mail merged. With Mail Merge, you can quickly merge common Microsoft Word templates with customer information and track those activities in salesforce.com. (See Chapter 8 for quick tips on how to build merge documents and log the activity in salesforce.com.)

- **Send an Email:** Logs an activity for an e-mail that you send to a contact or a lead. You can send e-mails from salesforce.com or from Microsoft Outlook and capture that information directly inside salesforce.com. (See Chapter 8 for all the tips and tricks on using e-mail in salesforce.com to impress and keep track of your customers.)

- **Request Update:** Sends a personalized reminder to your contact with a request to update personal contact information. By using this activity, you can keep your customer database accurate and up to date. (See Chapter 6 for details on requesting updates either automatically, *en masse*, or on the spur of the moment.)

Creating Activities

Before you can begin managing your time or activities in salesforce.com, you need to know the easiest and most reliable way to add events and tasks.

Creating an event

When you want to schedule activities that have a particular place, time, and duration, use event records. By doing this, you and your sales teams can keep better track of your calendars.

You can create an event from your home page, its calendar views, or the Open Activity related list of a record. The best method to choose often depends on what you're doing. If you're carving out meetings on a day, add events from your calendar's Day View. If you're working on a customer deal, you might create the event from an opportunity record. The end result is the same.

If you're just getting accustomed to filling out records in salesforce.com, create events from the record that's most directly associated to the event. By doing this, many of the lookup fields are prefilled for you. So when you save, you ensure that you can find the activity quickly because it's linked to all the right records

To create an event from a relevant record (such as the contact or account record) follow these steps:

1. **Enter names in the sidebar Search for the record you want to link the event to and click the Search button.**

   For example, if you wanted to schedule a meeting about an account, you would search for the account name. When you click Search, a Search results page appears.

2. **Click a link in the Name column to go to the record you want.**

   The record's detail page appears.

3. **Scroll down to the Open Activities related list on the page and click the New Event button, as shown in Figure 7-1.**

   A New Event page appears. If you created this event from a relevant record, notice that the name of the person or the related record is pre-filled for you.

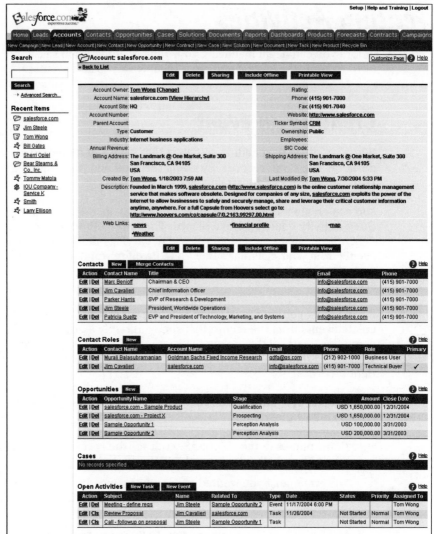

Figure 7-1:
Creating
an event.

4. Fill in the relevant fields.

Pay close attention to the required fields highlighted in red. Depending on your company's customization, your event record might differ from the standard, but here are tips on some of the standard fields:

• **Assigned To** defaults to you. Use the Lookup icon to assign the event to another user.

- **Subject** is the event's subject and appears on the calendar. Click the green pick box icon. A pop-up window appears with a list of your company's event types. When you click a selection, the window closes and your selection appears in the Subject field. Next to your selection, add a brief description. For example, you might click the Meeting link and then type **-Define Requirements** to explain the event's purpose.

- **Related To** drop-down lists and lookup fields. The standard event record shows two drop-down lists that you can use to link the event with relevant records, as highlighted in Figure 7-2. The first drop-down list relates to a person — a contact or lead. The second relates to other types of records — an account, opportunity, or case. First select the type of record, and then use the associated Lookup icon, to select the desired record. For example, if you selected Opportunity from the second drop-down list, you could use the Lookup icon to find a specific opportunity.

  Use the Related To fields on activities and you'll rarely have problems finding the activity later. For example, if you sell through channel partners, you might associate a meeting with a partner contact but you might relate the meeting to an end-customer account. When you save the event, it appears on the related lists of both records.

- **Location** provides you or other invitees with a hint on where the event will take place. Examples include conference rooms, cities, and office locations.

- **Time** lets you specify the time. You can use basic shorthand and avoid unnecessary key strokes. For example, type **9a** for 9:00 a.m. or **2p** for 2:00 p.m.

Figure 7-2: Linking the event to related records.

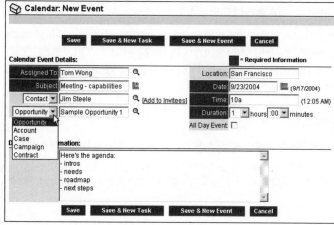

5. **When you're done, click Save.**

The page you started from reappears, and the event displays under the Open Activities related list for the associated records. The event also appears on the home page of the user assigned to the event.

Alternatively, click the Save & New Event or Save & New Task button if you want to immediately create another activity. A new activity record appears in Edit mode.

Inviting others

If you want to invite other people or resources to your event, use the Invite Others feature. You can check users' availability and send e-mail invitations to users, contacts, and leads.

To invite others, follow the steps in the "Creating an event" section, but perform these additional steps before you save the event:

1. **Click the Add Invitees button at the bottom of the New Event page.**

A pop-up window appears with a search box and list to select names.

If you're inviting only the lead or contact, instead of clicking the Add Invitees button, simply click the Add to Invitees link in brackets next to the Name field on the New Event page.

2. **Use the Search Within drop-down list to select the people or resources to invite.**

You have a choice of Users, Leads, Contacts, or Resources.

3. **If necessary, type a name in the search field to locate the person or resource, and then click Go.**

For example, if you're inviting a user, type the user's last name. When you click Go, a list of possible invitees appears in the window.

4. **Select the check boxes for your invitees and click the Insert Selected button, as shown in Figure 7-3.**

Your selections are displayed under the Selected List in the pop-up window.

5. **Repeat Steps 2 through 4 as needed until you finalize your Selected List.**

For example, you might need to repeat this three times if you're inviting contacts, users, and a public resource such as a conference room.

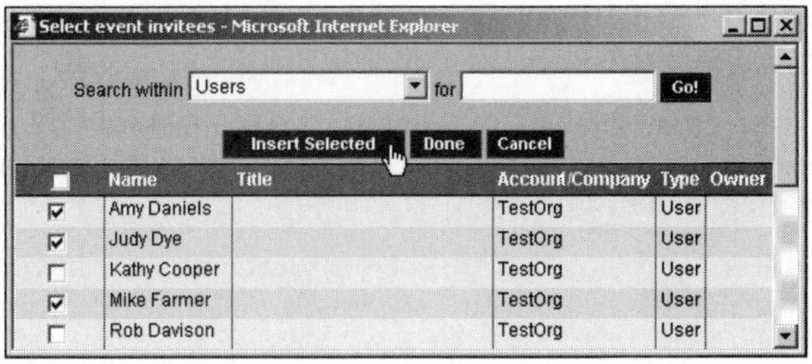

Figure 7-3:
Selecting
invitees.

Surprise! Yes, you can use salesforce.com to book public resources such as conference rooms. If your company has set this up for you, use the Search Within drop-down list to select Resources, and then click Go. Then follow the same steps just as if the resource were a user in order to book the resource.

6. **When you're finished, click Done.**

   The window closes, and the New Event page reappears with a list of your invitees and their availability on the date and time you scheduled. In circumstances where users or resources appear unavailable for the time you chose, adjust the Date and/or Time fields. If you change the date field, the page reappears to reflect the availability of invitees

7. **Review your event record and when you're done, click Save.**

   The page you started from reappears, e-mail invitations are automatically sent to invitees, and the event appears on users' calendars.

You can invite people to an event only if your records have valid e-mail addresses in salesforce.com. This applies to users, leads, and contacts.

Scheduling group events

By using your Multi User calendar view from your home page, you can schedule group events. The advantage here is that you can check availability immediately and drill down to the details if you have the right permissions.

To schedule a group event using the Multi User calendar view, follow these steps:

1. **Go to the home page and click the Multi User View icon (which looks like two people . . . sort of) below the calendar.**

   An All Users calendar page appears with a list of users and their apparent availability for the current day.

2. **In the calendar header, use the calendar icon or the Previous or Next directional arrows to select the date for the group event.**

The Multi User View changes to reflect times blocked out by users, as shown in the example in Figure 7-4. Grey means free, blue means busy, and purple means out of office.

With the Winter '05 release, in Multi User View, you now have the option of scheduling a group event from Day, Week, or Month Calendar Views.

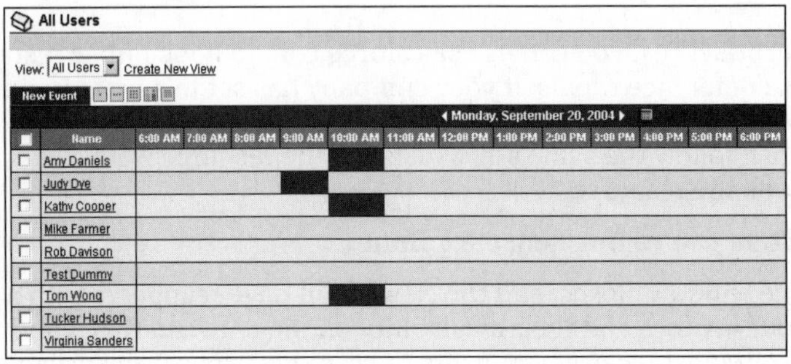

Figure 7-4:
Looking at
availability.

3. **Place your cursor over a blue area and click.**

Depending on sharing rules and user level permissions, an event record appears corresponding to the blocked-out period. You might also be able to see details in a ToolTip just by hovering your mouse over an area. If neither of these features happen, see Chapter 17 for details on configuring sharing and inquire with your administrator.

4. **Select the check boxes in the left column to select users to be invited, and then click the New Event button at the top of the calendar.**

A New Event page appears, and at the bottom of the page, invitees are listed.

5. **Complete the fields for creating an event and click Save.**

The Multi User View reappears and is modified to reflect the new group event.

Creating a task

Some sales reps refer to tasks as *ticklers;* others call them reminders or to-dos. Whatever your favorite term, use task records when you want to remind yourself or someone else of an activity that needs to get done.

You can create a task from the My Tasks section of your home page or from the taskbar on any page within salesforce.com. I find that I use both methods depending on whether I'm planning out my week or strategizing about a particular account, contact, or other record.

To create a task from the relevant record, follow these steps:

1. **Enter a name in the sidebar Search tool for the record you want to link the task to and click the Search button.**

   For example, if you want to set a task to review a proposal that related to an opportunity, search for the opportunity name. After you click Search, a Search results page appears.

2. **Click a link in the Name column to go to the record you want.**

   The record's detail page appears.

3. **Click the New Task link on the taskbar or click the New Task button on the Open Activities related list of a record, as shown in Figure 7-5.**

   Either way, the result is the same. A New Task page appears.

When creating tasks, go to the record that the task is most directly related to before adding the task. By taking this path, you ensure that your task is easy to find because it's automatically associated to the correct record and its account. For example, if I was creating a task to follow up on a letter to a contact, I would most likely add the task from the contact record.

4. **Fill in the relevant fields, as shown in Figure 7-6.**

   Like the event record, your fields may vary but here are some tips on adding a task:

   - **Assigned To** defaults to you. Use the Lookup icon to assign the task to another user.

   - **Subject** is the task's subject and appears on the My Tasks section of the Assigned To's home page. Click the green pick box icon. A pop-up window appears with a list of your company's activity types. When you click a selection, the window closes and your selection appears in the Subject field. Next to your selection, add a brief description. For example, you might click the Send Letter link and then type **-Introduction** to explain the task's purpose.

   - **Related To** drop-down lists and lookup fields. The standard activity record shows two drop-down lists to link the task with relevant records similar to the event fields shown previously in Figure 7-3. First select the type of record, and then use the associated Lookup icon to select the desired record.

   - **Priority** denotes the task's importance. High priority tasks display an exclamation mark (!) next to the activity on the assigned user's home page.

   - **Status** defines the status of the task.

- **Due Date:** This is the date you expect the task to be completed. This is typically an optional field but an important one, if you want to make sure a task gets done when it's supposed to. Click the Pick A Date icon and in the pop-up calendar window, select a date.

5. **Select the Send Email Notification check box if you want to notify the user that you're assigning this new task to.**

   You can't guarantee that every user will log in to salesforce.com daily, so e-mail notifications are an effective way to make sure that tasks are delivered to the right people in a timely fashion.

6. **When you're done, click Save.**

   The page you started from reappears, and the task displays under the Open Activities related list for the associated records. The task also appears in the My Tasks section of the home page of the user who is assigned to the task.

Always link your tasks with the relevant records in salesforce.com. Otherwise, you run the risk of losing valuable customer information that might have been captured in that task.

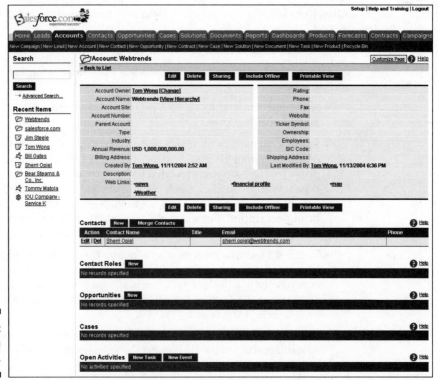

Figure 7-5: Creating a new task.

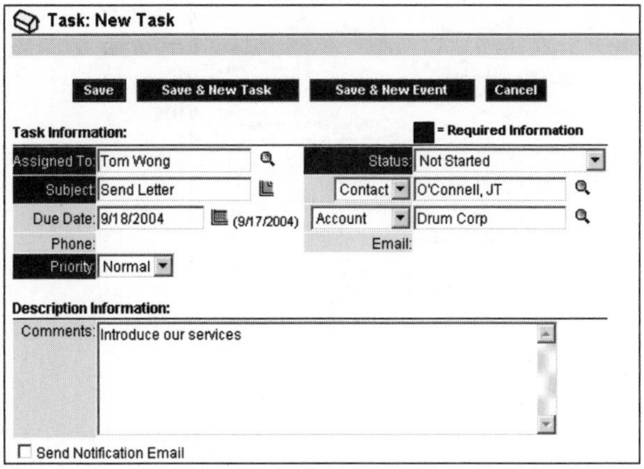

Task: New Task

| Save | Save & New Task | Save & New Event | Cancel |

Task Information:
■ = Required Information

Assigned To: Tom Wong

Status: Not Started

Subject: Send Letter

Contact ▼ O'Connell, JT

Due Date: 9/18/2004 (9/17/2004)

Account ▼ Drum Corp

Phone:

Email:

Priority: Normal ▼

Description Information:

Comments: Introduce our services

☐ Send Notification Email

Figure 7-6:
Completing
task fields.

Logging a call

Sometimes you perform a task and just want to log the activity after the fact. For example, a contact calls you on the phone or you get stopped in the coffee room by your boss to talk about a customer issue. In these situations, instead of creating a task and then completing it, use the Log a Call feature.

When you click the Log A Call button, you are simply creating a task record with a Completed Activity Status. To log a call, go to the record that the call relates to (an account or lead record, for example), and follow these steps:

1. **Scroll down to the Activity History related list and click the Log A Call button.**

   The Log a Call page appears with fields for a completed task at the top of the page and fields for a follow-up activity at the bottom of the page.

2. **Fill out or modify any of the fields to log the call.**

   Notice that the Status field is preset to Completed, as shown in Figure 7-7.

3. **If applicable, add another related task by filling out the fields below the Schedule Follow Up Task header.**

   Although certain fields are labeled as required, the follow-up task is optional.

4. **Select the Send Notification Email check boxes and click Save when you're finished.**

   The detail page that you started from reappears. Notice that the call record is displayed under the Activity History related list. If you set up a new follow-up task, that record appears under the Open Activities related list.

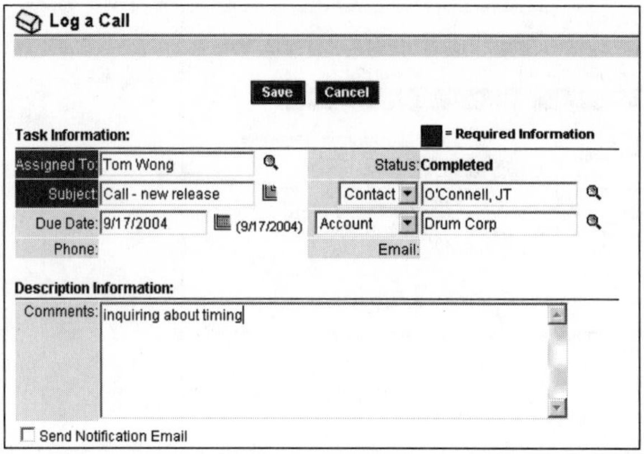

Figure 7-7:
Logging
a call.

Organizing and Viewing Activities

You can view your activities from the home page and a specific record's Open Activities or Activity History related lists. If you're planning out your calendar, use the home page. If you're working from a particular account, contact, or other item, you can get better context on pertinent activities from the related lists on the record.

After you create (or are assigned to) activities, you probably want to view them so that you can prioritize and complete them. In this section, I show you how to look at Open Activities and Activity History related lists and also the default views from your home page. Then I show you how to view other people's calendars, one user at a time or collectively. Then for more customized tracking of activities, see Chapter 15 on building activity reports.

Viewing activities from a record's related lists

If you're planning around a specific record such as a contact or opportunity, you can view linked activities from the Open Activities and Activity History related lists located on a detail page, as shown in Figure 7-8.

The two related lists work hand in hand. An event record automatically moves from the Open Activities related list to the Activity History related list when the scheduled date and time passes. A task record remains on the Open Activities related list until its Status is changed to Completed; then the record appears on the Activity History related list.

The two related lists work hand in hand. An event record automatically moves from the Open Activities related list to the Activity History related list when the scheduled date and time passes. A task record remains on the Open Activities related list until its Status is changed to Completed.

Viewing group calendars with Multi User View

When you click the Multi User View icon, you can now monitor the activities of multiple users. For example, if you're a sales manager, you might want to know what your team is doing. And you can add group events as well. See the "Scheduling group events" section in this chapter for details.

To try out the Multi User View, go to your home page and do this:

1. **Click the Multi User View icon beneath the calendar.**

   A group calendar page appears with a list of users and their apparent availability for the current day. Notice that the Multi User View and Day View icons appear green; that lets you know you're in that view.

2. **Click the Month View icon.**

   A group calendar page appears for the current month.

3. **Click the Week View icon.**

   No surprise; a group calendar appears for the current week.

4. **Click the Create New View link next to the View drop-down list.**

   With this feature, you can add a new view to look at a subset of users. Were you to save the view, it would be added to the View drop-down list for you and potentially other users. See Chapter 2 for details on customizing views.

5. **Click the Back button to return to the previous page.**

6. **Click the Single User View icon.**

   Your calendar reappears for the current week. Notice that the Single User View and Week View icons now appear green.

Looking at other users' calendars from the home page

If you want to look at another user's calendar or if your company has public calendars in salesforce.com for group events, you can view this information with just a few simple clicks.

To change your view to another user's or a public calendar, go to the home page and follow these steps:

1. **Click the Day, Week, or Month View calendar icon.**

   A calendar view page appears.

2. **Click the Change link, as shown in Figure 7-10.**

   A pop-up window appears with a search box and a list of users.

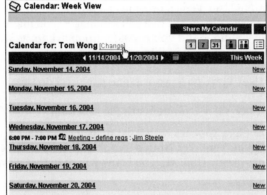

Figure 7-10: Viewing other users' or public calendars.

3. **Use the Search drop-down list to select either User Calendars or Public Calendars and Resources.**

   You can bypass this step if you already see the user you want displayed on the list. Otherwise, the list changes to reflect your search criteria.

4. **As needed, refine your search by typing words in the Search field and clicking Go.**

   If your company has many users in salesforce.com, you might find your selection quicker by searching rather than scrolling. Notice that the list changes based on the search criteria.

5. **Select the desired calendar by clicking the appropriate link.**

   The pop-up window disappears and a calendar view page reappears for the selected user or public calendar.

Sharing your calendar

If you weren't able to view another user's or a public calendar, your system administrator might have set up certain restrictions to limit this visibility across the entire company. See Chapter 17 for the how-to details on modifying your system-wide sharing rules. If you and your sales teams still want to share information on your calendars, you can still do this by granting sharing with the Share My Calendar feature, which I cover in the following steps.

To make your calendar available to another user, go to the home page and follow these steps:

1. **Click the Day, Week, or Month View calendar icon.**

   A calendar view page appears.

2. **Click the Share My Calendar button at the top of the page.**

   A Sharing Detail page appears with a User and Group Sharing list.

3. **Review instructions and click the Add button at the top of the list.**

   A New Sharing page appears.

4. **Specify the sharing by selecting the appropriate people in the Currently Not Shared column and adding them to the New Sharing column, as shown in Figure 7-11.**

   The Currently Not Shared drop-down list allows you to specify by user, role, or group. (See Chapter 17 for details on sharing.)

5. **Select an option from the Calendar Access drop-down list, and then click Save.**

   The Sharing Detail page reappears, and the list is modified to reflect the new sharing.

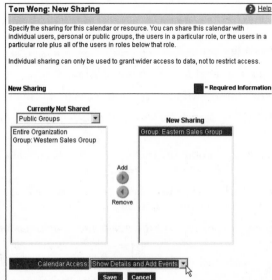

Figure 7-11:
Sharing
your
calendar.

Updating Activities

Things happen: Meetings get cancelled, and small tasks suddenly become big priorities. With salesforce.com, you can perform many of the actions that a normal time-management tool would allow you to do, including delegating activities to other users, rescheduling, editing information, deleting records, and so on.

You can do the following basic functions from buttons at the top of an activity record:

- ✔ Click **Edit** if you want to update information. Update the record and make sure you save.
- ✔ Click **Delete** if you want to delete the record. A pop-up window appears for you to confirm the deletion.
- ✔ Click **Create a Follow Up Task** if you need to generate a related task. A New Task page opens prefilled with information from the prior record.
- ✔ Click **Create a Follow Up Event** if you want to schedule a related meeting. A New Event page appears prefilled with information from the prior record.

Assigning activities

Sometimes you'll create activities and decide to delegate them later. Salesforce.com lets you easily reassign tasks and events and notify users of assignments.

To assign an activity, open the activity record and follow these steps:

1. **Click the Edit button.**

2. **Click the Lookup icon next to the Assigned To field.**

   A pop-up window appears with a list of your salesforce.com users.

3. **Use the Search field to search for the user or select the user from the list.**

   After you've made a selection, the pop-up window disappears and your selection appears in the Assigned To field.

4. **Select the Send Email Notification check box if you want to alert the user (see Figure 7-12), and then click Save.**

   The activity record reappears, and the Assigned To field has been modified.

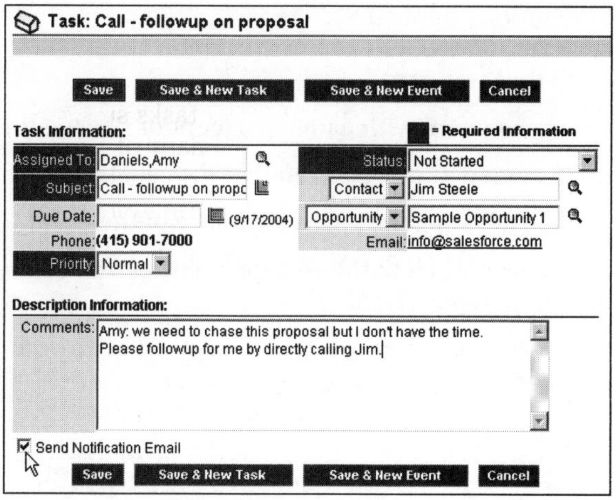

Task: Call - followup on proposal

Save | Save & New Task | Save & New Event | Cancel

Task Information: ■ = Required Information

Assigned To Daniels,Amy
Subject Call - followup on propc
Due Date: (9/17/2004)
Phone: **(415) 901-7000**
Priority Normal

Status: Not Started
Contact Jim Steele
Opportunity Sample Opportunity 1
Email: info@salesforce.com

Description Information:

Comments: Amy: we need to chase this proposal but I don't have the time. Please followup for me by directly calling Jim.

☑ Send Notification Email

Save | Save & New Task | Save & New Event | Cancel

Figure 7-12: Notifying a user of an assigned activity.

Completing a task

When you're done with a task, you'll want to gladly get it off the list of things to do. You can do this from your home page or from the Open Activities related list where the task link is displayed.

To complete a task, follow these steps:

1. **If you're viewing the task from an Open Activities related list, click the Cls link next to the task. If you're doing this from the home page, click the X link in the Completed column.**

   Both links create the same result: The task appears in Edit mode, and the Status field has been changed to Completed. (Your company might have your own terminology for the Completed status.)

2. **Type any last changes and click Save.**

   Some reps update the Comments field if they have relevant updates. The detail page reappears, and the completed task now appears under the Activity History related list.

Replying to an event invitation

When you're invited to an event, you have the ability to accept or decline the invitation. And you can keep a running track of who has responded directly inside salesforce.com.

To respond to an invitation, follow these steps:

1. **Open the e-mail that was sent to you.**

   An e-mail message appears with a link to accept or decline the meeting.

2. **Click the link to review the event details.**

   A Group Meeting page appears with a summary of the event.

3. **Type any comments and click the Accept Meeting or Decline Meeting button, as shown in Figure 7-13.**

   The home page reappears, and a notification e-mail with your response is sent to the inviter.

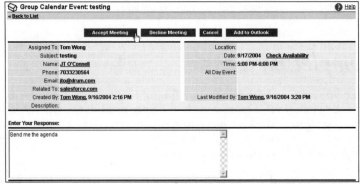

Figure 7-13: Responding to an invitation.

If you're an Outlook user, salesforce.com makes it easy for you to add events from salesforce.com directly into your Outlook calendar. To do this, go to an event record and click the Add to Outlook button. An Outlook dialog box appears. Review the information and click the Save & Close button. Then check your Outlook Calendar for the meeting record.

Displaying and updating a group event

A group event page appears slightly different from an event record because it displays related lists. These related lists show you the status of your invitations, as shown in Figure 7-14.

If you need to update a group event, follow these steps:

1. **Go to your calendar on the home page and open a group event record.**

   You can easily spot these meetings from your calendar because the item has a group icon, as shown in the Month View in Figure 7-14. When you click the name of the event, the Group Calendar Event page appears.

Figure 7-14:
Spotting a
group event
on the
calendar.

2. **Review the status of your invitations on the related lists.**

   For those listed under Not Decided, click the Send An Email link if you
   would like to send a reminder e-mail before rescheduling.

3. **Click the Edit button if you want to reschedule.**

   The event record appears in Edit mode.

4. **Modify the date and time if necessary.**

   If you change the date, the page reappears to reflect the availability of
   invitees.

5. **Click the Remove link if you want to eliminate certain individuals
   from the event.**

6. **Select an Email Option to notify individuals.**

7. **When done, click the Save or Save & Send Update button.**

   The group event page reappears, and if you clicked the Save & Update
   button, notifications are sent.

Synchronizing with Microsoft Outlook

With salesforce.com, you can synchronize your activities with Microsoft
Outlook so you don't have to input information twice.

To synchronize your tasks and events, follow these steps.

1. **Click the Intellisync for Salesforce.com icon on your desktop.**

   If you don't see the icon, choose Start⇨Programs. The Intellisync
   window appears. See Chapter 3 for details on installing and configuring
   Intellisync for Microsoft Outlook.

2. **Enter your salesforce.com user name and password.**

3. **Click the Configure button if you want to change your settings for
   tasks, events, or contacts.**

   I highly recommend that you test on a small sample of records if this is
   your first time. Be gentle with them.

4. **When you're ready, click the Synchronize button.**

   A window appears showing the progress of the synchronization.

   If Intellisync identifies conflicting records, a window appears and notifies you. Otherwise, skip to Step 6 of this list.

5. **In the event of conflict resolution, click the Accept or Cancel button to complete the process or click the Details button for more details.**

6. **Check salesforce.com and Outlook to verify the updates.**

Chapter 8

Sending E-Mail

E-mail is a fundamental method for communicating with customers, prospects, and friends. By using e-mail correctly you can manage more sales territory and be responsive to customers. However, by sending e-mail inappropriately you can leave a bad impression or lose a client.

If e-mail is an indispensable part of your business, you and other users can send e-mail from salesforce.com and track the communication history from relevant records like accounts, contacts, opportunities, and cases. This capability is helpful if you inherit a major customer account; you could potentially view all the e-mail interactions from a single account record.

Sending an e-mail is a cinch, and if that were all this chapter covered, I would have summarized it in just one section. But salesforce.com provides additional e-mail tools to help you better sell, service, and wow your customers. In this chapter, I show you all the tricks and best practices for sending a basic e-mail, mass e-mailing, using templates, and tracking responses. Then for Microsoft Outlook users, I show you how you can work in your current e-mail program but still track those messages instantly in salesforce.com.

Understanding E-Mail Fields in Salesforce.com

An e-mail in salesforce.com is an activity record compromising fields for the message and for the people you want to keep in the loop on the message.

The e-mail record comes standard with nine fields that people commonly use when sending e-mail. Here is a brief summary of those fields:

- **To:** The name of the contact or lead to whom the e-mail will be sent. You can enter only one name in this field.
- **From:** This field is automatically filled with the e-mail address of the user.
- **Related To:** Use this field to relate the e-mail to an account, opportunity, contract, campaign, or case record in salesforce.com. By completing this field, the e-mail is stored under the Activity History related list of that record.
- **CC:** The list of e-mail addresses that will be copied on the e-mail.
- **BCC:** The list of e-mail addresses that will be blind copied on the e-mail.
- **Subject:** This is the subject line of the e-mail.
- **Body:** This is the main content of your e-mail. You can type a maximum of 32K of data (which is a very long e-mail).
- **Signature:** Your personal signature that you define in your Personal Setup. See Chapter 3 for details on customizing your e-mail settings. The signature is automatically appended to individual e-mails. You have that option with mass e-mail.
- **Attachment:** You have the ability to attach files up to a maximum of 10MB per e-mail.

Setting Up Your E-Mail

Before you begin e-mailing people from salesforce.com, check out this section. I discuss a couple setup options that can save you time and headaches. In this section, I show you how to personalize your outbound e-mail and how to build personal e-mail templates for common messages that you send to people.

Personalizing your e-mail settings

When you send an e-mail from salesforce.com, the recipient can receive the message just as if you sent the e-mail from your current e-mail program. The e-mail message appears as if it came from your business e-mail address, and you can use a standard signature to go with your message. And if the recipient replies to your e-mail, the e-mail comes right back to your existing inbox. To pull this off, you need to personalize your e-mail settings in salesforce.com.

To set up your e-mail, follow these steps:

1. **Click the Setup link in the top-right corner of salesforce.com.**

   The Personal Setup page appears.

2. **Click the Change Your Outgoing Email Settings link under the Email heading.**

   The My Email Settings page appears in Edit mode, as shown in Figure 8-1.

3. **Modify the two required fields as necessary to specify the outgoing name and the return e-mail address.**

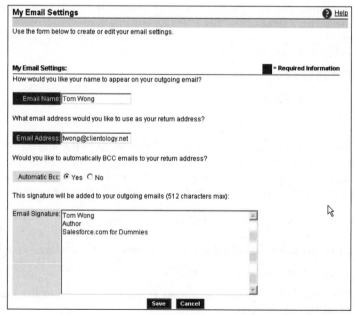

Figure 8-1:
Editing your
e-mail
settings.

4. **Select the Yes radio button if you want to send a blind copy to your existing e-mail inbox.**

   If, for example, you like to keep e-mails in customer folders in your Outlook or Lotus Notes, you don't have to give up this practice.

5. **Modify the Email Signature field.**

   If you're personalizing your e-mail settings for the first time, you might notice a default signature from salesforce.com. This message appears at the bottom of your e-mail in lieu of your signature unless you change it. I would change it.

6. **When you're done, click Save.**

   The Email page under Personal Setup appears, and your settings are modified.

Building personal e-mail templates

Ask your top sales reps about sending e-mail, and they'll probably tell you that they don't re-create the wheel every time they send certain messages to customers. It's a waste of their time, and time is money.

In your standard sales process, you probably send out a variety of e-mails to customers, including

- Letters of introductions
- Thank you notes
- Responses to common objections
- Answers on competition

Although you do need to personalize a message to fit the specific details of a customer, you probably use certain effective phrases and sentences over and over again. Rather than searching for a prior message and cutting and pasting, you can create personal e-mail templates and improve your productivity.

To create a personal template, follow these steps:

1. **Click the Setup link in the top-right corner of salesforce.com.**

   The Personal Setup page appears.

2. **Click the Create or Edit an Email Template link under the Email heading.**

   An Email Templates page appears.

3. **Click the New Template button.**

   Step 1 of the template wizard appears.

4. **Select the radio button for Text, HTML, or Custom to set the type of e-mail you want to create and click Next.**

   Note that the HTML and Custom options are both in HTML; the former uses letterhead and the latter doesn't.

   The next page of the wizard appears, and the content of the page depends on the choice you made. HTML has certain advantages from an appearance and tracking standpoint, but not all e-mail programs can receive HTML e-mail.

   When deciding whether to use HTML or text, consider your customer base. If your contacts or leads are primarily people at work who use Outlook, then HTML will typically work and can leave a stronger impression. Hopefully positive. If you know that you have customers who use old e-mail technology, who use technology that likes to strip out HTML, or who are vehemently opposed to HTML, well then text e-mail is just fine.

5. **If you selected Text in Step 4, complete the template fields provided (see Figure 8-2) and click Save.**

Figure 8-2:
Creating
a text
template.

   Note that you can use the template only after you select the Available for Use check box. After clicking Save, a Text Email Template page for your new template appears in Saved mode with an Attachments related list, which you can use if you want to attach a standard document. If you're only interested in creating text e-mail templates, your work is done.

6. **If you selected either HTML option (HTML or Custom) in Step 4, enter the properties for the e-mail template and click the Save & Next button.**

   If you chose to build your e-mail template with letterhead, you have to select the letterhead and layout by using the drop-down lists provided. After you click the Save & Next button, the Step 3 page of the wizard appears.

   You can create HTML or Custom e-mail templates only if you have profile permission to Edit HTML Templates. For Professional Edition users, only the system administrator or marketing user has this permission. For Enterprise Edition users, you need to have a profile with that permission.

7. **Create the HTML version by typing and formatting the content and copying and pasting merge fields.**

   See Step 5 of this list for the tip on using the merge field tool.

8. **Click Preview to review your work, and when you're done, click the Save & Next button.**

   The Step 4 page of the wizard appears.

9. **Enter the text version of the e-mail template.**

   Some of your customers cannot or choose not to receive HTML e-mails, in which case they would receive the text version. If the message is similar or identical to the HTML version, click the Copy Text from HTML Version button and modify the content as needed. For example, if you created a Custom e-mail template with an embedded drop-down list, its text-only version would display all the drop-down list values. (Imagine a drop-down list for State. A list of 50 states would not be a pretty sight.)

10. **When you're done, click the Save & Done button.**

    An HTML Email Template page for your new template appears in Saved mode with an Attachments related list, which you can use for attaching standard documents.

Sending E-Mail from Salesforce.com

You can send an e-mail to any lead or contact stored in salesforce.com with a valid e-mail address. By sending from salesforce.com, you can ensure that you and your team members can keep track of critical outbound communications to customers and prospects.

Creating and sending e-mail

You can initiate your outbound e-mail from many different records in sales-force.com, including opportunity, account, contract, case, campaign, lead, and contact records. To create and send an e-mail, go to the relevant record and follow these steps:

1. **Click the Send An Email button on the Activity History related list, as shown in Figure 8-3.**

   A Send an Email page appears.

Figure 8-3:
Sending an
e-mail.

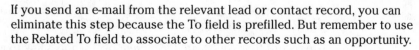

2. **Click the Switch to Text Only link if the message should not be sent in HTML. (In that event only, a dialog box appears to warn you that any HTML formatting will be removed. Click OK and the box disappears and the format is switched.)**

3. **Type the recipient's name in the To field and click the Lookup icon to search for the contact or lead.**

   A pop-up window appears with a search tool and a list of search results.

   If you send an e-mail from the relevant lead or contact record, you can eliminate this step because the To field is prefilled. But remember to use the Related To field to associate to other records such as an opportunity.

4. **Select the correct person by clicking the name or refine your search by modifying the name or using wildcards and click the Go button.**

   When you select the recipient, the pop up disappears and the To field is populated with your selection.

5. **Use the Related To drop-down list to associate the e-mail with the correct type of record, and then click the Lookup icon next to the adjacent field to find the exact record — similar to the process in Steps 3 and 4.**

   Depending on which record you started from, the Related To drop-down list might already be filled.

6. **Click the CC link or the BCC link to copy other contacts or users to the e-mail.**

A pop-up window appears with a drop-down list for co-workers at your company and for contacts of the account, as shown in Figure 8-4.

7. **Select a name in the Contacts list box and use the double arrows to include them as recipients, and when you're done, click Save.**

The pop up disappears, and the CC and BCC fields reflect your selections.

Figure 8-4:
Using the
CC and BCC
fields.

8. **Click in the CC or BCC fields and add additional e-mail addresses as needed.**

Salesforce.com allows you to send e-mails to other people who aren't contacts, leads, or users. Just type the e-mail address directly into this field. The CC and BCC fields have a limit of 2000 characters each, and e-mail addresses can be separated by commas, spaces, semicolons, or new lines.

9. **Complete the Subject and Body fields of the message, and when you're done, click Send.**

The record that you started from reappears, and a link to a copy of your e-mail appears under the Activity History related lists of the records that you linked. (See Chapter 12 for details on using the standard formatting tools.)

Using e-mail templates

In "Building personal e-mail templates" earlier in this chapter, I show you how to create a personalized template. In this section, you find out how to send an e-mail with a template that you've created. First create an e-mail as I describe in the preceding section, and then follow these additional steps before you send it:

1. **Before you modify the Subject and Body fields, click the Select Template button at the top of the page, as shown in Figure 8-5.**

   A pop-up window appears with a list of available templates.

Figure 8-5:
Using an
e-mail
template.

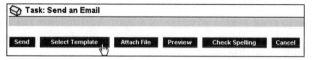

Task: Send an Email

Send | Select Template | Attach File | Preview | Check Spelling | Cancel

2. **Click the Folder drop-down list and select the desired folder.**

   The pop up refreshes with a list of available templates based on your folder selection. For example, you might have constructed personal templates in your personal folder, and the marketing department might have created other folders with templates that are publicly available for use.

3. **Select the desired template by clicking the relevant link in the Name column, as shown in Figure 8-6.**

   The pop up disappears and the page reappears with content based on the template that you selected.

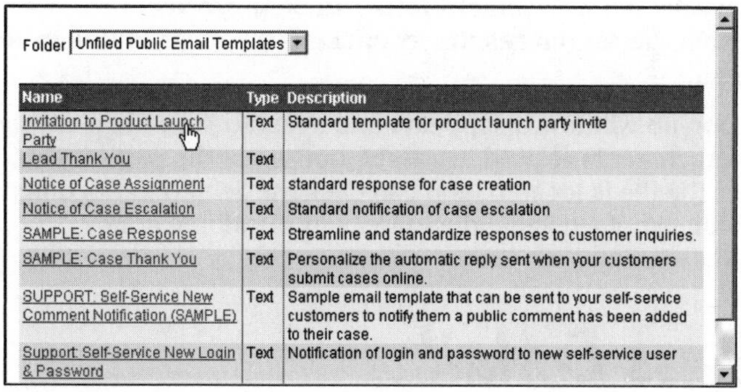

Figure 8-6:
Selecting
the
template.

Folder | Unfiled Public Email Templates ▼

Name	Type	Description
Invitation to Product Launch Party	Text	Standard template for product launch party invite
Lead Thank You	Text	
Notice of Case Assignment	Text	standard response for case creation
Notice of Case Escalation	Text	Standard notification of case escalation
SAMPLE: Case Response	Text	Streamline and standardize responses to customer inquiries.
SAMPLE: Case Thank You	Text	Personalize the automatic reply sent when your customers submit cases online.
SUPPORT: Self-Service New Comment Notification (SAMPLE)	Text	Sample email template that can be sent to your self-service customers to notify them a public comment has been added to their case.
Support: Self-Service New Login & Password	Text	Notification of login and password to new self-service user

4. **Modify the message to further personalize the e-mail, and when you're done, click Send.**

   The record you started from reappears and a link to a copy of your e-mail appears under the Activity History related lists of the records that you linked.

Attaching files to e-mails

You can attach files when sending e-mails from salesforce.com. Salesforce.com can locate files from your computer or from folders stored in the Documents area.

To attach a file to your e-mail, prepare an e-mail as usual (see the earlier section, "Sending E-mail from Salesforce.com"), but before you click Send, follow these additional steps:

1. **Click the Attach File button at the top of the Send an Email page.**

   Alternatively, scroll down the page to the Attachments related list and click the Attach File button. The result is the same. A pop-up window appears.

2. **Use the drop-down list to select the file location, and then click Go.**

   You can attach files located on your computer or in document folders of salesforce.com.

3. **If you selected My Computer in Step 2, browse your computer, attach the file, and click Done.**

   The pop-up window disappears, and a link to your file is displayed under the Attachments related list at the bottom of the page.

4. **If you selected a document folder in Step 2, select the appropriate file from the search results by clicking the desired link in the Name column.**

   The pop-up window disappears and a link to your file is displayed under the Attachments related list at the bottom of the page. If you don't know where the file is located, you can click the Search in Documents button for a full list of available documents in salesforce.com.

Sending Mass E-Mail

If you struggle to stay in touch with prospects or customers on a regular basis, you can use salesforce.com to send mass e-mails and shorten your workload. Mass e-mail is particularly helpful for sales reps who send common messages that don't require high levels of personalization. For example, if you're an institutional sales rep selling shares of a hedge fund, you might want to send a monthly e-mail newsletter to sophisticated investors specifically interested in your fund.

REMEMBER

When sending mass e-mail, you can send a maximum of 100 e-mails at a time. A company is limited to 1,000 e-mails a day.

You can send mass e-mail to contacts or leads — the method is basically the same.

To send out a mass e-mail, go to the Contacts home page or Leads home page and follow these simple steps:

1. **Click the Mass Email Contacts link or Mass Email Leads link (depending on which home page you're at) under the Tools section.**

   The Recipient Selection page appears.

2. **Use the View drop-down list to specify the recipients to include in the e-mail, and if you find what you want, skip to Step 5.**

3. **If you can't find the view that you want in the View drop-down list, click the Create New View link.**

   The Create New View page appears. In most circumstances, you need to create a custom view.

4. **To create the new view, fill in the information to filter the recipients for your mass e-mail and click Save.**

   For example, if you want to send an e-mail to all customer contacts that are located in New York, you could build a view, as shown in Figure 8-7. (See Chapter 6 for details on creating custom views for contacts.) When you click Save, the Recipient Selection page reappears with a list of contacts that meet your criteria.

Figure 8-7:
Building a
view for a
mass e-mail.

| Step 1. View Name: |
| Edit the name of this view |
| Name All New York City Customer Contacts |

Step 2. What to search in:
Restrict the set of information being searched
● All Contacts   ○ My Contacts

Step 3. Search Criteria:
Set the search conditions to further restrict the list.
• You can use "or" filters by entering multiple items in the third column.
• You can enter up to 10 items, separated by commas. For example: CA, NY, FL searches for CA or NY or TX or FL.
• Place quotation marks around data that includes commas. For example, "200,000","1,000,000" searches for 200,000 or 1,000,000.
• For fields that can be set on or off, use "0" for no and "1" for yes, e.g.,"Active equals 1" or "Converted equals 0."

Contact: Mailing City	▼	contains	▼	new york	and
Account: Type	▼	equals	▼	customer	and
--None--	▼	--None--	▼		and
--None--	▼	--None--	▼		and
--None--	▼	--None--	▼		

5. **Review the list and select the check boxes to designate the contacts for the mass e-mail, as shown in Figure 8-9.**

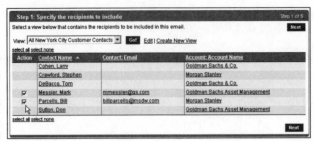

Figure 8-8:
Selecting
the
recipients.

Contacts or leads with missing e-mail addresses lack an available check box in the Action column.

If you know a contact's or lead's e-mail address but have yet to update the contact or lead record, right-click the link in the Contact Name or Lead Name column and choose Open in New Window. (Opening a new window enables you to make changes without leaving the wizard in progress.) Then update the contact with the e-mail address and click Save. Close the contact's window and refresh the Recipient Selection page to verify that the contact's e-mail address now appears.

6. **When you're satisfied with your selections, click Next.**

   A Template Selection page appears where you can select an e-mail template from the e-mail template folders and associate lists.

7. **Use the Folder drop-down list to locate the right folder and template.**

   You can skip this step if you already see the desired e-mail template on the list results.

8. **Select the desired e-mail template by clicking the appropriate radio button in the Name column and click Next.**

   A Preview Template appears.

9. **Review the content for the mass e-mail and click Next.**

   A Confirmation page appears, summarizing the number of contacts that will be sent the mass e-mail.

10. **Select the check boxes, if you want to receive a blind copy, store an activity, and/or use your signature. When you're done, click Send, as shown in Figure 8-9.**

    A Complete page appears, confirming the delivery of your mass e-mail.

Figure 8-9:
Confirming
the mass
e-mail.

Tracking E-Mail

By sending and storing important business-related e-mails in salesforce.com, you and your teams can get a more complete picture of what's happening with your accounts, contacts, and so on. In this section, I show you the basic ways to view your e-mail records and a special feature in salesforce.com that allows you to track HTML e-mails.

Viewing e-mails in Activity History

When you send an e-mail from salesforce.com or by using Outlook Edition, a copy of your message is logged as a task record on the Activity History related list of related records. For example, if you send an e-mail from an opportunity record in salesforce.com, you can view that e-mail from the related Opportunity, Contact, and Account detail pages. See Figure 8-10 for an example.

Figure 8-10:
Viewing
e-mail
records on
an Activity
History
related list.

Activity History	Log A Call	Mail Merge	Send An Email	Request Update	View All		? Help
Action	**Subject**		**Related To**	**Type**	**Due Date**	**Assigned To**	**Last Modified**
Edit | Del	Email: How about a football game?			Task	8/24/2004	Tom Wong	8/24/2004 1:53 AM
Edit | Del	Email: Stay-in-Touch Request			Task	7/30/2004	Tom Wong	7/30/2004 1:55 PM
Edit | Del	Demo - Morgan Stanley - Streaming Quotes		Morgan Stanley -	Task	1/27/2003	Tom Wong	8/24/2004 1:52 AM

On an Activity History related list, you can also click the View All button if you want to see all the completed activities (including e-mail) on a single page.

Tracking HTML e-mails

If you often wonder whether customers pay attention to e-mails that you send them, you can use the HTML Email Status related list for confirmation that the e-mail was opened. Sales reps can use this feature to see whether important e-mails on quotes, proposals, and so on are being opened and viewed by contacts and leads.

Simply put, when you send an HTML e-mail from salesforce.com, the e-mail is embedded with an invisible pixel that can be used for tracking.

You can view that e-mail not only on the Activity History related list but also on the HTML Email Status related list of a lead or contact record.

The HTML Email Status related list shows data on a number of key elements, including the date the e-mail was sent, first opened, last opened, and the total number of times it was opened. Although this isn't a sure-fire way to determine whether your customer wants to buy, some reps use this feature to measure interest on a single e-mail or even mass e-mails.

Integrating with Outlook E-Mail

If your company uses Microsoft Outlook for e-mail, you can work from Outlook and still track your e-mails in salesforce.com. Outlook users get accustomed to receiving and sending from Outlook, so this salesforce.com feature can help you capture both inbound and outbound e-mail on relevant records in salesforce.com.

To integrate Outlook e-mail with salesforce.com, you first have to install Outlook Edition, and then you need to know how to link the e-mail with the right records in salesforce.com. In the following sections, I cover all these tasks.

Installing Outlook Edition

Outlook Edition is a downloadable software application that essentially adds two additional tool buttons to your Outlook e-mail interface.

To download and install Outlook Edition, follow these simple steps:

1. **Shut down Outlook if you're currently running the application.**

2. **Log in to salesforce.com and click the Setup link in the top-right corner of the page.**

   The Personal Setup page appears.

3. **Click the Download Outlook Edition link under the Email heading.**

   An Outlook Edition page appears with instructions and tips.

4. **Click the Install Now button.**

   A dialog box appears.

5. **Click Yes to install the plug-in now.**

6. **Follow the prompts in the setup wizard to complete the installation.**

7. **When you're done, restart Outlook to begin using Outlook Edition.**

   When you log in to Outlook, you see a new Add to Salesforce.com button on your toolbar.

When you're using Outlook Edition, you will be prompted to enter your salesforce.com user name and password.

Moving sent or received e-mail

Outlook Edition provides you an easy way to move sent or received e-mails from Outlook into salesforce.com. You can link the e-mail to specific lead, contact, case, or opportunity records. This is particularly helpful for people who want to track inbound e-mail. You probably don't want to move all your daily e-mail messages from mom, so salesforce.com allows you to pick e-mails selectively. By doing this, you can track all your customer activities in one place and make important information available to other team members.

To append a sent or received e-mail to a salesforce.com record, open an e-mail in Outlook and follow these steps:

1. **Click the Add to Salesforce.com button on your toolbar.**

   A dialog box appears with three tabs.

2. **On the Contacts & Leads tab, type the name of a contact or lead in the field provided and click Search.**

   If you're logged in to salesforce.com, the dialog box re-appears with a list of contacts or leads that matched your search.

   Outlook Edition automatically searches salesforce.com for records that match the e-mail address in the To field of the sent e-mail or From field of the received e-mail. If you don't want to link the e-mail to a lead or contact, right-click the lead or contact and choose Deselect.

3. **Select the desired contact or lead record and if that's all you want to do, click the Add to Salesforce.com button, as shown in Figure 8-11.**

   The dialog box will close and your e-mail will be listed under the Activity History related list of the record. Alternatively, you will have situations when you also want to link the e-mail to a related opportunity or case. And you may even want to provide internal comments to an e-mail. In those situations, use the other tabs, prior to clicking the Add to Salesforce.com button.

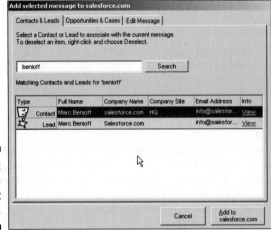

Figure 8-11: Linking to a contact record.

4. **If you want to, click the Opportunities & Cases tab on the dialog box.**

   Salesforce.com also allows you to append the record to a specific opportunity or case. For example, if the e-mail from a contact was pertinent to a specific potential sale, you would want to relate it to an opportunity record.

5. **Enter keywords in the search field to find the correct case or opportunity record, and click the Search button.**

   The dialog box reappears with a list of opportunities or cases that match your search.

6. **Select the desired opportunity or case.**

   If you're unsure of which opportunity or case to choose, click the View link next to the record to look at a printable view.

   You can also simply click the Edit Message tab and modify the message prior to adding.

7. **When you're completely done, click the Add to Salesforce.com button.**

   The dialog box closes and a small dialog box appears to confirm the update to salesforce.com. Click OK.

Sending outbound e-mail from Outlook

Outlook Edition enables you to send e-mails from Outlook and capture them automatically on specific contact, lead, opportunity, or case records in salesforce.com.

To send an e-mail from Outlook, follow these steps:

1. **Click New to compose an e-mail.**

2. **Write the e-mail.**

3. **Add recipients by typing in e-mail addresses or using your Outlook address book.**

4. **As needed, click the Salesforce.com Address Book button to search salesforce.com.**

   A dialog box appears, as shown in Figure 8-12. Type the person's name in the field provided and click the Search button to find that person's e-mail address.

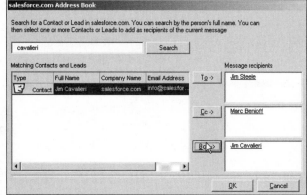

Figure 8-12: Using the address book.

5. **In the salesforce.com Address Book, select desired contacts or leads and use the To, CC or BCC buttons to select Message recipients. Click OK to close the salesforce.com Address Book.**

6. **When the e-mail is ready to be sent, click the Send and Add to Salesforce.com button on the e-mail toolbar.**

   A dialog box appears with tabs for linking to salesforce.com. See the section "Moving sent or received e-mail" for details on using the dialog box.

7. **When you're done, click the Send & Add to Salesforce.com button at the bottom of the dialog box.**

   The e-mail is sent and logged as an activity on the salesforce.com records that you specified from the dialog box.

Chapter 9

Tracking Opportunities

*Y*our sales pipeline is the lifeblood of your business. It's the list of deals that will help you achieve your sales targets. But try as you might, you will probably never close every deal on your pipeline. Things happen: Budgets get slashed, projects get tabled, roles change. So you must have enough deals to give yourself the chance to hit and exceed your goals in a given time frame.

An *opportunity* in salesforce.com is a sales deal that you want to track. The opportunity record has tools to help you efficiently track and close a sale. By using salesforce.com, you can manage more opportunities at the same time and pursue each opportunity with greater precision. For example, if you're a salesforce.com sales rep, you can use opportunities to follow a standard process, link distribution partners, associate products, strategize against competition, record your actions and other notes, and more. And you don't have to waste precious time updating a pipeline spreadsheet. Instead, you or your manager can generate the current pipeline with the click of a button.

In this chapter, I show you the techniques and best practices for using opportunities to track sales. First, you find out the most reliable way to create opportunities. Then I discuss how to view them in the manner that makes sense to you. You also discover how to update your records so that your information is current. Additionally, I describe several related lists unique to the opportunity record, as well as how to use those related lists to get an edge on your competition (or peers) in closing sales.

Getting Familiar with the Opportunity Record

The opportunity record is the collection of fields that make up the information on a deal you are tracking. The record has only two modes: The Edit mode allows you to modify fields, and the Saved mode lets you view the fields and the opportunity's related lists.

Customizing your opportunity fields

Companies rarely use the same sales strategy, so opportunity fields vary. One of the great benefits of salesforce.com is that your company's system administrator can quickly customize your opportunity record to mirror your desired sales process.

If you find your opportunity record not specific enough to your business, answer these questions to help design a more effective record:

✔ What are the stages within your sales process?

✔ What are the key activities that take place within each stage?

✔ What milestones signal the advancement from one stage to the next?

✔ What are the specific qualification criteria for an opportunity?

✔ Who are the people involved in an opportunity?

✔ What would you want to measure on a pipeline report?

✔ What information, if you had it, would consistently help you close more deals?

Based on the answers to these questions, your company might want to add custom checklists, sections, and fields to your opportunity page layout. Consult with your system administrator and see Chapter 18 for details on customizing salesforce.com.

One of the best ways to customize your sales process is to build a spreadsheet with your stages (or the salesforce.com default stages) laid out vertically and certain key columns laid out horizontally. Those columns could include stage description, probability, stage activities, milestone, who's responsible, and forecast category. Have your sales management and CRM team meet to discuss and ultimately agree on a set of stages that are well-defined so even your average sales rep could understand. Then have your administrator use the information on the spreadsheet to modify the opportunity layout.

Keep the record as simple as possible. If you add many fields, you might make the opportunity record harder to use. At the same time, you will have greater success with opportunities if you can easily capture what you want to track.

An opportunity record comes preconfigured with approximately 15 fields. Most of the standard fields are self-explanatory, but be sure to pay attention to these critical fields:

✔ **Amount:** The estimated amount of the sale. Depending on the way your company calculates the pipeline report, you might use numbers that include total contract value, the bookings amount, and so on.

✔ **Close Date:** Use this required field for your best guess as to when you will close this deal. Depending on your company's sales process, the close date has different definitions, but commonly this field is used to track the date that you have signed signatures on all the paperwork required to book the sale.

✔ **Expected Revenue:** This is a read-only field that's automatically generated by multiplying the Amount field by the Probability field.

✔ **Forecast Category:** This field is typically hidden but required. Each sales stage within the Stage drop-down list corresponds to a default forecast category so that higher probability opportunities contribute to your overall forecast after they reach certain stages. See Chapter 10 for details on forecasts.

✔ **Opportunity Owner:** The person in your organization who owns the opportunity. Although an opportunity record has only one owner, many users can still collaborate on an opportunity.

✔ **Opportunity Name:** This required text field represents the name of the specific deal as you want it reflected on your list of opportunities or a pipeline report.

When naming opportunities, you and your company should define a standard naming convention for the Opportunity Name field so that you can easily search for and distinguish opportunities. As a best practice, I recommend that the Opportunity Name should start with the Account Name, then a hyphen, and then the name of the customer's project or the product of primary interest.

✔ **Private:** If you want to keep an opportunity private, select this check box to render the record accessible only to you, your bosses, and the system administrator.

✔ **Probability:** The *probability* is the confidence factor associated with the likelihood that you will win the opportunity. Each sales stage that your company defines is associated to a default probability to close. Typically, you don't need to edit this field; it gets assigned automatically by the Stage option that you pick. In fact, your administrator might remove write access from this field altogether.

If you or your company are just getting started with salesforce.com, you might want to suggest that the Probability field be made read-only. Let your sales stages drive the probability, and over time you'll get a truer gauge on the accuracy of your sales stages.

✔ **Stage:** This required field allows you to track your opportunities following your company's established sales process. Salesforce.com provides a set of standard drop-down list values common to solution selling, but your system administrator can modify these values.

✔ **Type:** Use this drop-down list to differentiate the types of opportunities that you want to track. Most customers use the Type drop-down list to measure new versus existing business, but it can be modified to measure other important or more specific deal types like add-ons, up-sells, work orders, and so on.

Entering Opportunities

Before you can begin using salesforce.com to close opportunities, first you must get the records into salesforce.com. In this section, I discuss the best ways to create opportunities so that they link to the correct accounts, contacts, and other records.

Adding new opportunities

The best method for creating a new opportunity is to start from the relevant account or contact record. By doing this, you guarantee that the opportunity associates to the correct record so that the opportunity is easily trackable. And if you add the opportunity from a contact, you link both the account and contact at the same time.

To create an Opportunity, go to the relevant account or contact detail page and follow these steps:

1. **Click the New Opportunity link on the taskbar.**

   Alternatively, scroll down the detail page to the Opportunities related list and click the New button. The result is the same. The Edit mode of a new opportunity appears. Notice that the Account Name field is conveniently populated for you.

2. **Fill in the fields as much as you can or as required.**

   Remember that at a minimum, you must complete the required fields: Opportunity Name, Stage, Close Date, and whatever other fields your company has designated as required. Depending on how you've set up your opportunity record, you might have to fill in other required fields, which are highlighted in red. (See Figure 9-1 for an example of a record in Edit mode.) See "Getting Familiar with the Opportunity Record" earlier in this chapter for more detail on common required fields.

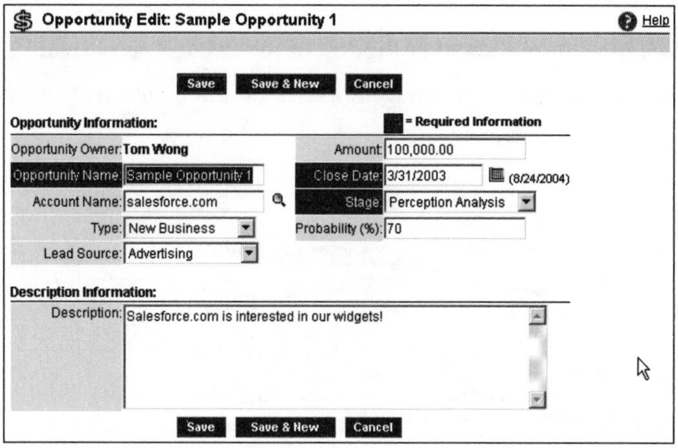

Figure 9-1: Completing opportunity fields.

| $ Opportunity Edit: Sample Opportunity 1 | ? Help |

Save Save & New Cancel

Opportunity Information: ■ = Required Information

Opportunity Owner: **Tom Wong** Amount: 100,000.00
Opportunity Name: Sample Opportunity 1 Close Date: 3/31/2003 (8/24/2004)
Account Name: salesforce.com Stage: Perception Analysis
Type: New Business Probability (%): 70
Lead Source: Advertising

Description Information:
Description: Salesforce.com is interested in our widgets!

Save Save & New Cancel

3. Click Save when you're done.

The Opportunity detail page appears. You can click the Edit button on this page at any time if you need to modify the record.

If you have the good fortune of needing to enter multiple opportunities, one after another, instead of clicking the Save button, click the Save & New button. A new opportunity record appears in Edit mode. You will have to fill in the Account Name field, but this technique might save you time.

Avoid using the Quick Create tool if it is displayed on your Opportunity homepage. While it is a fast way to add opportunities, it requires only three standard fields — Opportunity Name, Stage, and Close Date — which raises the chance of filling out your opportunity records incompletely.

Cloning an opportunity

If you commonly create opportunities that are similar to each other, use the cloning feature to reduce unnecessary retyping. For example, if you're an account manager who creates work order opportunities for additional purchases from the same customer, you might want to clone an existing record and change the details.

To clone an opportunity, go to the opportunity record that you want to clone and follow these steps:

1. **Click the Clone button at the top of the record, as shown in Figure 9-2.**

   A new Opportunity Edit page appears prefilled with all the data from the previous record.

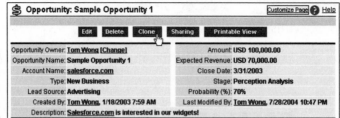

Figure 9-2: Cloning an opportunity.

2. **Modify the fields as necessary.**

   Pay close attention to content in required fields such as Close Date, Stage, and Opportunity Name — the information prefilled in those fields might be incorrect for the new opportunity. Review other data in fields to ensure that the information is applicable to this new opportunity.

3. **If your opportunity has products, select the Clone Products and Associated Schedules check box at the bottom of the page as needed.**

   If your company uses products in salesforce.com, you can use this check box to duplicate the products underlying an existing opportunity. See the "Adding products" section later in this chapter for more information.

4. **When you're done, click Save.**

   An Opportunity detail page for your cloned opportunity appears.

If your company has legacy databases with opportunities and you want this data in salesforce.com, you currently can't use an import wizard to migrate your records as you can with leads, accounts, and contacts. If this is a current challenge, seek out your technical staff, system administrator, or salesforce.com rep. With business guidance, a person with the technical know-how can use ETL (extract, transform, and load) tools to import opportunities and other records through the backend of salesforce.com, which could help you avoid wasting time manually re-inputting opportunities. See Chapter 19 for additional tips and tricks on migrating data.

Modifying Opportunity Records

After you add opportunities into salesforce.com, you can make changes to your records as deals progress, stall, or fade away. In this section, I cover three common practices: editing, sharing, and reassigning.

Updating opportunity fields

In the course of working with your opportunities, you inevitably collect information that you want to save directly in the opportunity record. Every time you capture important data on your opportunity, remember to update your record by doing the following:

1. **Click the Edit button on the opportunity.**

   Alternatively, if you're already on an account or contact record that's linked to the opportunity, scroll down to the Opportunities related list and click the Edit link next to the desired opportunity. The result is the same. The Opportunity Edit page appears.

2. **Update the fields as necessary, paying particular attention to keeping fields like Amount, Close Date, and Stage up to date.**

   Nine out of ten times, those fields play a key role in your company's sales pipeline reports. By keeping your information up to date, you and other users can get a true measure on the opportunity's progress.

3. **When you're done, click Save.**

   The opportunity reappears in Saved mode. Notice that the fields you edited have been changed.

You can keep track of certain critical updates to your opportunity record by using the Stage History related list. Any time you or one of your team members who has read-write access to your record modifies the Stage, Probability, Close Date, or Amount fields, you can see who modified the record and when. Sales managers can use this data in reports to measure progress and trends on opportunities. See Chapter 18 for further details on using and customizing opportunity reports.

Sharing opportunities with others

Depending on the way you sell and your company's overall sharing model, you might need to give other people in your company access to an opportunity on a case-by-case basis. A sharing model defines a user's access to other users' data. It can be highly restrictive (users can only see what they own), highly public (users have access to all data), or somewhere in between.

Giving access to your opportunities might not be an issue if you have a public sharing model. (See Chapter 17 for details on sharing information in salesforce.com.) If, however, your colleagues cannot immediately view or edit on your opportunity records, you can grant them permission by sharing an opportunity.

For Enterprise Edition customers, a good alternative to using the Sharing feature is to utilize Team Selling. Team Selling works particularly well for companies that commonly sell in teams where different people play defined roles. The Sharing feature works great for opportunity access on a case-by-case basis. But with Team Selling, you have even more flexibility. See the section "Establishing sales teams."

To share an opportunity with another user, go to the specific opportunity record and follow these steps:

1. **Click the Sharing button at the top of the opportunity record.**

   The Sharing detail page for the opportunity appears. On that page, you see simple instructions and a related list to share the opportunity with users or groups.

2. **Click the Add button on the related list.**

   A New Sharing page appears.

3. **Click the Currently Not Shared drop-down list and select the users, roles, or groups that you want to share your opportunity with.**

   For more details on users and groups, see Chapter 17.

4. **Click the Add arrow to move the person or group to the New Sharing column.**

5. **Modify the access rights by using the Opportunity Access drop-down list.**

   You use this drop-down list to provide your colleagues viewing privileges (Read Only) or viewing and editing rights (Read/Write) to the opportunity.

6. **When the task is completed, click Save.**

   The Sharing detail page reappears with your changes. Repeat these step as often as you need if you want different users or groups to have different access rights.

If you want to share all the opportunities for a particular account, see Chapter 5 for more detail on account sharing.

Reassigning opportunity ownership

You might find that after you set up your opportunities in salesforce.com, you need to give them to the right people. Or your sales teams might be set up in a hunter/farmer configuration where closed opportunities are reassigned from new business reps to account managers at a certain time.

If you want to reassign an opportunity, open the opportunity detail page and follow these steps:

1. **Next to the Opportunity Owner field, click the Change link, which appears in square brackets.**

   The Ownership Edit page appears.

2. **Select the user you're assigning the opportunity to.**

   By selecting the Send Notification Email check box on the page, you can choose to notify the recipient with an e-mail.

3. **Select the Keep Sales Team check box to retain the Sales Team.**

   In the event that your company isn't using Sales Teams, you won't see that particular check box. See Figure 9-3 for an example.

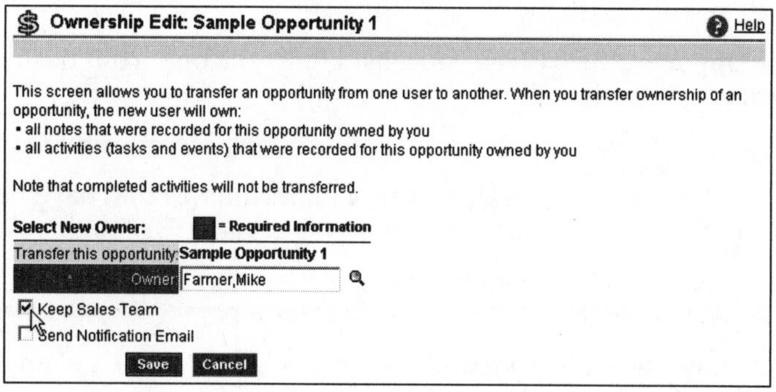

Figure 9-3: Reassigning an opportunity.

4. **When you're done, click Save.**

   The opportunity record reappears. Notice that the Opportunity Owner field has changed to the assigned user.

Organizing Your Opportunities

When you have all or a portion of your opportunities entered in salesforce.com, you can begin to organize them to suit the way that you sell.

In this section, you find out how you can use views and other tools from the Opportunities home page to provide greater focus for you and your sales teams. Then for even more robust organization of your opportunity information, check out Chapter 18 for specifics on how to use standard and custom opportunity reports.

Using opportunity views

An opportunity view is a list of opportunities that match certain criteria. When you select a view, you're basically specifying criteria to limit the results that you get back. The advantage of a view versus searching is that you can use this view over and over again. For example, if you're one of many sales reps, you probably want to see only your opportunities. On the Opportunities home page, salesforce.com comes preset with six defined views:

- **All Opportunities:** A list of all the opportunity records entered into salesforce.com. Depending on the way your company has set up your security model, you might not see this or its results.

- **Closing Next Month:** Displays opportunities where the close date falls in the following month.

- **Closing This Month:** Displays opportunities where the close date falls in the current month.

- **My Opportunities:** Gives you a list of just the opportunities that you own in salesforce.com.

- **New Last Week:** Just shows you opportunity records created last week.

- **New This Week:** Generates a list of opportunities that have been created since the beginning of the week.

- **Private:** Shows opportunities that you have access to that have been marked as Private.

- **Recently Viewed Opportunities:** Lets you look at a list of opportunities that you have recently viewed.

To try out a predefined view, do the following:

1. **On the Opportunities home page, click the down arrow on the Views drop-down list.**

   Depending on how your company has customized the views, you might see all or none of the options in the preceding bullet list and maybe some other choices that have already been created for you.

2. **Select the My Opportunities view.**

   A list page appears, showing opportunities that are currently owned by you. Notice that salesforce.com lays out the list with six standard columns that correspond to commonly used opportunity fields plus an Action column so you can quickly modify a record.

3. **Click a column header to re-sort the list page.**

   For example, if you click the Close Date header the list page re-sorts by the close dates entered on your opportunity records.

4. **Click into any opportunity by pointing and clicking an underlined link in the Opportunity Name column.**

   An Opportunity detail page appears.

5. **Click the Back button on your browser, and then click the Edit link on the same row as the opportunity you just clicked.**

   The opportunity record appears in Edit mode, and you can make changes to the data.

Creating custom opportunity views

If you want special lists for the way that you manage your opportunities, you should build custom views. For example, if you want to see only open opportunities closing this month at or above 50 percent, you can create a view that helps you focus on just that part of the pipeline.

To build a view from scratch, follow these simple steps:

1. **On the Opportunities home page next to the Views drop-down list, click the Create New View link.**

   The Create New View page appears.

2. **Name the view by entering text in the Name field.**

   For example, in the situation that I describe in the preceding section, you might call the view Closing This Month >= 50%.

3. **Select the appropriate radio button if you want to search All Opportunities or just My Opportunities.**

4. **Under the Search Criteria step, select your search criteria, as shown in Figure 9-4.**

   A basic criteria query is made up of three elements:

- **Field:** In the first drop-down list, you find all the fields on the opportunity record. An example would be the Probability field.

- **Operator:** The second drop-down list offers operators for your search. That might sound complicated, but it's easier than you think. Taking my example a step further, you would select the Greater or Equal option from the drop-down list.

- **Value:** In the third box, you type the value that you want in the search. For my example, you would type **50** because you want to see only those opportunities that are greater than or equal to 50 percent probability.

Figure 9-4:
Setting criteria for a custom view.

Step 3. Search Criteria:

Set the search conditions to further restrict the list.
- You can use "or" filters by entering multiple items in the third column.
- You can enter up to 10 items, separated by commas. For example: CA, NY, TX, FL searches for CA or NY or TX or FL.
- Place quotation marks around data that includes commas. For example, "200,000","1,000,000" searches for 200,000 or 1,000,000.
- For fields that can be set on or off, use "0" for no and "1" for yes, e.g., "Active equals 1" or "Converted equals 0."

Probability (%)	▼	greater or equal	▼	50	and
Close Date	▼	equals	▼	THIS MONTH	and
--None--	▼	--None--	▼		and
--None--	▼	--None--	▼		and
--None--	▼	--None--	▼		

5. **Select the columns that you want displayed.**

   Although salesforce.com's preset views take common fields such as Stage and Amount, you can select any of up to 11 opportunity fields to display on your custom list page.

6. **Decide whether you want others to see your custom view.**

   Your decision is made simple if you don't see the Visibility step. Otherwise, select the appropriate option if you want to share your view with others. Your options are basically all, none or limited. If you choose limited accessibility, use the two list boxes to select which users will see the view.

7. **When you're done, click Save.**

   A new view appears based on your custom view criteria. If you don't get all the results you would anticipate, you might want to recheck and refine the search criteria.

Salesforce.com doesn't currently provide ready views for opportunities shared by sales teams. So if your company is organized in sales teams and you aren't the owner of opportunities, you're out of luck. The good news is that you can use reports. In fact, salesforce.com provides a standard report under the Opportunity and Forecast Reports folder called Opportunity Sales Teams.

Making use of the Key Opportunities section

When you go to the Opportunities home page, just below the Views drop-down list you see a Key Opportunities section. This table comes with three columns: Opportunity Name, Account Name, and Close Date. These columns cannot be modified. You can see as few as 10 items and as many as 25 items at a time by clicking the Show # Items link at the bottom of the table.

Use the Select One drop-down list in the top-right corner of the table to quickly get to opportunity records based on the following:

- ✓ **Recently Created** shows the last 10 to 25 opportunities you created.

- ✓ **Recently Modified** shows the last 10 to 25 opportunities you modified.

- ✓ **Recently Viewed** shows the last 10 to 25 opportunities you looked at.

Performing Actions with Opportunity Related Lists

Fields on an opportunity record are useful for storing important data specific to a deal. But where do you go to capture all the critical interactions and relationships when you're working an opportunity? To keep track of these details, use the related lists located on the Opportunity detail page.

Many of the actions on opportunity related lists are common to other modules. For example, major modules such as Accounts, Contacts, and Opportunities all have related lists for Open Activities, Activity History, and Notes & Attachments. Rather than being redundant, see Chapter 7 for details on using related lists for tracking tasks and calendar events. Refer to Chapter 8 for the how-to's on creating notes and storing attachments. In the following sections, I describe certain related lists unique to opportunities.

Depending on the way that your company has customized or decides to customize salesforce.com, you might see all, more, or none of the related lists that I describe in these sections. Review your objectives, evaluate areas of interest, and then decide what works best for your sales process.

Defining contact roles

Depending on your sales process, at some early point you need to identify the decision makers who will influence the buying decision. Contacts and their titles often don't tell the whole story about decision makers and the chain of command within an opportunity.

To better define the buying influences on an opportunity, go to an opportunity record and follow these steps:

1. **Click the New button on the Contact Roles related list.**

    The Contact Roles page appears for that specific opportunity with a list of the available contacts linked to the related account.

2. **For each relevant contact, use the Role drop-down list to select the appropriate role, as shown in Figure 9-5.**

    Salesforce.com comes preconfigured with a standard list of contact roles but your company can customize this drop-down list if the list of values needs to be modified. You don't have to classify a role for every contact on the list; just leave the Role default value of None.

    If the right role for your contact doesn't appear, advise your system administrator to edit the roles.

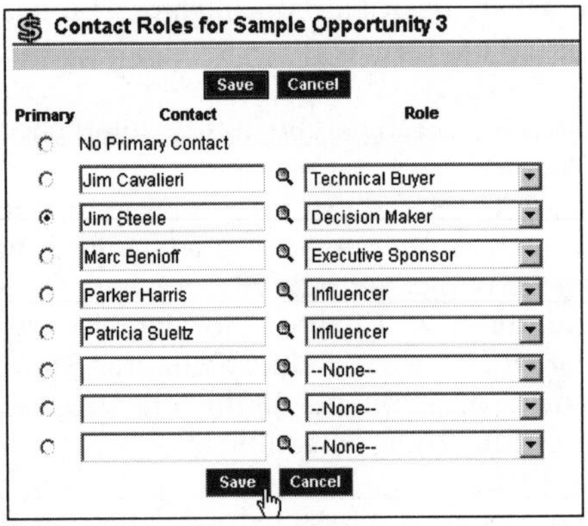

Figure 9-5:
Selecting
the contact
role.

3. **Select one radio button to designate the Primary Contact.**

    The Primary Contact typically refers to the person who currently is your point of contact. One of the benefits of selecting the Primary Contact is that you can list out who the primary contact is on a basic opportunity report.

4. **If necessary, click the Lookup icon next to empty fields in the Contact column to add other contacts who are critical to your opportunity.**

   If you work with multitier selling models or if you collaborate with business partners on your deals, use contact roles to add contacts who aren't employees of an account. For example, if your customer's legal gatekeeper works for an outside law firm, you can use the Contact Roles related list to highlight the attorney's role.

5. **When you're done, click Save.**

   The Opportunity detail page reappears, and your Contact Roles related list is updated to reflect contacts involved in the opportunity. If you need to add more contact roles, click the New button on the Contact Roles related list again.

Establishing sales teams

Many companies organize themselves in predefined sales teams because they believe their company can be more productive with team collaboration on particular opportunities. For example, some companies have account managers who own the overall customer relationship but leverage internal resources (including sales engineers, presales consultants, and sales specialists) to handle particular responsibilities.

If you want to set up a sales team for an opportunity, go to the opportunity record and follow these steps:

1. **Scroll down the Opportunity detail page to the Sales Team related list and click the Add button.**

   A New Sales Team Members page appears with a table to select users, opportunity access, and team roles.

   Depending on how your company has customized salesforce.com, you might be able to use two other buttons on the Sales Team related list: Add Default Team and Add Account Team. If you customize your Personal Setup with a default sales team, you can use the Add Default Team button and bypass all the following steps. See Chapter 3 for the details on setting up a default team. If the account linked to your opportunity has an account team, you can click the Add button to add the account team users to your sales team. Depending on the access privileges for the account team, this might be necessary. See Chapter 5 for details on setting up account teams.

2. **Type the name of a team member in the User field and click the Lookup icon.**

   A pop-up window appears with your search results.

3. **If you find the correct member of your team, select the member by clicking the link for the user name.**

   If your search didn't find the user, refine your search until you find your colleague and then select it. After you select the user, the pop-up disappears, and the User field is filled in.

4. **Use the Opportunity Access drop-down list to select the access level you want to grant to the user.**

   Depending on your sharing model, you can use the drop-down lists to grant read/write or read-only privileges to the team member for the opportunity.

5. **Use the Team Role drop-down list to select the appropriate role.**

   If the right role for your user doesn't appear, advise your system administrator to edit the roles.

6. **Repeat Steps 2 through 5 for each sales team member of your opportunity (see Figure 9-6), and then click Save.**

   The Opportunity detail page reappears, and your team is displayed on the Sales Team related list. If your opportunity team requires more than four users, click the Save & More button instead of clicking the Save button, and repeat Steps 2 through 5 to add more users.

Figure 9-6: Adding sales team members.

Tracking competitors

If you want to track competitors on your opportunities, salesforce.com provides a Competitors related list to help you strategize against the competition.

To track a competitor, go to the opportunity record and follow these steps:

1. **Click the New button on the Competitors related list.**

   An Opportunity Competitor page appears with three fields to name the competitor and specify strengths and weaknesses.

2. **Complete the Competitor Name field or click the green pick box icon to select a competitor, as shown in Figure 9-7.**

   The pick box icon opens a pop-up window with a list of your named competitors. Select a competitor and the window closes. You won't see the green pick box unless your company has created a list of named competitors.

   If you're going to use Competitors related list, always create a standard list of competitors. With a drop-down list, you can standardize naming conventions and use reports to better measure competitors on opportunities. For example, if you often run up against Company XYZ in vendor evaluations, you could run a report on all the opportunities linked to XYZ as a competitor.

3. **Fill out the competitor's strength and weaknesses relative to the opportunity, and then click Save.**

   The Opportunity detail page reappears, and the Competitors related list is modified to reflect the new competitor. Repeat this step if you need to add other competitors to the opportunity.

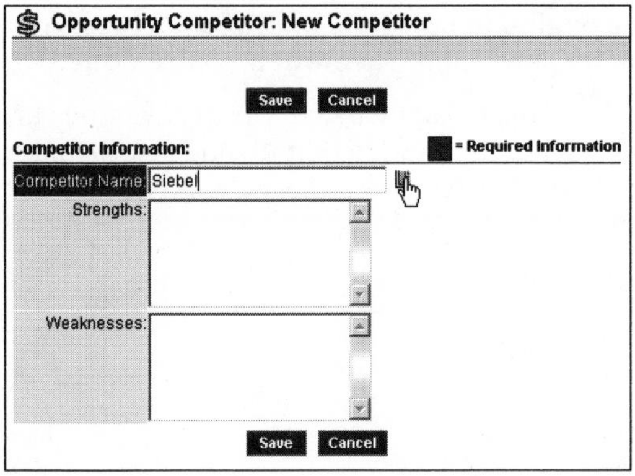

Figure 9-7:
Using a
standard
competitor
list.

> **Opportunity Competitor: New Competitor**
>
> [Save] [Cancel]
>
> **Competitor Information:**   = Required Information
>
> Competitor Name: Siebel
> Strengths:
> Weaknesses:
>
> [Save] [Cancel]

Associating partners

If you work for a company that depends heavily on partners for your marketing, sales, or service delivery models, use the Partners related list to link partners.

This feature is very useful in multitier selling models where you work with companies that could include resellers, distributors, and so on. to drive your business. For example, if you team with Accenture to sell or deliver services to end customers, the Partners related list would help you track both Accenture and related end customers.

To link a partner to a customer opportunity, go to the opportunity record and follow these steps:

1. **Click the New button on the Partners related list.**

   A Partners page appears.

2. **Type the name of your partner in the Partner field and click the Lookup icon.**

   A pop-up window appears with your search results.

3. **If you find the correct partner, select it by clicking the link with your partner's name.**

   If your search didn't find the partner, refine your search or click the New button to the right of the Search field to create an account record for your partner if you forgot to create it first. Then select it. After you select the partner, the pop up disappears and the Partner field is filled in.

4. **Select the role from the Role drop-down list.**

   If the right role for your partner doesn't appear, advise your system administrator to edit the partner roles.

5. **Repeat Steps 2 through 4 to associate multiple partners to the opportunity (see Figure 9-8) and click Save when you're done.**

   The Opportunity detail page reappears, and your selections are displayed under the Partner related list. Notice that if you click the partner link, the account record for your partner appears.

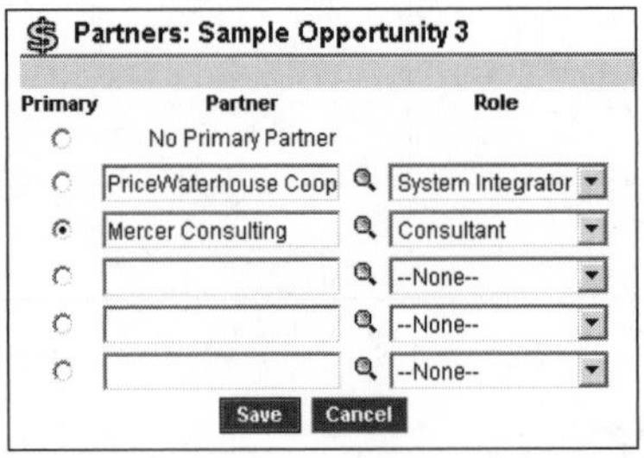

Figure 9-8:
Linking
partners to
opportu-
nities.

Measuring partner performance

A major communication services company drove its channel sales strategy by partnering with leading wireless equipment manufacturers. Sometimes the company was introduced to the end customer; other times the company was involved in opportunities completely managed by the manufacturer. But in all circumstances, the company's channel managers leveraged salesforce.com to track the partner sales performance, to improve mindshare with strategic partners, and to deepen its relationships with end customers.

Using Products with Opportunities

A product, as its name implies, is a product or service that you sell to customers. You can add products with specific prices to your opportunities and automatically calculate the Amount field on an opportunity record. If you're a sales rep selling multiple products and managing multiple opportunities at the same time, you can take the frustration out of remembering what you offered to a customer. If you're a sales manager, you can segment your pipelines and forecasts by product lines. And if you're in product management or marketing, products in salesforce.com can give you real insight into product demand from your markets.

Adding products

To take advantage of products, your company must first set up a product catalog and one or more price books. See Chapter 14 for the how-to details on setting up your products and price books. After this is done, you can add products to an opportunity by going to a specific opportunity and following these steps:

1. **Scroll down on the Opportunity detail page to the Products related list and click the Choose Price Book button.**

   A Choose Price Book page appears. If your company has made only one price book available to you, you can bypass this step.

2. **Select the appropriate price book from the Price Book drop-down list and click Save.**

   The Opportunity detail page appears again.

REMEMBER

On an opportunity, you can use only one price book at a time. If you have questions on the best ways to set up your products and price books, see Chapter 14 for the details.

3. Click the Add Product button on the Products related list.

A Product Selection page appears, as shown in Figure 9-9.

> $ **Product Selection**   ❓ Help
>
> Enter your keyword and filter criteria and click Find to begin your search. Click More filters to use more than one filter. Search results include all records that match both your keyword and filter entries.
>
> **Find Products**
>
> **By Keyword**
> [   ]
>
> **By Field Filter**
> [--None-- ▼] [--None-- ▼] [   ]
>
> [Find Product]
> More filters >>
>
>   ◀ Previous Page | Next Page ▶
>
>   [Select] [Cancel]
>
> | ☐ | **Product Name** △ | **Product Code** | **List Price** | **Product Description** | **Product Family** |
> |---|---|---|---|---|---|
> | ☐ | Widget 1 | | USD 3,000.00 | | |
> | ☐ | Widget 2 | | USD 15,000.00 | | |
> | ☐ | Widget 3 | | USD 1,000.00 | | |
>
>   ◀ Previous Page | Next Page ▶
>
>   [Select] [Cancel]

Figure 9-9: Finding your products.

4. If you need to, enter a keyword and filter criteria, and then click the Find Product button to begin your search.

The page reappears with your search results in a table at the bottom of the page. If you need more filters, click the More Filters link and refine your search until you find the products you want. In the event that you have a small product list and you immediately see the desired products under the search results table, you can bypass this step.

5. Select the check boxes next to the products that you want, and then click the Select button.

An Add Products page appears with your selections and fields for you to provide line item details, as shown in the example in Figure 9-10. The Sales Price field is prefilled with the default sales price from the price book that you selected.

>   ◀ Previous Page | Next Page ▶
>   [Select] [Cancel]
>
> | ☐ | **Product Name** △ | **Product Code** | **List Price** | **Product Description** | **Product Family** |
> |---|---|---|---|---|---|
> | ☑ | Widget 1 | | USD 3,000.00 | | |
> | ☑ | Widget 2 | | USD 15,000.00 | | |
> | ☐ | Widget 3 | | USD 1,000.00 | | |
>
>   ◀ Previous Page | Next Page ▶
>   [Select] [Cancel]

Figure 9-10: Selecting products.

6. Fill in the line item details, as shown in Figure 9-11.

You must at a minimum fill in the Quantity and Sales Price fields for each selected product. The Date field is typically used to reflect an expected ship or delivery date for the product, but you should check with your company on how you should use the Date field. Use the Line Description field if you need to supply details that can't be captured in the standard fields provided. For example, if your customer demands special pricing on a product at certain breakpoints, capture those details in this field.

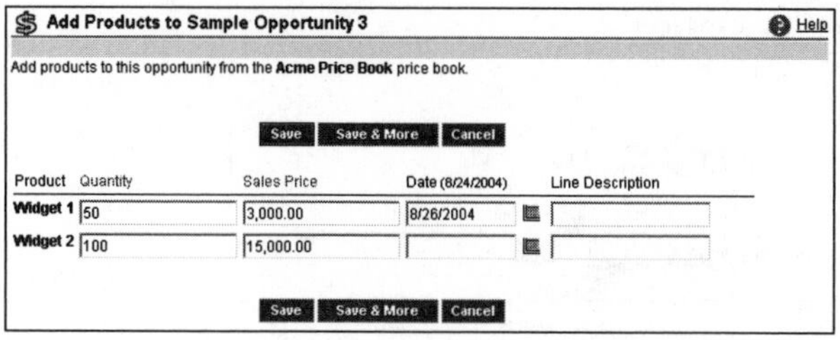

Figure 9-11:
Adding line item details to products.

7. When you're done, click the Save button or the Save & More button.

Clicking the Save & More button takes you back to the Product Selection page. If you click the Save button, the Opportunity detail page reappears. Notice that the Products related list reflects your selections and that the Amount field on the opportunity record has changed based on the total from the products you added.

Changing product details

If you need to change the details on your product selections in the course of the sale, you can do this easily on the Products related list. For example, if your customer wants to add another product, increase product quantities, or demand a better product discount, you need to know how to modify products.

To modify products on your opportunity, I suggest you do the following:

✔ To delete a product from the opportunity, click the Del link next to the product on the Products related list.

✔ To edit all the products on the opportunity, click the Edit All button. An Edit Products page appears in the same format as the Add Products page in Figure 9-11. Type in any changes and click Save.

✔ To edit one product at a time, click the Edit link next to the product on the related list. An Opportunity Product Edit page appears, as shown in

Figure 9-12. Depending on how your company has customized sales-force.com, your page might appear different. Make any changes and click Save.

✔ To reorder the products on your Products related list, click the Sort button. A page appears with your list of select products and arrow buttons to reorder the list. When you're done, click Save. (For example, if you need to look at your opportunity products from biggest to smallest ticket, use the sorting tool.)

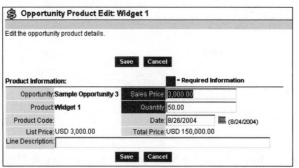

Figure 9-12:
Editing a
single
product
on an
opportunity.

Adding schedules for products

If you manage opportunities where your products or services are delivered over time, you can create schedules for your products by quantity, by revenue, or both. By using schedules, you and your users can benefit in multiple ways:

✔ If you're on a sales team, you get a gauge on revenue recognition, which could be significant if that affects compensation.

✔ If you're in product management, you can better forecast and plan for the amount of units that you'll have to deliver in future quarters.

✔ If you're part of a services organization, schedules updated by reps provide a real-time gauge in planning your resources and projects.

✔ Your system administrator must first set up your products with scheduling. (See Chapter 14 for more specifics on schedules and see Chapter 18 for the details on customizing salesforce.com.)

After scheduling is enabled for a product, set up a schedule by going to the Opportunity detail page and following these steps:

1. **Click the desired product in the Product Name column of the Products related list.**

   An Opportunity Product page appears with a Schedule related list.

2. **Click the Establish button on the Schedule related list.**

   An Establish Schedule page appears.

3. **Complete the fields and click Save.**

   Your fields might vary depending on whether the product is set up for quantity, revenue, or combined scheduling. For example, in Figure 9-13, Widget 2 is enabled for revenue scheduling. When you click Save, a schedule appears based on your choices.

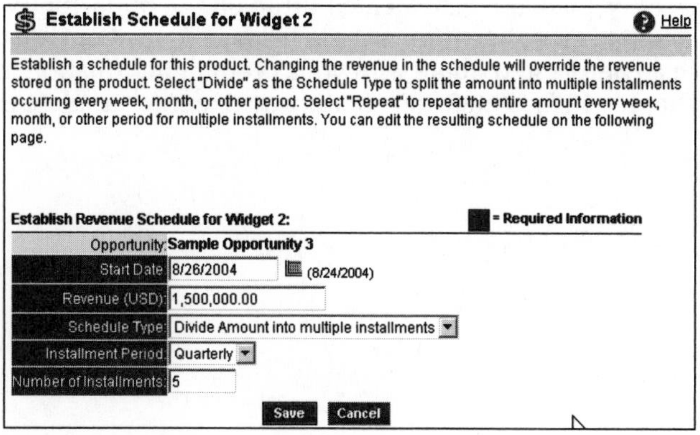

Figure 9-13: Establishing a schedule.

4. **Review and modify the schedule.**

   If the revenues or quantities aren't equal over the periods that you first established, you can type over the values in the schedule.

5. **When you're done, click Save.**

   The Opportunity Product page reappears with the schedule you established.

Making updates to schedules

Over the course of an opportunity, you can adjust the schedule on a product if terms change by clicking the buttons on the Opportunity Product page. To access an Opportunity Product page, go to the relevant opportunity record, scroll down to the Products related list, and click the desired product link from the Product column. The Opportunity Product page for the selected product appears with a Schedule related list.

- ✔ Click the Edit button if you want to modify the schedule.
- ✔ Click the Delete button if you want to delete the schedule.
- ✔ Click the Re-establish button if you want establish the schedule all over again.

If you typically generate quotes for customers and find yourself wasting precious time re-typing product detail into a form, you can use mail merge functionality to automate your quote generation. Your system administrator needs to first build and upload the quote template. When that's done, the quote generation is easy. Click the Mail Merge button on the opportunity's Activity History related list, complete three simple fields, and in about a minute, you can generate an automated quote with your product information in Microsoft Word. See Chapter 12 for details on creating mail merge templates.

Chapter 10

Calculating Forecasts

*W*ith salesforce.com, shaky forecasting can become a distant memory. Forecasts are generated from opportunities that all members of sales teams manage. And because salesforce.com understands that reps and managers sometimes need flexibility to make judgment calls on forecasts, salesforce.com allows for overrides on totals so that submitted forecast numbers are as accurate as possible.

By regularly using forecasts in salesforce.com, you and everyone in your organization can get a better measure on individual targets and goals as well as the overall health of your business.

In this chapter, I cover some basic terminology and the critical steps that your administrator should follow to set up forecasts. Then I show you, the sales reps and managers, how to create a forecast and enter your quotas. Finally, I go through the steps of displaying and updating your forecasts.

Getting Familiar with Forecasts

If you are in sales, a *forecast* in salesforce.com is your best guess of how much revenue you will generate during a forecast period, either monthly or quarterly. More than just a hunch, your forecast is tied to the opportunities that you create and update. So by managing your opportunities, you automatically contribute to your forecast.

For a sales manager, salesforce.com takes forecast that much further. A manager's forecast is the rollup (or combined total) of his team's forecast plus his or her individual contribution if applicable.

In salesforce.com, your forecasts can be compared against your quotas, to give you an up-to-date measure on how you are performing against your sales goals. See the later section "Assigning Quotas to Forecasts" for details on entering quotas.

Defining forecast categories

Salesforce.com automatically associates each opportunity to a forecast category through the Stage field on the opportunity record. The forecast categories are divided into the following five groupings, as shown in Figure 10-1:

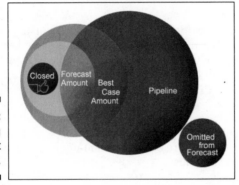

Figure 10-1:
Defining
forecast
categories.

If your company has been using Forecasts prior to 2005, be aware that the forecast category formerly known as "Forecast" has now been replaced with "Commit" to avoid confusion.

- ✔ **Closed:** The total amount of the opportunities you've won in a forecast period.

- ✔ **Commit:** The Forecast category, Commit is the amount that you confidently believe you can generate in a forecast period. (Commit is the Forecast Amount section in Figure 10-1.) The Commit category is made up of closed opportunities plus those opportunities that you're committing to win.

- ✔ **Best Case:** The total amount that you could bring in if all the stars aligned in the period. The Best Case amount is the total of opportunities that are categorized as Closed, Commit, and Best Case.

✔ **Pipeline:** This is the sum of all your open opportunities in a forecast period.

✔ **Omitted:** This category is made up of opportunities that you lost or that you want to omit from the forecast. For example, you might want to omit an opportunity from your forecast if your buyer informs you that the budget for the opportunity has just been cut.

So as you update the stages to your opportunities, you make corresponding changes to associated forecast categories.

Updating fiscal year settings

If you are the system administrator, you will want to re-check your fiscal year settings in salesforce.com. Fiscal year settings determine the forecast periods. If your administrator set it correctly when you first started using salesforce.com, this setting will probably not need to be modified.

To update the fiscal year settings, click the Setup link in the top-right corner of salesforce.com and follow these steps:

1. **Click the Forecasts heading under the Customize heading on the sidebar.**

   The Forecasts folder expands.

2. **Click the Fiscal Year link under the Forecasts heading.**

   The Organization Fiscal Year Edit page appears.

3. **Complete the fields in Step 1 on the page to apply fiscal year changes to customizable forecasting, as shown in Figure 10-2.**

   The fields are self explanatory, but here are some important tips:

   • Use the Forecast Period drop-down list to define if your company will forecast by month or by quarter.

   • In the Fiscal Year Start Month field, select the appropriate month.

   • Click the desired radio button to set the month that impacts the name of the fiscal year.

   When updating fiscal year settings, be aware that if you change the forecast period (or fiscal year start month when it's set to Quarterly), you delete previous overrides. See the section in this chapter called "Editing forecasts and applying overrides" for details on overrides.

4. **Select the check box in Step 2 on the page only if you want to apply your modified fiscal year definition to previously created forecasts.**

5. **When you're done, click Save.**

   The Forecasts page of Setup reappears.

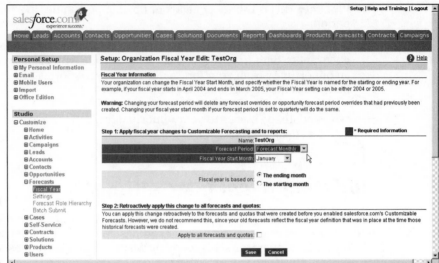

Figure 10-2:
Defining the
fiscal year.

Modifying the forecast settings

If you're an administrator, the success of your forecast solution might hinge on this section. But don't fret: If you don't use products in salesforce.com, modifying the forecast settings is a piece of cake. And if you do use products, changing the settings might be the long-awaited answer to your forecasting challenges and worth the effort.

To modify forecast settings, click the Setup link in the top-right corner of salesforce.com and follow these steps:

1. **Click the Forecasts heading under the Customize heading on the sidebar.**

   The Forecasts folder expands.

2. **Click the Settings link under the Forecasts heading.**

   The Forecast Settings page appears, as shown in Figure 10-3.

3. **Use the drop-down lists to complete the fields in the Settings section.**

   Here are some pointers:

   • In the **Forecast Date drop-down list,** select a date field to define how money from opportunities is allocated to time periods. If you don't use products, your choice is simply Opportunity Close Date. If you use products, you can select Product Date or Schedule Date (if scheduling is enabled).

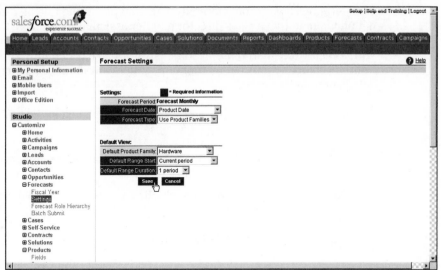

- Use the **Forecast Type drop-down list** to determine whether a rep carries one quota during a period (select the Use Overall Forecast option) or potentially multiple quotas separated by product family (select the Use Product Families option). For example, in a fresh produce company, a sales rep might have multiple quotas based on different product families that he sells (like a quota for vegetables and a quota for fruit). See Chapter 14 for details on using products and product families.

4. **Use the drop-down lists to complete the fields in the Default View section.**

   If your company used forecasts in salesforce.com prior to 2005, you'll soon notice that the Forecasts home page looks completely different. With these settings, you define the default view on the Forecasts home page, particularly the number of forecast periods a sales person can view and if the forecasts are broken out by product families.

5. **When you're done, click Save.**

   The Forecasts Setup page appears.

Adjusting the forecast role hierarchy

For administrators, the forecast role hierarchy provides a number of forecasting functions to better ensure that forecasts roll up correctly under the right people. Your company's forecast role hierarchy represents the same configuration as your role hierarchy. For example, in the role hierarchy, it's not uncommon that a sales director and her assistant might have the same role in salesforce.com, but the assistant probably doesn't have a forecast. With forecast role hierarchy, an administrator can easily remove the assistant from the company forecast but not impact her overall role. See Chapter 17 for details on role hierarchy.

To adjust the forecast role hierarchy, click the Setup link in the top-right corner of salesforce.com and follow these steps:

1. **Click the Forecasts heading under the Customize heading on the sidebar.**

2. **Click the Forecast Role Hierarchy link under the Forecasts folder.**

    The Forecast Role Hierarchy page appears.

3. **Click the Users link next to a role name.**

    A Forecast Users page appears for the selected role (see Figure 10-4).

4. **Use the Add and Remove buttons to move users from one list box to the other to create the Forecast Enabled Users list for the role, as shown in Figure 10-4.**

5. **When you're done, click Save.**

    The Forecast Role Hierarchy page appears. Repeat Steps 2 through 4 as often as necessary to define the forecast-enabled users for your company.

6. **Click the Edit link to designate a role's Forecast User, as shown in Figure 10-5.**

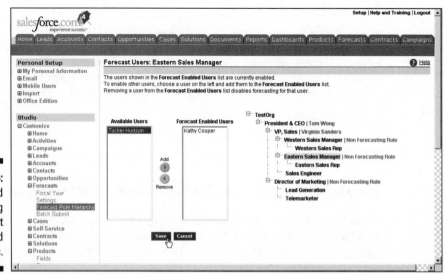

Figure 10-4: Adding and removing forecast enabled users.

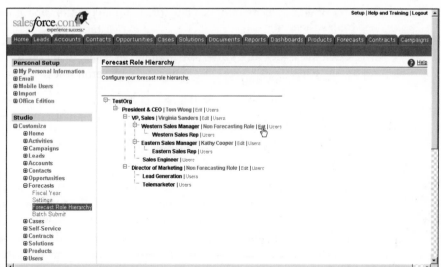

Figure 10-5:
Designating
a role's
forecast
user.

A Forecast User Assignment page appears.

Editing the Forecast User is also useful when you have two or more forecast-enabled users assigned to a role but only one carries that role's quota.

7. **From the Forecast User drop-down list, select one forecast user for the selected role, and then click Save.**

The Forecast Role Hierarchy page reappears.

Assigning Quotas to Forecasts

A quota is the revenue goal assigned to a user on a monthly or quarterly basis. Depending on your settings, a forecast-enabled user can carry one quota or multiple quotas within a forecast period. Administrators and users with appropriate profile permissions can enter and edit quotas that apply to forecasts. You add quotas to forecasts from a user's detail page.

When adding forecasts, assign quotas to all users in the forecast role hierarchy. By doing this, users — including reps and managers — can view the status of the quota.

To enter or edit a user's quotas, click the Setup link in the top-right corner and follow these steps:

1. **Click the Users link under the Manage Users heading on the sidebar.**

   A user list page appears.

2. **From the View drop-down list, select Active Users.**

   The Active Users list page appears.

3. **Click a user listed in the Full Name column.**

   A User detail page appears.

   If you're updating your own quotas, you can access your User detail page by clicking the Setup link and then clicking the Personal Information link under the My Personal Information heading on the sidebar.

4. **In the Quotas related list, select the time range and product family (if applicable) that you want to set quotas for, and then click the Edit button.**

   A *Username* Quota page appears.

5. **For the periods listed, enter the user's quotas and click the Submit button, as shown in Figure 10-6.**

   The User detail page appears.

6. **Repeat Steps 3 through 5 as necessary to enter quotas for your users.**

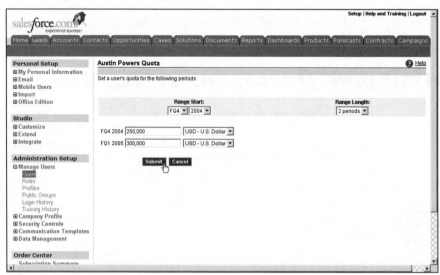

Figure 10-6: Entering quotas to forecasts.

Updating Forecasts

If you're a sales rep or manager in the forecast role hierarchy, you can update opportunities on your forecasts, override forecast amounts at your discretion, and formally submit your updated forecasts.

Viewing your forecasts

If you used salesforce.com prior to 2005, you'll notice the difference in forecasts immediately. Even if you're new to salesforce.com, the pages accessible from the Forecast tab appear different from your typical view or detail pages in salesforce.com.

Do this right now: Click the Forecasts tab. A forecast summary page appears, as shown in Figure 10-7. From this page, you can do the following:

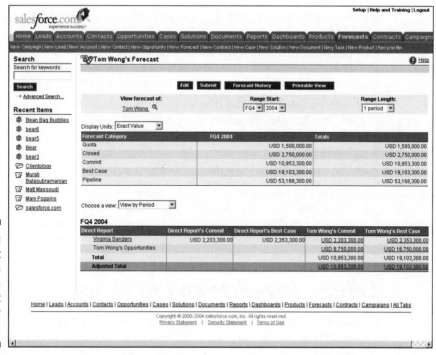

Figure 10-7: Looking at your options from the forecast summary page.

✔ Click the Edit button if you want to update your forecast.

✔ Click the Submit button when you are ready to formally submit your forecast.

✔ If you want to review the history of your forecasts, click the Forecast History button.

✔ Use the Printable View button if you want to print your forecast in a formatted version.

✔ Under View Forecast Of, click the Lookup icon or user name to select another user's forecast. For example, if you want to view the forecast of sales reps that report to you, click the Lookup icon and select a user from the pop-up window. When the window closes, the summary page reappears for the selected user.

✔ Use the Product Family drop-down list, if applicable, to summarize the forecast by a specific product family. You won't see this drop-down list if your company isn't using products in salesforce.com or your administrator has not set up forecasts for product families. See the earlier section "Modifying the forecast settings" for details.

✔ Modify the Range Start if you want to look at a different forecast period.

✔ Use the Range Length drop-down list to change the amount of periods to be summarized on the summary page at one time. For example, if you chose 2 periods from the drop-down list, the summary page reappears with two forecasts based on the Range Start.

✔ Select a value from the Display Units drop-down list to alter the display of your forecast summary. For example, if you select the % Quota option, the view reappears summarized according to percentage attainment of quota.

✔ Use the Choose a View drop-down list to view your forecasts either by period or by subordinates.

✔ Click links under the *Username*'s Commit or *Username*'s Best Case columns to drill into the opportunity detail for the particular forecast category.

Editing forecasts and applying overrides

As you update Stage, Probability, Amount, and/or Close Date fields on your opportunities, your amounts corresponding to the different forecast categories automatically adjust. At the same time, not every seasoned sales rep and manager wants her forecast to necessarily reflect the total amount of opportunities in a forecast period. The actual forecast that you submit for you or your team might be higher or lower depending on your judgment.

You have basically four ways to adjust your forecast:

✔ Modify the opportunity fields: Stage, Probability, or the applicable forecast date (Close Date, Product Date, Schedule Date). See Chapter 9 for details on opportunity fields.

✔ Override at the opportunity level by changing the default forecast category on opportunities or their products.

✔ Override the forecast of users who report to you.

✔ Override the adjusted totals.

Updating opportunities on the forecast

To make changes to your forecast, click the Forecast tab and follow these steps:

1. **Use the View Forecast Of, Range Start, and Range Length filters to find your desired view.**

   The forecast summary page changes based on your selections.

2. **Click the Edit button to alter your forecast.**

   A page for your forecast appears, as shown in Figure 10-8.

3. **From the Opportunities tab on your forecast page, click the Edit link next to an opportunity you want to update.**

   An Opportunity Forecast Edit page appears.

4. **Modify the opportunity fields to adjust the forecast.**

   Here are some important tips to keep in mind:

   • Changes that you make to Stage Name or Close Date will update the opportunity record.

   • Select a different value from the My Forecast Category drop-down list if you want to override the default forecast category associated to the stage, as shown in Figure 10-9.

   • Use My Forecast Comments to provide rationale for your changes.

5. **When you're done, click the Save button or Save and Refresh button.**

   If you click Save & Refresh, the Opportunity Forecast Edit page appears with your changes reflected in the Commit and Best Case columns displayed at the top of the page.

   When you click the Save button, your forecast page appears and an ! flag appears next to the opportunity you have overridden.

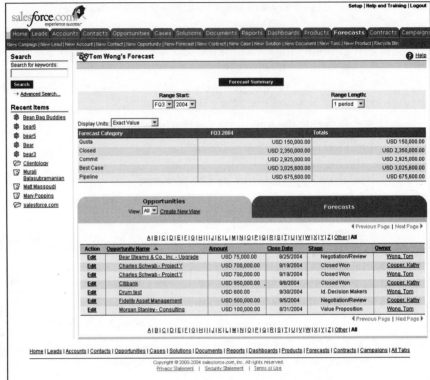

Figure 10-8:
Looking over your forecast.

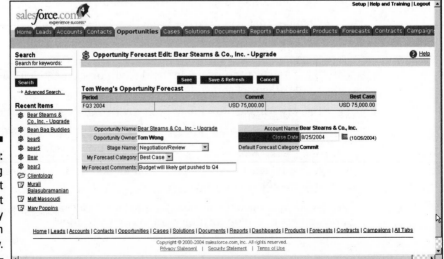

Figure 10-9:
Overriding the default forecast category on an opportunity.

If you need to review or edit the full opportunity record, right-click an opportunity listed in the Opportunity Name column, and open the page in another window. By doing this, you can modify the opportunity without leaving the forecast. This would be useful, if for example you wanted to update the Amount field on an opportunity to impact the forecast. Remember to close the window when you're done.

If your forecasts are set up with product families and you add products to opportunities, you can override forecast categories at the product line item level of the opportunity, as shown in Figure 10-10. This feature gives you the option of forecasting only certain pieces of an opportunity that you feel have a high likelihood of closing, while holding back on other pieces.

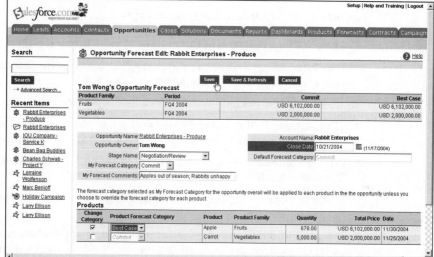

Figure 10-10: Overriding the forecast category at the product line item level.

Overriding your individual forecast totals

If you're a sales rep with no direct reports (you know, someone who reports directly to you), and you want to make overrides to your forecast totals, you can apply additional judgment through the Forecasts tab located at the bottom of your forecast page. To override individual forecasts, follow these steps:

1. Click the Forecasts tab at the bottom of your forecast page.

Your forecast appears with a table summarizing the Forecast Period, Commit, and Best Case amounts.

2. **Click an amount link in the Commit or Best Case columns.**

   A pop-up window opens where you can apply the override.

3. **Enter your override in the My Forecast Override field, add comments, and click the Save button.**

   The window closes and your overrides appear on the forecasts.

4. **Repeat Steps 2 and 3 until you're satisfied with your forecast.**

Overriding forecasts at the management level

If you're a sales manager with direct reports who have forecasts, your forecast is the aggregate of their forecasts plus your contribution. You can override both the forecasts of direct reports plus the adjusted totals.

To override forecast totals, follow these steps:

1. **Click the Forecasts tab at the bottom of your forecast page.**

   Your forecast appears with a summary that includes the forecasts of your direct reports and your aggregate forecast.

2. **Select View by Period on the Forecasts drop-down list.**

3. **Click a name in the Direct Report column if you want to view a direct report's forecast and then click the Back button when done.**

4. **Click an amount link for a direct report in the My Commit or My Best Case columns if you want to override an amount.**

   A pop-up window appears displaying options for overriding the forecast category's amount.

5. **Use the radio buttons and the amount field, if applicable, to select the override option, and then click Save, as shown in the example in Figure 10-11.**

   The window closes, and your changes appear on the forecast totals below the special Forecasts tab.

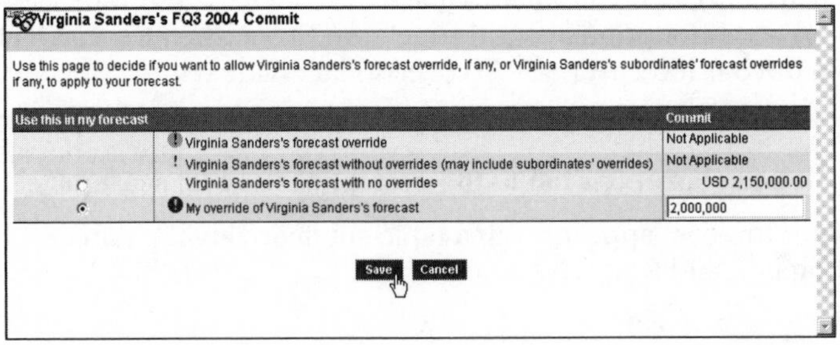

Figure 10-11:
Overriding
the forecast
of a direct
report.

6. **If you want to override your adjusted totals, click an amount link in the Adjusted Totals row in the My Commit or My Best Case columns.**

   A pop-up window appears summarizing your quota and rollup and allowing you to provide your forecast override.

7. **Enter your forecast override and any comments if necessary, and then click Save.**

   The window closes, and your override appears on the forecast totals below the special Forecasts tab, and it's also displayed in the forecast summary at the top of your forecast page.

   Salesforce.com displays colored "!" flags to indicate amounts or opportunity line items that have been overridden. The color coding is explained above the special Forecasts tab when you click the tab. If you hover your cursor over the flag, comments appear explaining the override.

8. **When you're done, click the Forecast Summary button to return to the forecast summary page.**

Submitting your forecast

The final step in the forecast process is for you to formally submit your forecast. Many companies enforce an internal policy that reps and managers who carry quotas must update the forecast by a certain time each week. By using the Submit button, a user places a time stamp on what he or she is committing to at that particular time. And after the forecast is submitted, the submission is logged in the forecast history.

To submit your forecast, click the Forecasts tab and follow these steps:

1. **Review the forecasts that you intend to submit.**

2. **When you're satisfied, click the Submit button.**

   A pop-up window appears to confirm the submission.

3. **Click OK.**

   The window closes, and your Forecast History page appears with a summary of your submitted forecast.

   At the conclusion of every forecast period, move any open opportunities from the closed forecast to a new, open forecast by modifying close dates, product dates, or schedule dates, as applicable.

Part III
Optimizing Marketing

The 5th Wave   By Rich Tennant

BUS STOP

"Well, here's what happened—I forgot to put it on my 'To Do' list."

In this part . . .

You can expect to ask the most out of your sales teams only if you're capable of providing all the raw materials necessary to make them successful. They need effective marketing to help generate leads so they don't have to do it all on their own. Sales reps also need to know the products and services that are available, the way to position those offerings, and they must have the documentation that customers require to make buying decisions.

As you can imagine, these raw materials rely not only on sales managers, but on other people in your company: marketing, product management, finance, and so on. With salesforce.com, those people can manage their sales-related activities, coordinate with sales teams, and instantly provide the raw materials in one convenient interface. And because users can access salesforce.com anywhere at anytime, you don't have to worry about getting calls from reps sitting in airports in the middle of the night.

This part is devoted to the unsung heroes of marketing (although sales people will find these chapters useful, too). I show you how to set up a Document Library where you can store the latest and greatest sales collateral. You discover how easily you can build e-mail and Word templates that sales reps can use instead of having to re-create the wheel each time they need to send information. Next, I cover the exciting world of marketing campaigns and how you can use salesforce.com to manage and measure campaigns and demonstrate your contribution to the bottom line. I also take you through the details of setting up your product catalog and price books in salesforce.com so that reps can easily link products to opportunities and even generate quotes.

Chapter 11

Driving Sales Effectiveness with Documents

*I*f you, as a sales or marketing manager, expect to get the most out of your sales reps, you have to put the best tools at their fingertips. Aside from a desk, chair, phone, and some caffeine, reps need accurate and compelling documentation: sell sheets, white papers, case studies, and so on. In today's competitive environment, they need this backup information to speak intelligently about your company and services and to be properly armed when they identify a selling opportunity. Sales reps can't afford to waste time searching for the right document when your customer asks. All too often, however, sales documents reside in multiple places: network drives, intranets, e-mails, desktops, and so on.

If your reps are losing business because they can't access the right documents, take advantage of the salesforce.com Document Library, which you can use to store the latest and greatest sales collateral in easy-to-use, organized folders. And so long as you have an Internet connection, reps can access the Document Library, even if they're sitting in an airport in Omaha, Nebraska.

What does an easily accessible library mean for you? If you're a sales rep or manager, you can spend more time in front of your customer and spend less time chasing information. If you're in marketing or product management, you can better control the message to customers with the confidence that sales reps are providing customers the most up-to-date information available. And regardless of your role, you can individually store documents in your own personal folder.

In this chapter, I show you how to organize folders, load and maintain the Document Library, and search for documents so that your reps can put them to work to sell more effectively.

Understanding the Document Library in Salesforce.com

The Document Library in salesforce.com is much like a network drive that you use to store critical documents. You can create folders to organize sales documents and index those documents so that they're easily retrievable by sales teams.

Depending on your desire for document control, you can store your documents directly in salesforce.com or simply use Web links if you prefer that your documents be maintained internally. Whichever method you decide to use, the point is that you want to make sales information quickly accessible to your sales people wherever they are and whenever they need it.

A document record comes standard with a set of fields that help you find, retrieve, and maintain your documents.

Organizing Your Documents

If you want documents to be a highly effective sales tool for your staff, you have to organize your documents so that people can easily find them. By using folders, you can sort documents into logical groupings.

Building folders

I've seen many different and effective approaches to organizing document folders in salesforce.com. Some companies like to separate documents by product family; others prefer to take a vertical approach. The only right answer is the one that works for your company, but the following is a list of common folders that work for many organizations:

✔ Sell sheets

✔ Sales presentations

✔ Product data sheets

✔ Proposal templates

✔ White papers

✔ Press releases

✔ Case studies

✔ General marketing

✔ Salesforce.com training

To create a document folder, go to the Documents home page and follow these steps:

1. **Click the Create New Folder link under the Document Folders heading.**

   A New Document Folder page appears.

2. **Type a name for the folder in the Document Folder field.**

3. **Use the Public Folder Access drop-down list to select the access rights.**

4. **Use the radio buttons to select who should have access to the folder.**

   See Figure 11-1 for an example of creating a document folder.

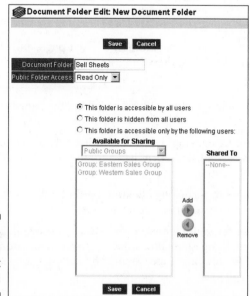

Figure 11-1:
Creating a
document
folder.

5. **When you're done, click Save.**

   The Documents home page reappears, and your folder is added to the Document Folders drop-down list.

REMEMBER

As you plan out your document strategy, keep in mind that not all sales documents need to be in the Document Library. Some might be better suited as attachments on an account record; others you might not even want in salesforce.com. As a general rule, documents that might be re-useable or have wide applicability are well suited for the library. Documents that relate to a specific account are typically more relevant as attachments to Account detail pages.

Viewing document lists

A document list shows a list of documents contained in a folder. To view a list, select a folder from the Document Folders drop-down list on the Documents home page. A list page appears, as shown in the example in Figure 11-2.

Documents: Sell Sheets
Help
Folder Sell Sheets
Edit | Create New Folder
Previous Page | Next Page
New Document
A | B | C | D | E | F | G | H | I | J | K | L | M | N | O | P | Q | R | S | T | U | V | W | X | Y | Z | Other | All
Action
Name
Description
File Size
Last Modified
Type
Author
Edit | Del | View | Email
Widget 1 Sell Sheet
This document summarizes all the features and pricing for Widget 1.
81KB
8/24/2004 1:02 PM
doc
TWong
Edit | Del | View | Email
Widget 2 Sell Sheet
This document summarizes all the features and pricing for Widget 2.
81KB
8/24/2004 1:04 PM
doc
TWong
Edit | Del | View | Email
Widget 3 Sell Sheet
This document summarizes all the features and pricing for Widget 3.
81KB
8/24/2004 1:04 PM
doc
TWong
Previous Page | Next Page

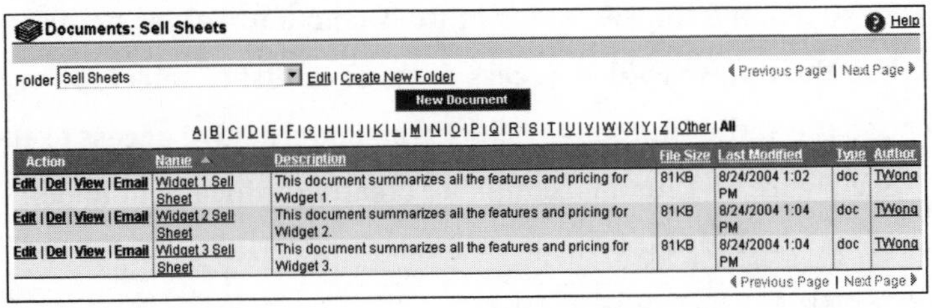

Figure 11-2: Viewing a document list.

You can perform a variety of functions common to a list page, and some actions unique to document folders. (See Chapter 2 for tips on list pages.) Unique actions include

- **Adding** another document to the folder by clicking the New Document button.
- **Deleting** a document by clicking the Del link adjacent to a document listed. (You must have read/write privileges to do this.) Deleted documents go to the Recycle Bin.
- **Editing** a document's properties by clicking the Edit link next to a document listed (if you have read-write access to the file).
- **Sending** an e-mail with the document automatically attached. To e-mail a document, simply click the Email link adjacent to a document and complete the e-mail before sending. (See Chapter 8 for details on sending e-mail.)

✔ **Viewing** a document. To view a document, you click the View link next to a document listed in Name column, which opens the file in its associated application.

If salesforce.com can't recognize the file type of the document or you don't have the right application on your computer, a dialog box appears, prompting you to save the document to your computer. Save the document and then seek out help from someone in your company's desktop support group.

Adding Documents

Before reps can begin using documents in salesforce.com, you or someone in your company must first add the documents to the Document Library.

You basically have two options for adding documents to the library: by uploading the actual file or by creating a link that points to where the document is stored on your network or intranet. You can do both depending on which approach is appropriate for a particular file. In this section, I show you how to perform both functions and the advantages and disadvantages of each option.

Uploading a document

If you've been searching for a solution for document management of sales collateral and you're not overly concerned with storage, you might prefer to upload your files into salesforce.com. (See the later section, "Maintaining the Document Library," for details on standard document storage limits.) The huge advantage of the upload option is that users can access the actual documents anywhere and at anytime as long as they can connect to the Internet.

When uploading files, the file size limit on any individual file is 5MB. For some companies, this might be the average size of a PowerPoint presentation or a PDF file with graphics, so plan accordingly.

To add a document and upload its file, log in to salesforce.com and follow these steps:

1. Click the New Document link on the taskbar.

An Upload New Document page appears.

If you don't see the New Document link, see your system administrator about whether you have the Edit Documents permission.

2. Type a name for the file in Document Name field.

You don't have to make it the actual name of the file, but you should use a name that is obvious to you and your users.

If you want the document name to be an exact match of the filename, leave this field blank. After you select the file, the filename automatically populates the empty Document Name field.

3. Select the For Internal Use Only check box only if you want this document to be confidential.

If you select this check box, you don't alter its access, but you flag your end users not to send the file outside the company.

4. Use the Folder drop-down list to select a folder.

If you haven't yet created the appropriate folder or you don't have read-write access to the correct folder, you can first store the file in the My Personal Documents folder and re-file the document later.

When setting up your Document Library, create folders before adding documents so that you don't have to re-file documents later.

5. In the Description field, type a brief description of the document.

Write a description that provides clarity to users and can be used for search criteria.

6. In the Keywords field, type keywords that will help your end users find the document.

Salesforce.com provides a Find Documents search tool on the Documents home page so you should select keywords that you think your users will enter.

For example, if you're adding a case study, you might enter keywords that include relevant products, customer names, challenges, and so on that sales reps could use for cross-referencing.

7. Under the Select the File step, the Enter the Path radio button is selected by default, so you just need to click the Browse button to select the desired file.

A Choose File dialog box appears.

8. Select a file from the folders on your computer and click Open.

The dialog box closes and the document path is entered in the File to Upload field.

See Figure 11-3 for an example of uploading a document to salesforce.com.

9. When you're done, click Save.

A pop-up window appears, showing progress on the upload. When the upload is completed, the document record page reappears in Saved mode with information on the document and a link to view the document.

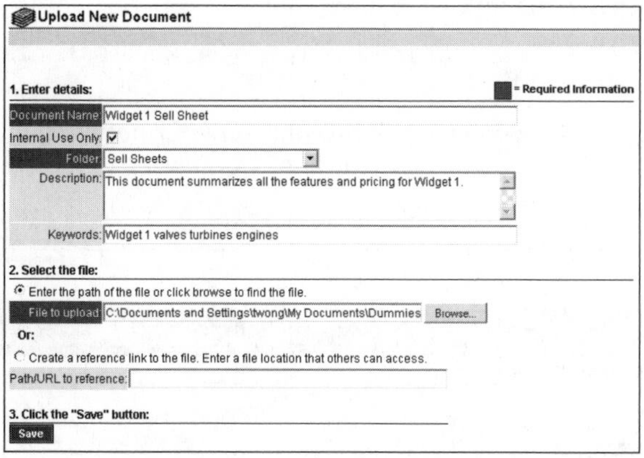

Figure 11-3: Uploading a document.

Linking to an external file

Some companies get concerned about storage constraints in salesforce.com. Other companies already have a robust network drive for sales collateral and don't want to maintain two repositories. Still other companies have marketing people who are responsible for sales collateral although they might not yet have access to salesforce.com. If these or other concerns might impact uploading your files, you can still use the Document Library and point to external documents by adding a Web link or a path and a filename.

To use a Web link to a document in lieu of uploading, the document must first be Web-accessible. For example, if your current sales collateral resides on a network drive that isn't currently accessible from a browser, you're still out of luck. Consult with your MIS department if this is still the path you want to take.

To add a document and reference its location with a path or URL, follow these steps:

1. Create a document record as you normally would, but pause at the Select the File step.

For the steps on creating a document record, see the preceding section.

2. **Under the Select the File step, select the Create a Reference Link to This File radio button.**

3. **In the Path/URL to Reference field provided, type the path or URL, as shown in Figure 11-4.**

   For example, if I want to create a link to salesforce.com's forecast tip sheet, I could use the following link:

   ```
   https://na1.salesforce.com/help/doc/en/salesforce_
                forecast_cheatsheet.pdf
   ```

   In addition to URLs, you can point to files on your network with links that look like *file:\\\\networkdrive\\\\folder\\\\filename*.

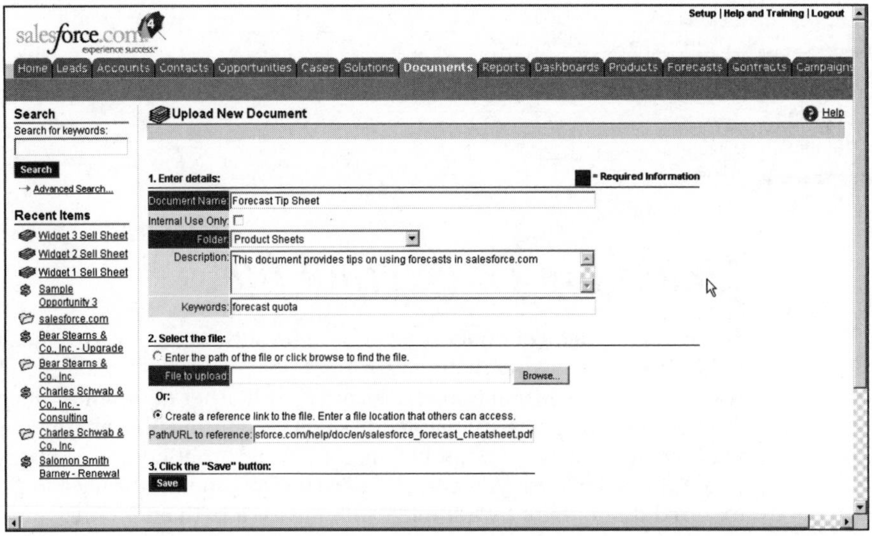

Figure 11-4: Adding a document with a Web link.

4. **When you're done, click Save.**

   A pop-up window appears, showing progress on the upload. When the upload is complete, the document record page reappears in Saved mode with information on the document and a link to the location of the document.

   If you decide to use Web links instead of uploading the actual file, your end users can't attach those documents to e-mails sent from salesforce.com.

Using Documents

After you create documents in salesforce.com, you can use various tools to search and utilize documents in the course of your selling. In this section, I show you how to use the Documents home page to search for documents with the Document Folders drop-down list and the Find Documents search box. Then, I cover the simple practice of attaching a document to an e-mail before sending it to a customer from salesforce.com.

Searching for documents

You can search for documents with keywords from the search box located on the Documents home page. To perform this action, click the Documents tab to go to the Documents home page and follow these steps:

1. **In the Find Documents search box, type search terms, as shown in Figure 11-5.**

   Salesforce.com doesn't search the actual contents of the document itself, just the Document Name, Keywords, and Description fields. So it's important to enter good keywords and descriptions to enable good searches.

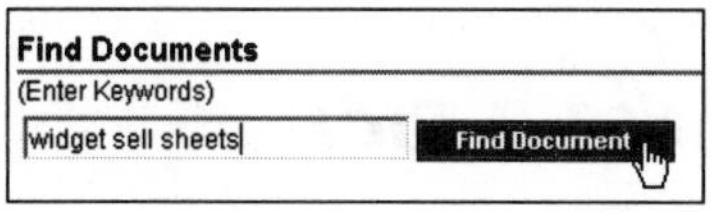

Figure 11-5:
Searching
for a
document.

> **Find Documents**
> (Enter Keywords)
> | widget sell sheets | **Find Document** |

2. **Click the Find Document button.**

   A Document Search page appears with a list of documents based on your search. The results are ordered by closest matches, as shown in Figure 11-6. Salesforce.com uses Document Name and Keywords fields to rank the closest matches.

3. **Click a View link in the Action column if you want to make sure that you've found the correct document.**

   A window opens with your selected document.

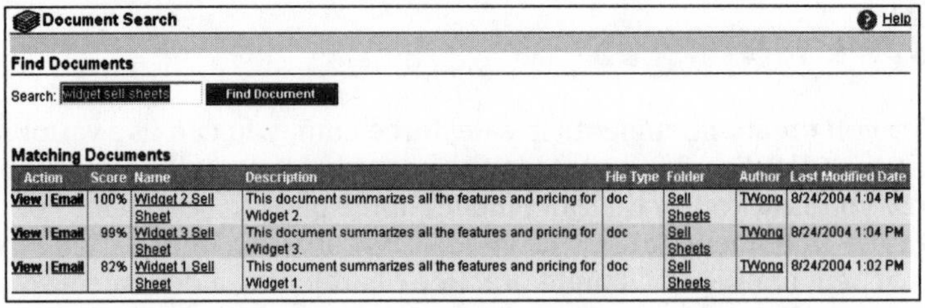

Figure 11-6:
Viewing
document
search
results.

Searching through folders

If you think you know the name of the folder where the document is located, you can also use the folders from the Documents home page. To search through folders, click the Documents tab to go to the Documents home page and follow these steps:

1. **Use the Document Folders drop-down list to select a folder.**

   A list page appears with the list of documents that have been placed in the folder.

2. **Click the View link to look at the actual file or click a link in the Name column to see information on the document.**

   See the "Viewing document lists" section earlier in this chapter for other details on using list pages.

Sending documents via e-mail

In Chapter 8, I discuss how to attach a document to an e-mail to send to a contact or lead. From a document list that results from a folder or a search, you can also directly send an e-mail as long as the document is uploaded in salesforce.com. If you're focusing on a specific document and you want to send it out to people, you can save a lot of time and effort. For example, if marketing prepares a new product launch and announces that a new product sheet is available, you might want to go directly to the document list or detail page and e-mail the document to a set of customers.

To send an e-mail with a document attached, go to a document list or the Document detail page and follow these steps:

1. **Click the Email link from a document list or click the Email Document button from a record, as shown in Figure 11-7.**

The result is the same. A Send an Email page appears. You can see that your document is attached by scrolling down to the Attachments related list.

Document: Widget 1 Sell Sheet

Figure 11-7:
E-mailing a
document.

2. **Fill out your e-mail as you would normally.**

   See Chapter 8 for details on sending an e-mail from salesforce.com.

3. **When you're done, click Send.**

   The document page that you initiated the e-mail from reappears. You can view a record of the e-mail and the document sent from the Activity History related lists of the records that you linked in the e-mail. For example, if you send a document and e-mail to a contact, you can view the e-mail under the Activity History related list on the Contact detail page.

When you send an e-mail with an attachment, salesforce.com doesn't store a copy of the attachment with the e-mail record, but salesforce.com does reference the name of the file sent. By doing this, you conserve your storage space, but you have to go back to the document if you want to review its content.

Maintaining the Document Library

Anyone who has ever managed a document repository for themselves or their company can tell you that repositories need to be maintained to remain effective. If you sell a variety of products, for example, your product sheets need to updated as specs change, deleted if you retire products, and added as you release new products.

You have to face the challenge of keeping the Document Library up to date regardless of whether you use salesforce.com. But salesforce.com provides easy-to-use tools to help you manage the workload of document control.

Editing document records

When I talk about editing documents in salesforce.com, I mean editing the document record — not the file itself. Whether you're a sales rep updating documents in My Personal Documents or you're the director of marketing communications responsible for all sales collateral, you might periodically need to change the properties on documents.

To edit a document record, search for a document, open a Document detail page and follow these simple steps:

1. **Click the Edit Properties button.**

   A Document Edit page opens for the selected document, as shown in Figure 11-8.

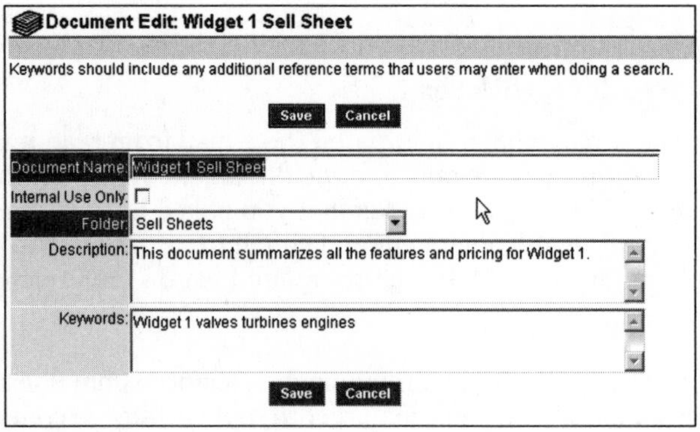

Figure 11-8:
Editing
document
properties.

Document Edit: Widget 1 Sell Sheet
Keywords should include any additional reference terms that users may enter when doing a search.
Save   Cancel
Document Name: Widget 1 Sell Sheet
Internal Use Only: ☐
Folder: Sell Sheets
Description: This document summarizes all the features and pricing for Widget 1.
Keywords: Widget 1 valves turbines engines
Save   Cancel

2. **Modify any of the information.**

   You can edit five fields: Document Name, Internal Use Only, Folder, Description, and Keywords.

3. **When you're done, click Save.**

   The Document detail page reappears, displaying any changes you've made.

Updating documents

If you want to update an actual document, you must replace the current file either by pointing to a different URL or uploading a replacement file.

To update a document, go to the document record and follow these steps:

1. **Click the Replace Document button, as shown in Figure 11-9.**

   A Replace page appears for your selected document.

Figure 11-9:
Replacing a
document.

2. **Under the Select the File step, choose an option for replacing the file:**

   • **If you want to upload a file, click the Browse button and locate the file.** See the section "Uploading a document" for details.

   • **If you want to use a Web link, select the Click to Reference a URL radio button and enter the new URL in the field provided.**

3. **When you're done, click the Replace Document button.**

   The Document detail page reappears with the replacement changes that you made.

If you're in sales or marketing management, consider using Web links on the main home page to promote new or updated sales documents. By doing this, you can foster greater adoption of the Document Library and keep users informed of important document developments.

Deleting documents

In the course of managing your documents, you might want to delete documents that you no longer want in salesforce.com.

To delete a document, go to the document record and follow these steps:

1. **Click the Delete button.**

   A pop-up window appears, warning you that deleting could affect associated e-mail templates or letterheads.

2. **If you want to proceed, click OK.**

   The Document home page appears, and the deleted document is stored in your Recycle Bin for 30 days.

Chapter 12

Improving Communication with Standard Templates

*T*he wonderful thing about creating communication templates (as the name implies) is that it allows you and your end users to reuse what works instead of repeatedly reinventing the wheel. In so doing, your company can use templates to communicate to so many more people than you otherwise could, and your users can sell and service more productively.

With salesforce.com, you can build reusable templates both for documents and e-mail messages. And templates in salesforce.com can make use of mail merge, a feature that allows you to combine a template with information from another data source with the use of merge fields. (More on merge fields in the next section.) But the point is that your end users can quickly generate documents or emails that are both professional and highly personalized.

In this chapter, I show you how to create standard e-mail templates, install and use Office Edition for Microsoft Word, and set up and use mail merge to generate customized Word documents.

Understanding Standard Templates

In the normal course of using salesforce.com, you will collect pertinent information (like names, titles, addresses, and so on) on accounts, contacts, leads, and other records. Wouldn't it be great if you didn't have to retype that information in every time you send an e-mail or create a quote or proposal in Microsoft Word? A template allows you to do this by combining reusable content with merge fields for your customized content.

In salesforce.com, you can use two types of standard template tools:

- ✔ E-mail templates for sending an e-mail or using mass e-mail.
- ✔ Mail merge for generating Word documents such as proposals, agreements, quote forms, and letters.

I won't bore you with the technical details of merge fields. What you should know is that each salesforce.com field label, such as Account Name, is associated with a behind-the-scenes database field name (Account_Name) that is used for the merge field. And you should also relax in knowing that salesforce.com provides you easy-to-use tools to automatically generate merge fields so that you don't make mistakes creating a merge field.

To create standard templates for general, wide use, you must be an administrator or be a user with permission to manage public templates and edit HTML templates. See your system administrator if you need help and request access to these permissions. Even if you can't create public templates, all users can create personal e-mail templates. (See Chapter 3 for details on your personal setup.)

Planning Your E-Mail Templates

You don't have to get the e-mail template strategy fully baked the first time. Many successful companies that use salesforce.com e-mail templates began with simple e-mail templates that created immediate benefit to the sales teams. Then as the adoption grew, these companies got more creative with e-mail templates, plus they got better because they learned what worked. To be successful, however, you should understand the possibilities and begin to organize e-mail templates in ways that would make their uses obvious to your end users.

Understanding the possibilities

If you haven't done so already, go to a whiteboard and draw out all the processes involved in marketing, selling, and satisfying customers. Then list all the standard communications that relate to particular stages of the processes.

If this seems too complicated, I recommend that you assemble a small SWAT team of sales reps and revisit a recent, typical customer win — especially if the win originated from marketing. Ask the team to describe the sales process and types of outbound communication that were critical to the sale.

You will probably come up with your own unique list, but many salesforce.com customers create e-mail templates that give their sales teams a head start on composing such items as company introductions, product background, customer references, and thank you notes, to name a few.

Write down your list, prioritize the list, and review the list items with sales reps to get their buy in and suggestions. Ask your top reps to send you examples of e-mails they commonly use. You might be pleasantly surprised by what you can reuse.

Setting up e-mail template folders

You can create folders for e-mail templates in salesforce.com so that the right templates are easy to find and maintain. After the template folders are created, you can just select a template the next time you're sending an e-mail. I've seen many options for organizing folders, but I recommend keeping it simple and obvious. Common approaches might include folders for the following:

- ✔ Sales team e-mail templates
- ✔ Customer service e-mail templates
- ✔ Product-specific e-mail templates
- ✔ Marketing campaign e-mail templates

To create an e-mail template folder, log in to salesforce.com and follow these steps:

1. **Click the Setup link in the top-right corner of any salesforce.com page.**

   The Personal Setup page appears.

2. **On the sidebar (on the left) under the Administration Setup heading, click the Communication Templates heading.**

   The Communication Templates page appears.

3. **In the sidebar under the Communication Templates heading, click the Email Templates link.**

   The Email Templates page appears.

4. **Click the Create New Folder link next to the Folder drop-down list.**

   A New Email Template Folder page appears, as shown in Figure 12-1.

   If you've already created templates that are unfiled, you can use the Add/Remove tool to move templates into your new folder as you're creating the folder.

5. **Type a folder name and select a radio button to determine access rights for users; if you choose limited access (the third radio button), use the two list boxes to select the roles or groups that should have access.**

   For those you granted access, you can select Read Only or Read/Write.

6. **When you're done, click Save.**

   The Email Templates page reappears, and your new folder displays on the Folder drop-down list.

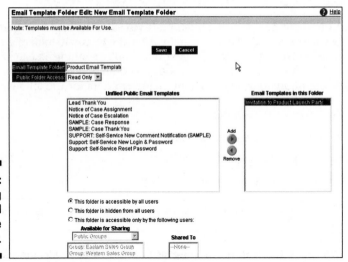

Figure 12-1:
Creating
an e-mail
template
folder.

Creating E-Mail Templates

With salesforce.com, your company can create e-mail templates in three different formats:

- ✔ Text
- ✔ HTML (with letterhead)
- ✔ Custom (without letterhead)

Regardless of which format you use, you can construct your e-mail templates with standard content, attachments, and merge fields.

Creating a text e-mail template

All users can create text e-mail templates. If you're concerned that fancy HTML would annoy customers, you can always use text as a reliable option.

To create a text e-mail, log in to salesforce.com and follow these steps:

1. **Click Setup in the top-right corner of any salesforce.com page**

   The Personal Setup page appears.

2. **On the sidebar under the Administration Setup heading, click the Communication Templates heading.**

   The Communication Templates page appears.

3. **On the sidebar under the Communication Templates heading, click the Email Templates link.**

   The Email Templates page appears.

4. **Click the New Template button, as shown in Figure 12-2.**

   Step 1 of the template wizard appears.

Figure 12-2:
Starting the
e-mail
template
wizard.

5. **Select the Text radio button and click Next.**

6. **Complete the template fields.**

   The following are some pointers for Step 2 of this wizard:

   • **Folder:** Select the folder for your e-mail template.

   • **Available For Use:** Select this check box if you want to make your e-mail template immediately available.

   You must check the Available For Use Box if you want users to be able to see the template when sending an e-mail.

- **Template Name:** Create a name that will be obvious to your users.

- **Encoding:** Select the encoding for the e-mail. If you don't know the right option for your company, select the General US & Western Europe option (which works for most English-speaking countries) or check with your MIS department.

- **Description:** Use this field to provide additional details to your users. It is for internal purposes only.

- **Subject:** Compose a standard subject line and use merge fields to personalize. See the sidebar "Generating merge fields for e-mail."

- **Email Body:** Type the standard message for your e-mail template. Insert merge fields where appropriate to personalize the message.

7. **When you're done, click Save.**

   A Text Email Template page for your new template appears in Saved mode with an Attachments related list, which you can use to attach a standard document.

Generating merge fields for e-mail

Instead of trying to decipher merge fields, use the merge field tool displayed during the Add Content step of the e-mail template wizard to generate accurate merge fields for your e-mail template.

To generate a merge field, go to the grey box labeled Available Merge Fields and follow these steps:

1. **Select the field type from the first drop-down list.**

   For example, if you're looking for the merge field for a contact's title, you would select Contact Fields from the drop-down list.

2. **Select the field by from the second drop-down list.**

   To follow the same example, you would choose Contact: Title. After you select a field, a merge field value appears in the third box, as shown in the figure.

3. **Copy and paste the merge field value into the e-mail template.**

Creating a standard HTML letterhead

To get the most out of extending your brand image, use an HTML template with a standard letterhead. With a letterhead, you can embed your logo and other creative images into a template to promote your corporate identity. And one of the exciting benefits of using a letterhead is that if your company brand changes (colors, logos, taglines, and so on), you can change the letterhead once and all templates built on the letterhead are changed, too.

Before you can create this HTML template, you first have to create a letterhead for your company. Then you can use the template wizard with additional formatting tools.

With letterheads, you can control the look and feel of your outbound e-mails. In addition to the logo, you can adjust background colors, text settings, and basic layout.

To create a letterhead, log in to salesforce.com and follow these steps:

1. **Click the Setup link in the top-right corner of any salesforce.com page.**

   The Personal Setup page appears.

2. **On the sidebar under the Administration Setup heading, click the Communication Templates heading.**

   The Communication Templates page appears.

3. **On the sidebar under the Communication Templates heading, click the Letterheads link.**

   The Letterheads page appears.

4. **Click the New Letterhead button.**

   The first time you use this tool, an Understand Letterheads page appears. When you understand the basics of letterheads, you can select the Don't Show Me This Page Again check box to bypass this page in the future.

5. **Click Next.**

   The Step 1 page of the letter properties wizard appears, as shown in Figure 12-3.

6. **Fill in the properties including name, description, and availability, and then click the Save & Next button.**

   The Step 2 page appears to customize look and feel.

7. **Click layout buttons to adjust the look and feel.**

   With these buttons you can essentially select or remove your logo and edit the properties of the different sections of the letterhead including header, body and footer, and so on.

If you're going to insert your logo into the letterhead, you must first save the logo as a document in salesforce.com.

8. When you're satisfied, click the Save & Done button.

The Letterhead page reappears in Saved mode with a summary of the properties you chose and a visual of the letterhead.

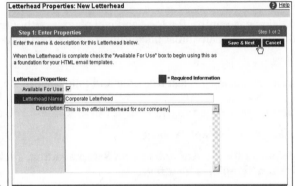

Figure 12-3:
Entering
properties
for a
letterhead.

Creating an HTML template with a letterhead

You can use a completed letterhead for HTML templates.

To create an HTML template by using a letterhead, follow the first four steps of the section "Creating a text e-mail template," and then and add these steps.

1. Select the HTML (Using Letterhead) radio button and click Next.

Step 2 of the template wizard appears.

2. Enter the properties for the HTML e-mail template (see Figure 12-4), and then click the Save & Next button.

See the bullets under Step 6 of the section "Creating a text e-mail template" for details. The following are two additional required fields:

- **Letterhead:** Use this drop-down list to select the desired letterhead.

- **Email Layout:** Use this drop-down list to select the desired layout or click View Email Layout Options and use the popup window to select the layout.

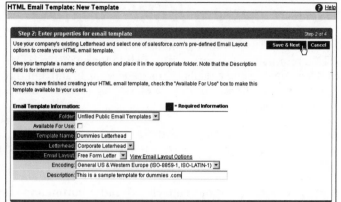

Figure 12-4:
Filling in
template
properties
when using
letterhead.

After you click the Save & Next button, the Step 3 page of the template wizard appears.

3. Create the HTML version by composing the message and copying and pasting merge fields.

See the sidebar "Generating merge fields for e-mail."

4. Use the Formatting Controls tool to format your e-mail template.

You use the Formatting Controls tool just as you would the Formatting toolbar in Microsoft Word.

If you need to figure out the function of a button or drop-down list on the Formatting Controls tool, simply hover your cursor over the button or drop-down list and a ToolTip description appears.

5. Click Preview to review your work, and when you're done, click the Save & Next button.

The Step 4 page of the wizard appears.

6. Type in the text version of the e-mail template.

Some of your customers cannot or choose not to receive HTML e-mails, in which case they would receive the text version. If the message is similar or identical to the HTML version, click the Copy Text from HTML Version button and modify as needed.

7. When you're done, click the Save & Done button.

An HTML Email Template page for your new template appears in Saved mode with an Attachments related list for attaching files.

Creating a custom HTML template

If you're a system administrator or you have the permissions in salesforce.com to edit HTML templates, you can create custom templates in HTML. You can create professional-looking e-mails that extend your brand and that you can track after you've sent them. For details on tracking HTML e-mails, see Chapter 8 on sending e-mail.

To create a custom e-mail template without a standard letterhead, follow the first four steps of the section "Creating a text e-mail template," and then add these steps:

1. **Select the Custom (Without Letterhead) radio button and click Next.**

   The Step 2 page of the template wizard appears, as shown in Figure 12-5.

2. **Enter the properties for the e-mail template and click the Save & Next button.**

   The Step 3 page of the template wizard appears.

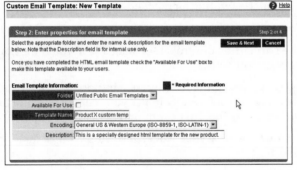

Figure 12-5: Entering properties for a custom HTML template.

3. **Create the HTML version by composing the message and copying and pasting merge fields.**

   If you're experienced with HTML, you can insert traditional HTML code into the Subject and Email Body fields to better control the look and feel of your template.

4. **Click the Preview button to review your work, and when you're done, click the Save & Next button.**

   The Step 4 page of the wizard appears.

5. **Type in the text version of the e-mail template.**

   Some of your customers cannot or choose not to receive HTML e-mails, in which case they would receive the text version. If the message is similar or identical to the HTML version, click the Copy Text from HTML Version button and modify as needed.

6. **When you're done, click the Save & Done button.**

   An HTML Email Template page for your new template appears in Saved mode with an Attachments related list for attaching files.

Setting Up Your Mail Merge Templates

You can automatically create documents by using your data with Microsoft Word templates. To perform this function, your system administrator first has to set up and load the templates for the mail merge tool.

In this section, I show you the easiest way to build templates with Office Edition, upload your templates, and then generate a personalized mail merge document. (See Chapter 3 for details on installing Office Edition.)

Building a mail merge template

With Office Edition installed, you can quickly build mail merge templates. Even if you don't have permission to upload the files, you can always build the templates and forward them to your system administrator for loading.

To build a mail merge template by using Microsoft Word, follow these steps:

1. **Open Microsoft Word.**

   Office Edition adds a new menu (labeled *salesforce.com*) to the menu bar.

2. **Choose salesforce.com➪Login.**

   A dialog box opens, prompting you for your salesforce.com user name and password.

3. **Enter your user name and password in the fields and the click the Login button.**

   When the dialog box disappears, you have successfully logged in.

4. **Open a document that you want to become a template.**

   For example, you might open a standard contract.

5. **Identify any variable information in the document.**

   Variable information are the blanks — the areas of your template that change each time you begin a new document. Following the same example, a contract might have blanks to be filled in for the account, the account's address, the contact, the contact's title, and so on. Those variable sections might be perfect places to insert a merge field.

6. **Place your cursor where you want to insert a merge field in the document.**

   If your template currently has actual underlines for blanks, you will want to delete the blanks.

7. **Choose salesforce.com⇨Insert Merge Field.**

   An Insert Merge Field dialog box appears.

8. **Select the field type by selecting a value in the first list box.**

   For example, if you want to insert a company-related field, select the Account Field option.

9. **Select the merge fields that you want to insert by clicking a value in the second list box.**

   You can select multiple fields at one time by holding down your Shift key before clicking.

10. **When you're done, click the Insert button.**

    The dialog box disappears, and your selected merge fields appear within your document. Repeat Steps 5 through 9 as often as needed until you are done with your template.

11. **When you're done, you save your document under a new filename.**

    You could save the mail merge template over the existing document, but by taking this extra step, you can always go back to the previous document, and you know which one is the mail merge template.

Uploading your mail merge templates

If you're your own system administrator, you can load mail merge templates into salesforce.com. If you don't have the permissions to do so, you might want to send the templates to the administrator.

To upload mail merge templates, log in to salesforce.com and follow these steps:

1. **Click the Setup link in the top-right corner of any salesforce.com page.**

   The Personal Setup page appears.

2. **On the sidebar under the Administration Setup heading, click the Communication Templates heading.**

   The Communication Templates page appears.

3. **On the sidebar under the Communication Templates heading, click the Mail Merge Templates link.**

   The Microsoft Word page appears with details on mail merge, plus a bonus link to download default templates.

   With the default templates you can get a quick start to creating templates, including one of the most requested templates: the quote form! One of the big uses of mail merge templates with salesforce.com is to generate custom quotes from opportunities especially if your reps use products. Creating this template requires some extra steps, but for a great shortcut, click the Download the Default Templates link on the Microsoft Word page. Open the templates and copy and paste the last template — entitled Quote with Products — into a new document. Then modify the content to suit your needs before uploading it. By doing this, you can provide a solution to your sales teams that will be a big time-saver when generating quotes.

4. **Click the Manage Your Document Mail Merge Templates link.**

   An All page appears with a list of currently loaded mail merge documents.

5. **Click the New Template button.**

   A New Template page appears, as shown in Figure 12-6.

Figure 12-6: Adding a mail merge template.

All						❓ Help
This is a list of the mail merge templates available to your users. To upload a new mail merge template, click on the "New Template" button below.						
			New Template		◀ Previous Page	Next Page ▶	
		A|B|C|D|E|F|G|H|I|J|K|L|M|N|O|P|Q|R|S|T|U|V|W|X|Y|Z| Other | **All**				
Action	Name ▲	Description	Filename	Size	Created By Alias	Created Date
Edit | Del | Preview	Appointment Request	Appointment Request	Appointment Request.doc	23KB	TWong	1/18/2003
Edit | Del | Preview	Lost Sale	Lost Sale	Lost Sale.doc	24KB	TWong	1/18/2003
Edit | Del | Preview	Phone Call Follow Up	Phone Call Follow Up	Phone Call Follow Up.doc	23KB	TWong	1/18/2003
Edit | Del | Preview	Referral Request	Referral Request	Referral Request.doc	26KB	TWong	1/18/2003
Edit | Del | Preview	Reminder for Function	Reminder for Function	Reminder for Function.doc	24KB	TWong	1/18/2003
Edit | Del | Preview	Reminder To Buy	Reminder To Buy	Reminder To Buy.doc	24KB	TWong	1/18/2003

6. **Complete the fields and click the Save button to locate your mail merge template, as shown in Figure 12-7.**

   A dialog box appears, which you can use to locate your file.

7. **Use the dialog box to locate your file, and then click Open.**

   The dialog box closes and the filename appears in the File field.

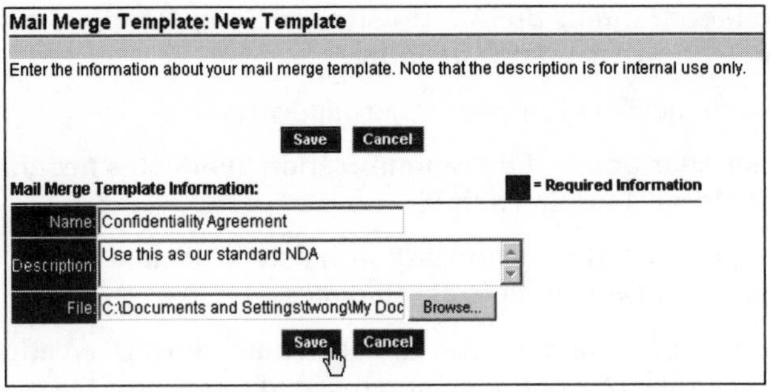

Figure 12-7:
Completing
the mail
merge
upload.

> **Mail Merge Template: New Template**
>
> Enter the information about your mail merge template. Note that the description is for internal use only.
>
> [Save] [Cancel]
>
> **Mail Merge Template Information:** [ ] = Required Information
>
> Name: Confidentiality Agreement
>
> Description: Use this as our standard NDA
>
> File: C:\Documents and Settings\twong\My Doc [Browse...]
>
> [Save] [Cancel]

8. **When you're done, click Save.**

   A Mail Merge Template page appears with a record of your new mail merge template.

Running a Mail Merge

If your administrator has loaded mail merge templates, you can generate personalized documents that combine templated content with your sales force.com data. You can run this tool from any lead, contact, case, contract, or opportunity record.

To run a mail merge, go to a relevant record, such as an opportunity, and follow these steps:

1. **Click the Mail Merge button on the Activity History related list.**

   A Mail Merge page appears, as shown in Figure 12-8.

2. **Specify the contact.**

   If you started from a lead or contact record, this field is prefilled. If not, click the Lookup icon and use the search window to find and select the appropriate contact or lead.

3. **Select the template by clicking a template in the Specify the Template list box.**

   Salesforce.com commonly prepopulates this list with sample templates.

4. **Select the Log an Activity check box if you want to log an activity.**

   If you want to record the activity on the Activity History related list, select the check box.

5. When you're done, click the Generate button (see Figure 12-8).

If you selected the Log an Activity check box, a Log a Call page appears where you can record comments about the activity. See Chapter 7 for details on logging an activity. At the same time, Microsoft Word opens with your mail merge document.

Figure 12-8: Generating a mail merge document.

The first time you run mail merge, a dialog box prompts you to install a plug in for the mail merge utility. Click Yes in the dialog box to proceed with the installation.

6. Make any changes to the mail merge document and save the file.

You can then print the document or e-mail the document as an attachment. Some sales reps also prefer to store the document as an attachment on the relevant record so that they can refer to it for future reference. See Chapter 9 for tips on attaching documents to records such as opportunities.

Chapter 13

Driving Demand with Campaigns

In This Chapter
- ▶ Creating campaigns
- ▶ Creating a target list
- ▶ Executing a campaign
- ▶ Assessing campaign effectiveness

Companies want to increase revenue by spending marketing dollars intelligently. However, because of the disconnect between sales and marketing teams, managers have a harder time executing campaigns, let alone tracking and measuring the results of their marketing programs.

If this sounds familiar to you, campaigns in salesforce.com can help you manage and track your marketing programs more effectively, resulting in lower costs, better leads, and potentially greater sales.

A *campaign* is any marketing project that you want to plan, manage, and track in salesforce.com. Depending on your current or planned strategies, types of campaigns include tradeshows, direct marketing (including e-mail), seminars, Web events, and print advertising, although this is by no means a complete list.

In this chapter, you find out how to create and manage campaigns, segment target lists, execute campaigns, track responses, and analyze campaign effectiveness.

To administer campaigns, you must be a system administrator or a user with permission to manage campaigns. See Chapter 22 for details on configuring your user information and profile to manage campaigns.

Understanding Campaigns

The Campaign module in salesforce.com is a set of tools that enable you to manage, track, and measure your outbound marketing programs. Its foundation is the campaign record, but the campaign record can be manually or automatically linked to lead, contact, and/or opportunity records to provide real metrics on campaign effectiveness.

A Campaign record comes standard with a set of fields that help you manage and track your campaigns. The following list describes the fields you use most often to measure campaign effectiveness:

- **Campaign Name:** This is the name of your marketing project. Choose a name that is readily obvious to sales reps and other users whose leads or contacts might be included in the campaign.

- **Type:** This drop-down list includes the types of campaigns you run within your marketing mix (Direct Mail, Email, and so on).

- **Status:** This drop-down list defines the statuses of a campaign. Salesforce.com provides a simple default drop-down list of statuses to measure a campaign's progress.

- **Start Date:** A date field you use to track when a campaign begins.

- **End Date:** A date field you use to track when a campaign ends.

- **Expected Revenue:** Use this currency field to estimate how much revenue the campaign will generate.

- **Budgeted Cost:** This is the amount that you have budgeted for the marketing project.

- **Actual Cost:** This is the amount that the project actually cost.

- **Expected Response:** This percentage field is your best guess of the response rate on a campaign.

- **Num Sent:** This is the amount of people targeted in the campaign. For example, if you executed an e-mail campaign to 10,000 e-mail addresses, that would be your Num Sent.

- **Active:** Use this check box to mark whether a campaign is active or not.

- **Description:** This field allows you to describe the campaign so that other users who want more detailed information on the campaign can get a solid snapshot.

Depending on your marketing processes, terminology, and goals, you or your system administrator should modify the drop-down list values and change the fields on the record. (See Chapter 18 for details on customizing salesforce.com.)

If you're a marketing manager, you can plan and manage the majority of your campaign preparation inside salesforce.com. You can

✔ Lay out your entire marketing plan of projects.

✔ Build the basic framework and business case for a project.

✔ Define statuses and success metrics for campaign responses. By *success metrics,* I mean how you determine if the campaign was worth your company's time, money, and effort. Each company has their own metrics, but with salesforce.com you can define and measure those numbers.

✔ Develop a detailed project plan so that important tasks get accomplished.

In this section, I show you where and how to accomplish these tasks.

Creating a new campaign

To create a campaign, log in to salesforce.com and follow these steps:

1. **Click the New Campaign link on the taskbar.**

   A New Campaign page appears, as shown in Figure 13-1.

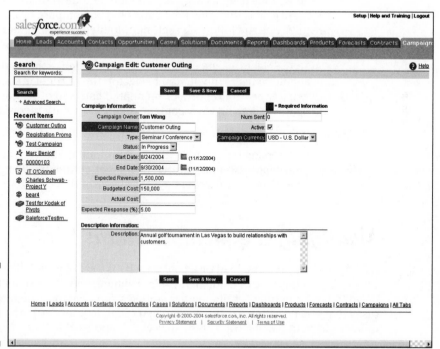

Figure 13-1:
Filling in the campaign record.

2. **Fill in the fields as much as possible or as required.**

   If you currently manage marketing programs for your company, you should see few surprises in the campaign fields. Here are some pointers on completing some of the critical fields, and you can refer to the previous section for a summary of the standard entry fields:

   - **Campaign Name:** Use this for the name of your project. If you operate similar types of campaigns, make the name descriptive enough so that it's obvious to you and your users. For example, if you send out monthly e-mail newsletters, you might distinguish each campaign by month, as in "Newsletter — May" and "Newsletter — June."

   - **Type:** Use this drop-down list to select the type of project.

   - **Status:** Use this drop-down list to select the current status of the campaign. By using this field, you and others can make sure that the campaign is on track.

   - **Expected Response:** Use this percentage field to create a baseline metric for a campaign. For example, if your direct mail campaigns typically receive a 2 percent response rate, you might use this value to benchmark the effectiveness of the campaign. You define what actions from a campaign member actually constitute a response, and then this field can help you compare against the results. See the following section, "Modifying the member status," for the details on campaign members and defining a response.

   - **Active:** Select this check box if you want to make the campaign available to users. If you don't select it, the particular campaign doesn't appear in reports or on related lists and other campaign drop-down lists on lead, contact, and opportunity records.

3. **When you're done, click Save.**

   The campaign page reappears with the information you've entered, as well as additional system-generated fields that automatically update as your company makes progress on a campaign.

Modifying the member status

A campaign member is a lead or a contact who is part of a specific campaign. Depending on the type of campaign you're running, you can modify the campaign to have a unique set of member statuses. For example, the member statuses that you track for an e-mail campaign (Sent, Responded) are typically different from those of a tradeshow that you're sponsoring.

To customize member statuses for a specific campaign, follow these steps:

1. **Go to the campaign record and click the Advanced Setup button.**

   The Campaign Member Status page for your campaign appears. When you first begin to create campaigns, salesforce.com sets up a default set of member status values of Sent and Responded, as shown in Figure 13-2.

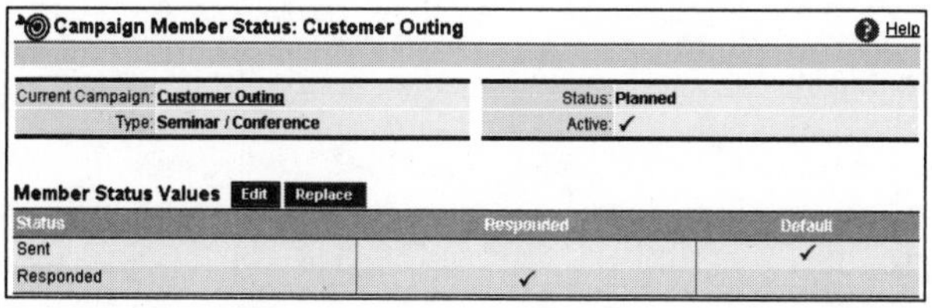

Figure 13-2: Viewing the default member status.

2. **On the Member Status Values related list, click the Edit button.**

   The Campaign Member Status page appears in Edit mode.

3. **Modify statuses by clicking into a field in the Member Status column and entering a new value.**

   For example, suppose that you're sponsoring a booth at a conference, the preregistrants list is part of the package, and you want to invite attendees to visit your booth. In such a case, you might type member statuses of Registered, Invited, Attended, Visited Booth, and Met at Show.

4. **Select the check box in the Responded column to classify a status as responded.**

   By using this field, you can track the Expected Response Rate field against the actual response rate. Following the previous example, both Visited Booth and Met at Show might constitute a response in your success metrics (as shown in Figure 13-3).

5. **Use the Default column to select a default value, and then click Save.**

   The Campaign Member Status page reappears with your changes.

If you want to make sure that all the activities involved in pulling off a campaign get done, you can use campaign related lists for your project planning. Not only can you use the campaign detail page to keep everyone on the team in the loop, but you can use its related lists to assign and track activities to other team members to ensure that no one drops any balls. (For details on creating and updating activity related lists, see Chapter 7.)

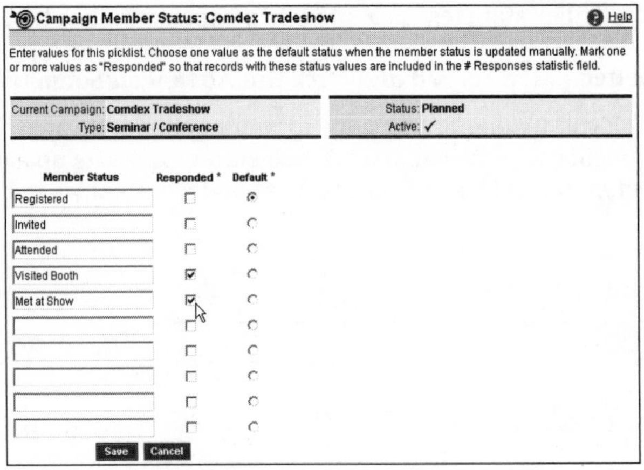

Figure 13-3:
Editing a
campaign's
member
statuses.

Building Target Lists

One of the biggest challenges that marketing managers face is developing
the right target lists for a campaign. *Target lists* are the lists of people you're
targeting in your campaign. Depending on the type of campaign that you're
planning, your lists might come from different sources, such as rented or purchased lists from third-party providers or existing lists of leads and contacts
already entered in salesforce.com. If your target list is composed of the latter,
you can create your target list directly from the salesforce.com Reports tab
and associate specific campaigns to those leads and contacts.

Using rented lists

With a rented list, your options are limited. Depending on the circumstances,
sometimes you don't know who's on the list because the list is controlled by
the vendor. Other times you enter into limited use terms, such as one-time
usage. In these circumstances, simply use the external list as the target list
rather than importing the list into salesforce.com.

You can use salesforce.com to improve the quality of rented lists. Many third-
party vendors de-duplicate their database against your customer database
when they're generating the record count for a rented list. As long as you can
trust the vendor, you can quickly use salesforce.com to generate a file of your
existing contacts to compare. By getting rid of duplicates first, you can stretch

your marketing dollars by making sure that you're not paying for contacts you already have. And if you're doing a mixed campaign of rented and owned lists, you stand a better chance of not upsetting a customer with duplicate mail.

Importing new campaign members

If you own or purchase a list and you intend for your teams to follow up on all the records, you can import the list into salesforce.com as lead records and automatically link the records to a campaign.

To import a list and attribute to a campaign, follow these steps:

1. **On the campaign record, click the Advanced Setup button, verify that the member statuses are accurate, and then return to the campaign record by clicking the Back button on your browser.**

2. **Click the Member Import button.**

   A pop-up window appears for the Campaign Member Import Wizard.

3. **Click the Import Leads button.**

   Step 1 of the Lead Import Wizard appears, as shown in Figure 13-4.

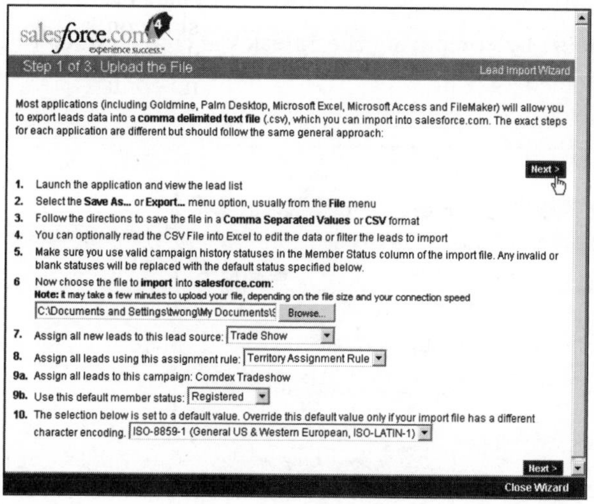

Figure 13-4: Completing the first page of the Lead Import Wizard.

4. **Prepare your file, following the instructions that the wizard gives you.**

   Here are the main steps to perform:

   - Add and fill in a column for Member Status unless all records will use the default member status.
   - Add and fill in a column for Lead Owner unless you will be the owner or you are applying lead assignment rules.
   - Save the file in a .csv format on your computer.

5. **In the wizard, click the Browse button to select the file from your computer.**

   A Choose File dialog box appears.

6. **Locate your file and click Open.**

   The dialog box closes and the file name appears in the field.

7. **Use the drop-down list to select a lead source.**

8. **Use the next drop-down list if you want to select an assignment rule.**

9. **Verify the default member status.**

10. **Leave the character encoding unchanged unless necessary.**

11. **When you're done, click Next.**

    Step 2 of the wizard appears, as shown in Figure 13-5.

12. **Map the fields by comparing the Salesforce.com Field columns against the corresponding drop-down lists in the Import Field columns.**

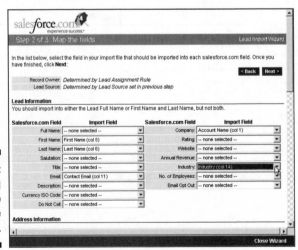

Figure 13-5:
Mapping
fields to
complete
Step 2.

13. **When you're done, click Next.**

    Step 3 of the wizard appears.

14. **Review and confirm the import, and when you're done, click the Import Now button.**

Targeting existing records in salesforce.com

Assuming your company has already imported users' leads and contacts, you can build your target lists directly in salesforce.com by using custom reports. Then in a two-step process, you can link your desired leads or contacts to target them for a specific campaign. See Chapter 18 for all the details on building and exporting custom reports.

To do a member update of existing leads and contacts in salesforce.com, you first have to export the list and then upload the list from the campaign detail page. When you export the list, remember to include the field for either Lead ID or Contact ID.

To associate existing leads or contacts to a campaign you're planning, follow these steps:

1. **From the Reports home page, click a custom report of the leads or contacts that you'll be targeting.**

   A Reports page appears. Make sure that you've customized your report to include a column for the Lead ID or Contact ID, as shown in the example in Figure 13-6.

2. **Click the Export to Excel button.**

   A page appears prompting you to select the file format.

3. **In the Export File Format field, select the Comma Delimited .csv option and click Export.**

   A dialog box opens for the file download.

4. **Click Open.**

   The dialog box disappears, and the Excel file appears.

5. **Add and fill in a Member Status column only if the records will have different statuses.**

   If you're just associating records to a campaign, you will probably choose the default status for all members.

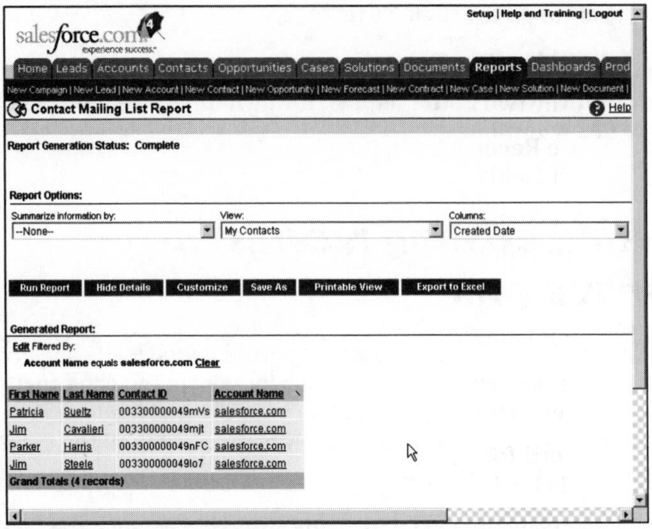

Figure 13-6:
Viewing a
contact
report with
a Contact ID
column.

6. **Delete any unnecessary columns and save the file to your computer.**

   In practice, you need to include only the Lead ID or Contact ID, but I recommend that you retain the First Name, Last Name, and either the
   Account or Company fields.

7. **Go to the specific campaign detail page and review the record to
   verify that the Active check box is selected. If it's deselected, click the
   Edit button, select the Active check box, and click Save.**

   The campaign detail page reappears.

8. **Click the Member Import button.**

   A pop-up window appears with the campaign member import wizard.

9. **Click the Update Campaign History button.**

   Step 1 of the wizard appears.

10. **Complete the fields.**

    You've already done the prep work, so the following are pointers on
    completing this step:

    • Click the Browse button and select the file from your computer.

    • For the Use This Default Member Status drop-down list, select a
      status.

    • Change the encoding selection only if necessary.

11. **Click Next to go to Step 2 of the wizard.**

12. **Map the fields.**

    You have only two fields to consider:

    - For the **Record ID**, select either Lead ID or Contact ID from the Import Field drop-down list.

    - For the **Status**, select an Import Field if you added a column for member status in your file.

13. **Click Next to go to Step 3 of the wizard.**

14. **Review the Review and Confirm page and click the Import Now button.**

    A confirmation page appears, and within minutes your selected leads or contacts are members of your campaign.

15. **Go to a record for a lead or contact that was part of the member update and check the Campaign related list to verify the update.**

    If you can't view the related list, see Chapter 18 for details on customizing the page layout.

Executing Campaigns

Most often you will execute your campaigns outside of salesforce.com. Depending on the type of campaigns you're running, you might be performing those campaigns online or offline or in combination. And based on the complexity of the campaign and your resources, you can use salesforce.com to assist the execution of parts of your campaign.

Delivering an online campaign

If you send out e-mail campaigns as part of your marketing strategy, you can use salesforce.com for elements of the execution. Those elements might include:

✔ Exporting an e-mail list from salesforce.com for delivery to your e-mail execution vendor or internal resource.

✔ Building an automated Web form to capture leads as part of your e-mail or Webinar campaign. (See the section "Capturing leads from Web forms" for details on building Web-to-Lead forms.)

You can use salesforce.com to deliver mass e-mails, but salesforce.com was not designed nor intended to be used for large-scale mass e-mail marketing. Some salesforce.com customers utilize the mass e-mail tool for small campaigns. You can send only 100 e-mails at a time, and your company is limited to 1,000 e-mails a day through this feature. See Chapter 8 for specifics on sending mass e-mail.

Several e-mail vendors have integrated their campaign execution tools with salesforce.com. With this integration, marketing managers can more seamlessly deliver e-mail campaigns from salesforce.com. The costs and functionality vary across the e-mail marketing vendors, but four proven salesforce.com solution partners are Eloqua, Got Corporation, ExactTarget, and VerticalResponse.

Executing an offline campaign

If you execute offline campaigns, you can also use salesforce.com in a variety of ways to simplify the process. How you use salesforce.com depends on the type of campaign, but here are some suggestions:

- ✔ If you're sponsoring a conference, set up a Web registration form for your booth computers to capture information on attendees who visit your booth.

- ✔ If you're sending out direct mail pieces, use salesfore.com to generate lists for your fulfillment vendor. If you're running the direct mail internally, you can use Office Edition to generate labels and personalized mail merge Word documents. (See Chapter 12 for tips on mass mail merge.)

- ✔ If you host Web seminars, with salesforce.com's Winter '05 release, WebEx customers can manage their Web meetings from salesforce.com. If you use another service for hosting Web events, run the Webinar from the other service and see the following section on tracking responses.

Tracking Responses

After you launch a campaign, you can use salesforce.com to track responses. In salesforce.com, you have three basic types of tracking mechanisms, which I describe in the following sections.

To track responses on a campaign, you need to be able to view the Campaign related list on lead and contact records. If you can't view this list, see Chapter 18 on customizing page layouts or see your system administrator for help.

Capturing leads from Web forms

Web-to-Lead is a salesforce.com feature that enables your company to easily capture leads from your Web sites and automatically generate new leads in salesforce.com. With Web-to-Lead, you can collect information from your Web sites and generate up to 500 new leads a day. You might already have a registration or a lead form on your public Web site. With salesforce.com, you can, in minutes, generate HTML code that your Webmaster can apply to your existing form. Then when people fill out the form on your Web site, the information is routed instantaneously to users in salesforce.com. By using Web-to-Lead, your reps can follow up on leads in a timely manner.

Specifically for campaign tracking, you can also create forms for Web pages designed for a unique campaign to capture information on a campaign member who responds.

Before you can capture leads from an external Web page, you need to enable Web-to-Lead, add any additional custom fields to your lead record, generate the HTML code, and add the code into a Web page.

All salesforce.com customers can capture leads from Web forms. First you need to turn it on for your company.

To enable Web-to-Lead, log in to salesforce.com and follow these steps:

1. **Click the Setup link in the top-right corner of any salesforce.com page.**

   The Personal Setup page appears.

2. **Click the Customize heading on the sidebar on the left.**

   The Customize menu appears.

3. **Click the Leads heading on the sidebar.**

   The Leads page for customization appears.

4. **Click the Web-to-Lead link on the sidebar.**

   The Web-to-Lead instructions page appears. Under the Steps to Capturing Leads from your Web Site heading, look to see if Web-to-Lead is already enabled. If so, you're done with these steps.

5. **If Web-to-Lead isn't enabled, click the Enable Web-to-Lead link.**

6. **Fill out the page.**

   Salesforce.com provides three fields:

   - **Web-to-Lead Enabled:** Select this check box.

   - **Default Lead Creator:** Use the Lookup icon next to this field to select the default creator for when a lead is generated from a Web form. You must select a user who has the Modify All Data and Send Email permissions in his or her user profile. You usually select the user who manages marketing campaigns for your organization.

- **Default Response Template:** Select a default e-mail response template. (See Chapter 11 on creating e-mail templates, and see Chapter 4 for details on lead assignment rules.)

7. **When you're done, click Save.**

The Capturing Leads from your Web Site page reappears.

Generating HTML

You can use a tool in salesforce.com that takes the guess work out of generating HTML code for your Web forms.

To generate a general or a campaign-specific Web-to-Lead form, log in to salesforce.com and follow these steps:

1. **Click the Setup link in the top-right corner of a page.**

The Personal Setup page appears.

2. **On the sidebar, click the Customize heading.**

The Customize page appears.

3. **On the sidebar under the Customize heading, click the Leads heading.**

A Leads page appears with a menu for customization.

4. **Click the Web-to-Lead link under the Leads heading on the sidebar.**

A Capturing Leads for your Web Site page appears.

5. **Click the Generate the HTML link.**

A page appears with all the available fields for the lead record.

6. **Select the check boxes for the fields that you want on your Web form, as shown in the example in Figure 13-7.**

If your organization has many lead fields, you can click the Select None link first and then deselect fields at your discretion.

If you're creating a Web form specific to a campaign, create the campaign first and make sure that you've selected the Active check box for that campaign record. By doing this, you can select the fields for Campaign and Campaign Member Status, which enables you to track the specific campaign.

7. **In the URL field, enter a return URL if known, and then click the Generate button at the bottom of the page.**

   The return URL corresponds to the landing page that appears after the lead has submitted his information online. Some companies create a specific confirmation or thank you page for a campaign or the public Web site. When you click the Generate button, a page appears with HTML code inserted in a box.

8. **Copy and paste the HTML code into a text file and send it to your Webmaster.**

   Depending on your applications, you can use Notepad, Word, or simply paste the HTML code into an e-mail.

Capture Leads	
Enter the URL that the user will be returned to:	
URL http://dummies.com	
Select the fields to include: select all | select none	
☐ Salutation	
☑ First Name	☑ Last Name
☑ Title	☑ Company
☐ Website	☑ Email
☑ Phone	☐ Fax
☐ Mobile Phone	☑ Description
☑ Address	☐ City
☑ State/Province	☐ Zip
☐ Country	☑ Lead Source
☑ Industry	☐ Rating
☐ Lead Currency	☐ Annual Revenue
☐ Employees	
☑ Campaign	☑ Campaign Member Status
☐ Email Opt Out	☐ Do Not Call

Figure 13-7: Selecting lead fields for your Web form.

Viewing and testing the form

You can view and test the HTML code as an actual form by using your favorite Web publishing application and a browser.

To view and test the form, follow these steps:

1. **Open a new file in your favorite Web publishing program.**

   Many companies use popular programs such as FrontPage, Dreamweaver, or HomeSite.

2. **Copy and paste the HTML code in the HTML mode.**

3. **Save the Web page on your computer.**

4. **Open a browser and choose File⇨Open to open the Web page.**

   A Web form appears with the lead fields that you selected. The form is relatively unformatted, but your Webmaster can apply code to make the form fit with your desired look and feel.

5. **Fill out the basic form and click the Submit button.**

   If you inserted a return URL, that page appears. If not, a page appears that displays the information that was sent to salesforce.com.

6. **Log in to salesforce.com and click the Leads tab.**

7. **Select Today's Leads from the Views drop-down list.**

   The leads list for today appears. If the test lead isn't listed, click the refresh button on your browser until the test lead appears.

8. **Click the test lead's link under the Name column to validate the information from your test lead.**

   The lead record appears and displays the information that you submitted.

9. **Scroll down to the Campaign related list.**

   You should see a link to the campaign and the default member status. If you selected the Campaign Member Status field when generating the HTML code (refer to Figure 13-7), you can apply a member status to all leads derived from the Web form.

Manually updating member statuses

If your campaign is designed to have recipients respond by phone or e-mail, your reps can manually update records as they interact with campaign members. Reps might have to create lead or contact records first if you didn't build your target list from salesforce.com. For example, if you rent a third-party list for an e-mail campaign, the respondent might not yet be recorded in salesforce.com.

To manually update a lead or contact responding to a campaign, follow these steps:

1. **In the sidebar Search, search for the lead or contact.**

   See Chapter 2 for details on using Search.

2. **If you can't find the lead or contact record, create it.**

   See Chapters 4 and 5 for details on creating lead and contact records, respectively. If you find the record, skip this step.

3. **Go to the specific lead or contact record page.**

4. **Click the Edit button to make any changes to the record, and then click Save.**

   For example, you might use the fields to type in additional information supplied by the respondent.

5. **Use the related lists to log any related information or future activities.**

Adding a member to a campaign

In those circumstances when your target list was built externally, reps should add the member to the campaign.

To manually add a member to a campaign, go to the lead or contact record and follow these steps:

1. **On the Campaign History related list, click the Add Campaign button.**

   The Add Campaign page appears.

2. **Select the appropriate campaign from the Campaign Name drop-down list and click Next.**

   The Add Campaign page reappears.

3. **Select the appropriate member status from the Status drop-down list and click Save.**

Updating the status of a current member

If the lead or contact is already linked to the campaign in salesforce.com, you'll want to update the member status when he or she responds.

To update member status manually, go the lead or contact record and follow these steps:

1. **On the Campaign History related list, click the Edit button next to the relevant Campaign Name, as shown in Figure 13-8.**

   The Add Campaign page appears.

2. **Use the Status drop-down list to change the status and click Save.**

Figure 13-8:
Updating
the status
of a
campaign
member.

Campaign History	Add Campaign						❓ Help
Action	Campaign Name	Start Date	Type		Status	Responded	Last Modified
Edit | Del	Custom Outing	8/24/2004	Seminar / Conference		Invited		8/24/2004 5:15 PM

Updating campaign history in batch

If leads or contacts that are part of a campaign respond in batch, you can do a mass update of campaign members. For example, if you sent out a direct mail campaign to existing contacts and you received a batch of business reply cards, you could perform a mass update.

To update campaign history in batch, log in to salesforce.com and follow these steps:

1. **Click the Reports tab and scroll down to the Campaigns Reports heading.**

2. **Click the Campaign Call Down Report link.**

   A page appears, allowing you to select a specific campaign.

3. **Use the Lookup icon to choose a campaign and click the Run Report button.**

   A Campaign Call Down Report for your campaign appears.

4. **Click the Customize button.**

   The report wizard opens.

5. **Choose Select Columns from the Jump To Step drop-down list.**

   A page appears that allows you to select the columns for the report.

6. **Select the Member ID check box and click the Export to Excel button.**

   A page appears to select the encoding and export file format. You probably don't need to alter the default selection under the Export File Encoding drop-down list.

7. **Under the Export File Format drop-down list, select the Comma Delimited .csv option and click the Export button.**

   Your report opens in Excel.

8. **In Excel, update the Member Status field for applicable leads or contacts.**

   For example, if a portion of your campaign members that have a status of Invited need to be updated to Attended, change the status in Excel.

9. **When you're done, save your file to your computer as a `.csv` file.**

10. **Go to the specific campaign record and click the Member Import button.**

    The Member Import page appears.

11. **Click the Update Campaign History button.**

    Step 1 of the wizard appears.

12. **Complete the fields.**

    Here are some pointers:

    - Click the Browse button and select the file from your computer.

    - For the Default Member Status drop-down list, select a status.

    - Change the encoding selection only if necessary.

13. **Click Next to go to Step 2 of the wizard.**

14. **Map the fields, as shown in Figure 13-9.**

    You have only two fields to complete:

    - For the **Record ID,** select the Member ID import field.

    - For the **Status,** select the Member Status import field.

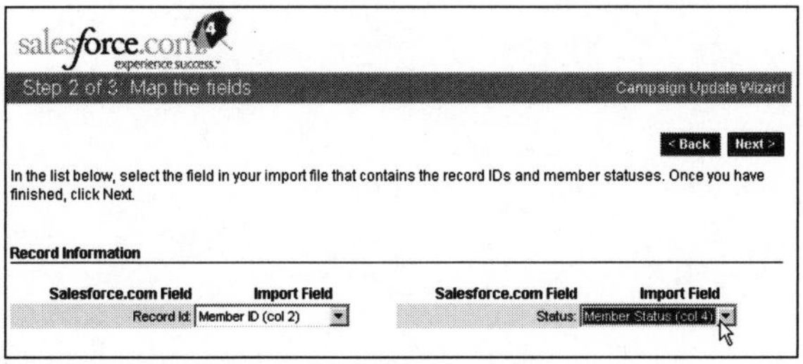

Figure 13-9:
Mapping
fields to do
a member
update.

15. **Click Next to go to Step 3 of the wizard.**

16. **Look over the Review and Confirm page to make sure everything is correct, and then click the Import Now button.**

    A confirmation page appears, and within minutes your selected leads or contacts have been updated.

Chapter 14

Managing Products and Price Books

*P*roducts are the individual line items that make up an opportunity. Depending on your goals for salesforce.com, you might not need to incorporate salesforce.com's product-type features into your opportunities. But if you do sell multiple products and services and you struggle with product-level visibility, salesforce.com provides powerful and easy tools to implement solutions.

Using products in salesforce.com benefits sales reps and people in product marketing, management, and development throughout your organization. Sales reps can quickly locate the price of a product and select products to calculate an opportunity's amount. Marketing, management, or development professionals can get vital sales information to support strategic business planning, new product development, and product lifecycle management.

Before your sales teams can begin adding products to opportunities, your administrator — with the help of marketing — needs to do some advance planning. In this chapter, I show you how to create a product catalog, set up schedules, and build price books. I then show you how to maintain products and price books on an ongoing basis to facilitate your sales and marketing goals.

Discovering Products and Price Books

You need to know two key terms and two interrelated terms before you can begin planning your product strategy in salesforce.com.

- ✔ **Products:** Individual items that you sell on your opportunities. All products belong to one universal product catalog. After you create a product, you can associate it to one or multiple price books with identical or different prices.

  A product can have an associated *schedule* based on quantity, revenue, or both. If you currently sell products and break out schedules to forecast revenue recognition or for planning, you can use salesforce.com to reflect important schedules for products linked to opportunities.

- ✔ **Price book:** A collection of products and their associated prices. A product with its associated price is called a *price book entry*. You can also create custom price books based on your unique sales model.

  You can associate a price book, add products, and build schedules on an opportunity through the *Products related list* on an Opportunity detail page.

When adding products to opportunities, you can select only one price book at a time. So plan your price books accordingly. For example, some companies create price books based on what's available in a region. Others create price books based on direct sales versus channel sales.

Defining standard product fields

A product record consists of a number of fields that you use to capture information about a product you sell. If you're involved in shaping products for your company, most of the standard fields are obvious. If you want specific definitions, click the Help and Training link in the top-right corner of salesforce.com.

The following are a couple important pointers on understanding the standard product record fields:

- ✔ **Product Name:** This is the name of your product. If you have ambitions to use this field for mail merge documents (such as quote forms), use titles that are clear and familiar to your sales reps and customers.

- ✔ **Product Code:** An internal code or product ID used to identify your product. If your existing products and product codes reside in a financial database and you want to plan for integration, make sure the product codes are consistent.

✔ **Product Description:** Text to distinguish products from each other. If you're in product management or marketing, describe your products so that they're obvious and useful for your sales teams.

✔ **Product Family:** The category of the product. Use this drop-down list if you plan to build reports that reflect sales data by product category. For example, if you work for a technology value-added reseller (VAR), you might want to reflect your pipeline by families that include hardware, software, services, training, and maintenance. You can set up products in salesforce.com so that each product automatically maps to a product family.

✔ **Active:** This check box must be selected to make the product available to your users.

✔ **Quantity Scheduling Enabled:** Use this check box to enable quantity scheduling for a product.

✔ **Revenue Scheduling Enabled:** Use this check box to enable revenue scheduling for a product.

Understanding the different types of pricing

Salesforce.com lets you customize your pricing based on the way you sell. If you use products in salesforce.com, your company has three different options for pricing:

✔ **Standard Prices** are the default prices that you establish for your products when you set up your standard price book.

✔ **List Prices** are the prices that you set up for custom price books.

✔ **Sales Price** is the price of a product determined by the sales rep when he or she adds a product to an opportunity. See Chapter 9 for details on adding products to opportunities.

Planning products and price books for success

If you have a vested interest in your product strategy, be aware and take advantage of all the options that salesforce.com provides for customizing products and price books. The more you plan ahead, the better you can implement products and price books for the way your sales teams sell.

For products, consider the characteristics of your products outside the standard realm that you want to analyze. In most companies, the product management or marketing teams own and maintain these records. You should pull together a cross-functional team made up of sales, marketing, finance, and product management users to decide what you want to achieve from products in salesforce.com. Then work with your system administrator to customize the product record to meet your specific needs. For more details on customization, see Chapter 18.

Here are a couple additional ideas based on what I've seen with various companies:

✔ **Families of Families:** I've worked with some companies that need to roll their product reporting to view them in higher categories. For example, a value-added reseller (VAR) might offer many models of routers and switches. Although those products might associate to product families of "routers" or "switches," some companies roll product families to an even more general classification (such as "hardware") by using a custom field such as Product Category.

✔ **Standard margin:** Actual margins on products and opportunities might vary as sales reps negotiate pricing, but some companies want to understand the standard margin on products.

✔ **Vendor or Supplier:** Some companies want to be able to report on which of their vendors or suppliers are strategic to them at the product level. I've also seen companies that send reports back to vendors, detailing the amount of product purchased in a given period.

For pricing, consider whether you have set pricing on your products or whether you'd prefer to keep the pricing simple at the beginning. Many customers of salesforce.com, for example, set the prices on their products at $0 or $1 and depend on their sales reps to fill in the sales prices when they prepare an opportunity. Other companies invest time and effort in creating actual standard or list prices on products to provide guidance to their sales reps.

Building the Product Catalog

Before your sales reps can begin linking products to their opportunities, you need to add the products into salesforce.com.

To add a product, log in to salesforce.com and follow these steps:

1. **Click the New Product link on the taskbar.**

   A New Product page appears.

2. **Complete the fields, as shown in Figure 14-1.**

   Your exact fields might vary, but see the earlier section, "Defining standard product fields," for info on the standard fields.

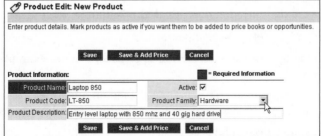

Figure 14-1:
Adding a
product.

3. **When you're done, click Save.**

   The Product detail page for your new product appears with related lists for standard prices and price lists.

Setting Up Schedules

If your company wants to track annuity streams, stay aware of key shipping dates, or estimate when revenue will be recognized on products, you can also set up schedules on all or some products.

Enabling schedules for your company

Your administrator first needs to enable schedules before you can add them on specific products.

If your company wants to track shipping dates with salesforce.com, you need to enable quantity scheduling. If your company wants to measure revenue recognition or anticipate upcoming payments, be sure to enable revenue scheduling. If your company wants to do both, you would enable both types of scheduling.

To set up schedules, follow these steps:

1. **Click the Setup link in the top-right corner of any salesforce.com page.**

   The Personal Setup page appears.

2. **Click the Customize heading in the left column.**

   The Customize page appears.

3. **Under the Customize heading, click the Products heading.**

   The Products page appears.

4. **Under the Products heading, click the Schedule Setup link.**

   The Schedule Setup page appears.

5. **Select the appropriate check boxes, as shown in the example in Figure 14-2.**

   You can choose to enable schedules based on quantities, revenue, or both. You can also choose to enable schedules for all products.

6. **When you're done, click Save.**

   The Products page reappears.

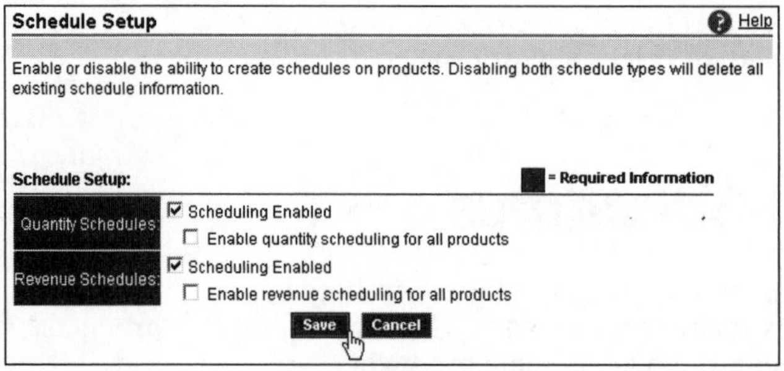

Figure 14-2:
Enabling
schedules
for your
company.

> **Schedule Setup**   ❓ Help
>
> Enable or disable the ability to create schedules on products. Disabling both schedule types will delete all existing schedule information.
>
> **Schedule Setup:**   ▮ = Required Information
>
> Quantity Schedules
> ☑ Scheduling Enabled
> ☐ Enable quantity scheduling for all products
>
> Revenue Schedules
> ☑ Scheduling Enabled
> ☐ Enable revenue scheduling for all products
>
> [Save] [Cancel]

Adding a default schedule

After schedules have been enabled, you can create default schedules on existing products or as you're adding new products.

By creating default schedules, you can simplify repetitive tasks for sales reps. With this setting, a default schedule is created when a sales rep adds a product to an opportunity. A sales rep can still re-establish a product schedule on an opportunity. The product date determines the start date for the installments.

If you sell a basic service with different payment plans, you might consider creating a unique product for each payment plan and then utilizing default revenue schedules. By doing this, you can simplify the data entry for the rep and reduce the chance of error.

To create a default schedule, follow these steps:

1. **Click the New Product link on the taskbar or click the Edit button on a product record.**

   A Product page appears in Edit mode. If scheduling is enabled, you see additional fields for quantity and/or revenue scheduling, as shown in Figure 14-3.

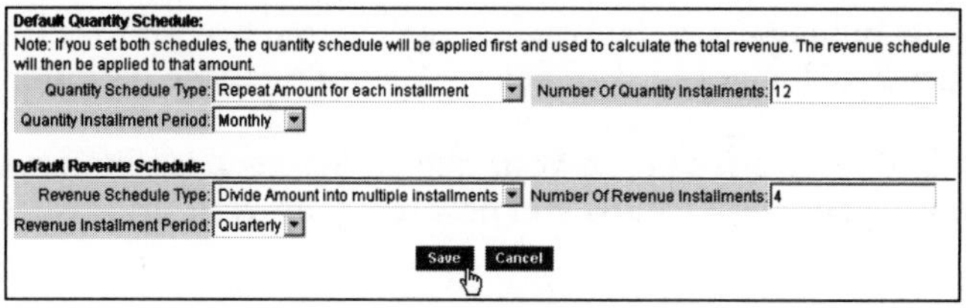

Figure 14-3:
Adding a
default
schedule.

Default Quantity Schedule:
Note: If you set both schedules, the quantity schedule will be applied first and used to calculate the total revenue. The revenue schedule will then be applied to that amount.

Quantity Schedule Type: Repeat Amount for each installment Number Of Quantity Installments: 12
Quantity Installment Period: Monthly

Default Revenue Schedule:
Revenue Schedule Type: Divide Amount into multiple installments Number Of Revenue Installments: 4
Revenue Installment Period: Quarterly

Save Cancel

2. **Complete the fields as appropriate.**

   Here are some tips on completing the default schedule:

   - For the **Schedule Type,** select Divide if you want to divide the amount into installments. Select Repeat if you want to repeat the quantity or revenue on each installment.

   - Use **Installment Period** to define the frequency.

   - Use **Number of Installments** to define the duration.

3. **When you're done, click Save.**

   The Product detail page appears.

If your product has both quantity and revenue default scheduling, quantity scheduling is calculated first and drives the total amount. Then revenue scheduling divides the amount.

Devising Price Books

Some companies require just one universal price book. Many other companies, however, want custom price books based on their unique selling needs. Examples include price books that are

 Based on geography: For a global company, the Japanese sales team might sell a subset of the products sold by their North American counterparts (and at different prices and in different currencies).

✔ **Based on partner tiers:** In some companies that sell through partners, strategic partners might get preferential pricing.

✔ **Based on sales teams:** If your company is divided into sales teams that sell different products, you can use custom price books to simplify the product selection for groups.

✔ **Based on volume discounts:** Some companies build price books based on volume purchases.

✔ **Based on seasonality:** Some companies change their pricing based on seasonal buying patterns. You can use custom price books to communicate pricing changes to your sales reps during these periods.

If the standard price book meets your objectives, keep it simple. Otherwise, in the following sections, I show you how to set up your price books.

Adding to the standard price book

Every time you add a standard price to a product, you automatically associate it to the standard price book. You can do this while you're creating products or you can add the standard prices after you've built the product records.

Adding standard prices while creating products

The easiest way to add a standard price is while you're creating products. To use this method, start creating a product record as you normally would (see the earlier section "Building the Product Catalog") but instead of clicking Save, follow these steps:

1. **Click the Save & Add Price button, as shown in Figure 14-4.**

   An Add Standard Price Page appears.

Figure 14-4:
Adding a product and price at the same time.

2. **Complete the field and click Save.**

   The Product detail page appears, and a standard price displays on the Standard Price related list.

Adding or editing standard prices for existing products

If you want to create the products first and add prices later, you can do so. To add or edit a standard price, go to the desired Product detail page and follow these steps:

1. **Click the Add button on the Standard Price related list, as shown in Figure 14-5.**

   In the event that standard prices exist already, you can click Edit or Edit All. The result is the same: An Add or Edit Standard Price page appears.

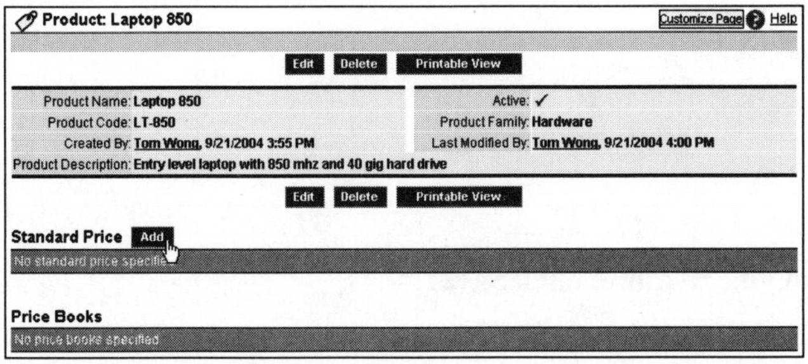

Figure 14-5: Adding a standard price from a product page.

2. **Complete or modify Standard Price field as necessary and click Save.**

   The Product detail page reappears with any changes reflected on the Standard Price related list.

Creating a custom price book

If you want to create a price book, you need to be an administrator or have permission to manage price books.

To create a price book from scratch, go to the Products home page and follow these steps:

1. **Click the Manage Price Books link under the Maintenance section.**

   A Price Book page appears with related lists for active and inactive price books.

2. **Click the New button on the Active Price Books related list.**

   A New Price Book page appears in Edit mode.

3. **Complete the fields, as shown in Figure 14-6.**

   Remember to select the Active check box if you want to make the price book available.

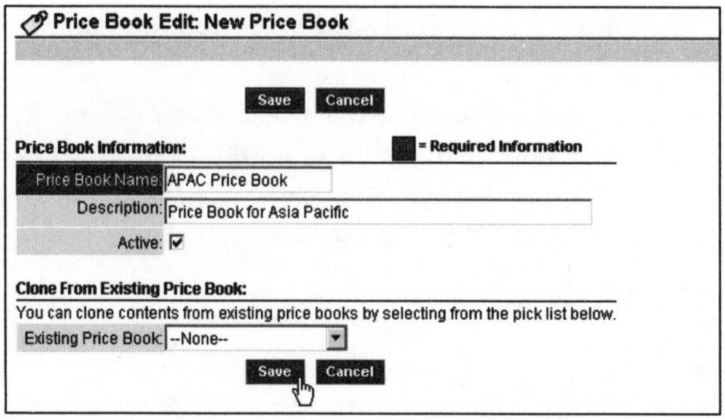

Save   Cancel

Figure 14-6:
Creating a
price book.

4. **When you're done, click Save.**

   The Price Book detail page for your new price book appears with a Products related list.

Adding products to a custom price book

After the price book has been established, you can add products to it. A product listed on a price book is also referred to as a price book entry. To add products to an existing price book, go to a price book and follow these steps:

1. **Click the Add button on the Products related list.**

   A Product Selection page appears with a search tool and list of products.

2. **Enter keywords and filter criteria, and then click the Find Product button to narrow your search.**

   The Product Selection page reappears with a list of products based on your search criteria.

   You can click the More Filters link if you want to use more filters on your search. You can skip this step if you prefer to scroll through the product list at the bottom of the page.

3. **Use the check boxes on the search results to choose products and click the Select button, as shown in Figure 14-7.**

   An Add List Price page appears.

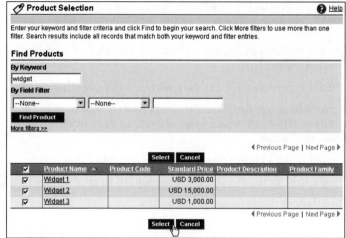

Figure 14-7:
Selecting
products for
the price
book.

4. **Complete the fields.**

   Select the check boxes if you want to use the standard price for the list price of a product or just enter a list price. You can use the Active check boxes to make products immediately available in the price book.

5. **When you're done, click Save or Save & More if you want to find more products.**

   After you save the product, the Price Book detail page reappears, and your selected products have been added to the Products related list.

Finding Products and Price Books

Let the Products tab be your friend. On the Products home page are all the tools that you need to find, view, and manage your products and price books.

Searching for products

You can search for specific products easily by using the Find Products search tool on the Products home page.

Instead of searching from the Products home page, you can now search for products from your main home page. Your administrator must set this up for your company. For details on adding this home page tool, see Chapter 18 for customizing salesforce.com and consult with your administrator.

To search for a product, go to the Products home page and follow these steps:

1. **Enter keywords in the Find Products search tool and click the Find Product button.**

   A Product Search page appears with a list of possible selections.

2. **If necessary, use the Find Products search tool to enter more keywords or filters to refine your search and again click the Find Products button.**

   The list results change based on your criteria.

3. **Click a link in the Product Name column to go directly to the product.**

   The Product detail page appears.

If you're adding products to an opportunity, you can also search for products from the Product Selection page accessible from the Products related list of an opportunity. See Chapter 9 for details on adding products to opportunities.

Viewing products and price books

If you need to look at products and price books in list form, you can also use the drop-down lists located on the Products home page.

- ✓ **To view products within a price book,** choose a price book selection from the Price Books drop-down list and click Go. A list page appears for your selected price book where you can add, edit, or delete price books or go directly to price book entries.

- ✓ **To view product lists,** select a view from the Product Views drop-down list and click Go. A product list page appears, and you can add, edit, or deactivate products or go directly to specific product records.

Creating custom views for products and price lists

If the existing lists don't provide the views that you want, you can create custom views for products and price lists. You can define your views to see additional standard or custom fields in list form. See Chapter 2 for details on creating custom views.

Maintaining Products and Price Books

In the lifecycle of a company, products and their details change all the time. Salesforce.com provides many tools to help you keep your products and price books up to date. Because you have so many options to make updates based on your intentions, I divide the actions into individual versus global changes in the following sections.

Updating specific products and price book entries

You can make most of your changes to a product from its detail page. Go to a specific product (as shown in Figure 14-8) and take a look at this list of actions that you can perform:

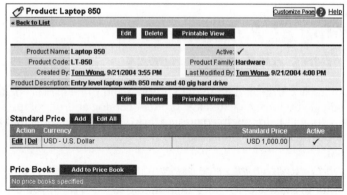

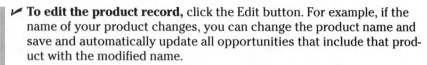

Figure 14-8: Viewing update options from a product page.

✔ **To edit the product record,** click the Edit button. For example, if the name of your product changes, you can change the product name and save and automatically update all opportunities that include that product with the modified name.

If you're editing the default schedule on a product, your changes won't affect existing opportunities that include the product.

✔ **To delete the product,** click Delete, and then click OK on the dialog box that appears. For example, you'd delete a product if you created a product record as a test and you wanted to keep your database clean. (In circumstances where you're no longer offering a product but it's linked to opportunities, I recommend that you deactivate or archive the product rather than deleting it.)

✔ **To deactivate the product,** click the Edit button, deselect the Active box, and then click Save. You can also do this in one step by clicking the Deactivate link next to a product on a product list. Take this path if you might offer the product in the future.

✔ **To delete and archive,** click Delete, and then click OK on the dialog box that appears. In the event that your product is linked to opportunities, a Deletion Problems page appears with suggested options. Click the Archive link if you're still intent on deleting the product but not altering the existing opportunities.

✔ **To create price book entries,** click the Add to Price Books button on the Price Books related list. Then select the price books and enter the list prices before saving.

You can also create a price book entry from a Price Book detail page, as I describe earlier in the section "Adding products to a custom price book." But performing this action from the product detail page is a more efficient method if, for example, you're adding a product to multiple price books at the same time.

Making global changes to products and price books

Maintaining accurate and up-to-date product and price lists is challenging, especially if you have an extensive product catalog and/or complex pricing. If you're responsible for such a daunting task, you can use tools that are located on the Products home page to save time.

Changing activation on price books

If you want to make a price book unavailable to sales reps, you can deactivate one or more price books almost instantly.

To deactivate a price book, go the Products home page and follow these steps:

1. **Click the Manage Price Books link under the Maintenance section.**

   The Price Book detail page appears with related lists for active and inactive price books.

2. **On the Active Price Books related list, click the Deactivate link next to a price book that you want to make unavailable, as shown in Figure 14-9.**

   The Price Book detail page reappears, and the selected price book now appears on the Inactive Price Books related list.

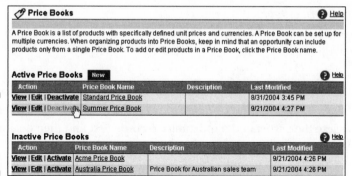

To activate price books, you follow a similar process, the difference being that you would click the Activate link adjacent to a price book listed on the Inactive Price Books related list.

Cloning price books

On occasion, you might want to create a price book that closely resembles an existing price book. Rather than starting from scratch, you can clone from an existing price book and then make changes as necessary. For example, if your products remain constant but prices vary based on the quarter, you could clone the Q4 price book from the Q3 price book and then modify the entries.

To clone a price book, follow these steps:

1. **Click the Manage Price Books under the Maintenance section.**

   The Price Book page appears with related lists for active and inactive price books.

2. **Click the New button on the Active Price Books related list.**

   A New Price Book page appears.

3. **Complete the fields and use the Existing Price Book drop-down list to select a price book to clone.**

4. **When you're done, click Save.**

   The new Price Book page appears with a Products related list cloned from the existing price book.

5. **If needed, click Edit or Edit All on the Products related list to change the list prices.**

6. **If needed, click Add or Delete on the Products related list to add or delete price book entries.**

Deleting price books

You can delete price books, but if the price book is associated to existing opportunities, beware. In those circumstances, I recommend the following actions:

- ✔ Deactivate (rather than delete) the price book so that the linkage between opportunities and products stays intact.
- ✔ Delete the associated opportunity records first and then delete the price book.
- ✔ Archive the price book entries prior to deleting. Then even if you delete the price book record, the associated products on opportunities are retained.

If you still want to delete a price book, follow these steps:

1. **On the Products home page, click the Manage Price Books link under the Maintenance section.**

   The Price Book detail page appears with related lists for active and inactive price books.

2. **Click the link for the desired price book.**

   The specific Price Book page appears.

3. **Click Delete and then OK on the dialog box that appears.**

   If you selected a price book that wasn't associated with opportunities, you're returned to the Price Book detail page with the lists of price books. If a Deletion Problems page appears, follow the suggestions provided in the preceding bullet list and on the Deletion Problems page.

Mass deleting products

You can now mass delete products. This tool is particularly helpful if you've created test records as part of your salesforce.com implementation. Be aware that the same implications for deleting price books apply to deleting products.

To delete products *en masse,* follow these steps:

1. **On the Products home page, click the Mass Delete Products link under the Maintenance section.**

   The Mass Delete page for products appears.

2. **Review salesforce.com tips in Step 1 and 2 of the Mass Delete page.**

   Among their suggestions, I recommend that you back up your data just in case. See Chapter 19 on managing your data.

3. In Step 3 of the Mass Delete page, enter criteria to find the products you want to delete, as shown in Figure 14-10 and click the Search button.

See Chapter 2 for general details on using fields, operators, and values to create views. When you click the Search button, the page reappears with a list of products that match your criteria.

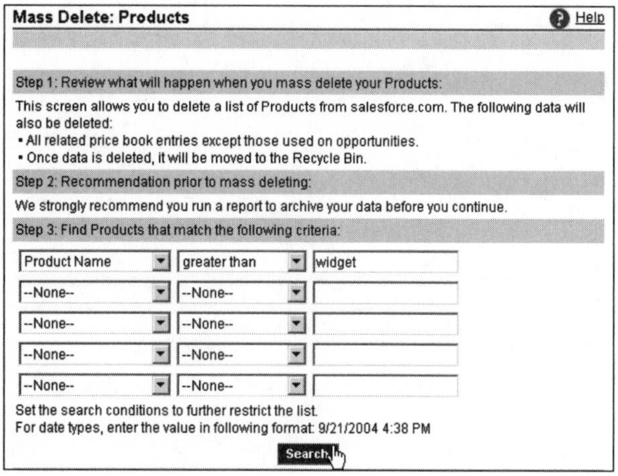

Figure 14-10:
Using the
wizard to
mass delete
products.

Mass Delete: Products   ❷ Help

Step 1: Review what will happen when you mass delete your Products:

This screen allows you to delete a list of Products from salesforce.com. The following data will also be deleted:
• All related price book entries except those used on opportunities.
• Once data is deleted, it will be moved to the Recycle Bin.

Step 2: Recommendation prior to mass deleting:

We strongly recommend you run a report to archive your data before you continue.

Step 3: Find Products that match the following criteria:

Product Name ▼	greater than ▼	widget
--None-- ▼	--None-- ▼	
--None-- ▼	--None-- ▼	
--None-- ▼	--None-- ▼	
--None-- ▼	--None-- ▼	

Set the search conditions to further restrict the list.
For date types, enter the value in following format: 9/21/2004 4:38 PM

Search

4. If desired, select the check box to archive your opportunity product data.

By doing this, you at least ensure that opportunities with associated products won't lose critical product data.

5. Use the check boxes in the Action column to select products to be deleted.

You can also use the Select All or Select None links if you have an extensive list.

6. When you're satisfied, click Delete and then OK in the dialog box that appears.

If you selected products that weren't associated with opportunities, the Mass Delete page reappears. If a Deletion Problems page appears, follow the suggestions provided in the "Deleting price books" section and on the Deletion Problems page.

As you make products and price books active, your sales reps can start associating products to their opportunities. See Chapter 9 for details on how sales reps can select price books, add products, and develop schedules as they manage their opportunities.

Part IV
Measuring the Overall Business

The 5th Wave   By Rich Tennant

"Oh wait — this says, 'Lunch Ed from Marketing,' not 'Lynch', 'Lunch'."

In this part . . .

You stand a better chance of achieving and surpassing your sales goals if you know exactly where you are and how fast you're going. By using reports and dashboards in salesforce.com you can get real-time insight into your sales, customers, and overall business. Manual reporting will be a thing of the past. Sound too good to be true? It's not. As long as you and other users are updating records in salesforce.com, the data is at your fingertips.

In this part, I explain everything you need to know about reports and dashboards. I show you how to use the standard reports and create your own custom ones by using the salesforce.com report wizard. If for some reason you still need to work with your data in spreadsheets, I show you just how simple it is to export your data into Excel. And you discover how to build powerful dashboards to visually depict key parts of your business.

Chapter 15

Analyzing Data with Reports

· ·

· ·

*H*ow much time do you waste every week trying to prepare reports for your manager, your team, or yourself? You have to chase the information down, get it into a useful format, and then hopefully make sense of the data. By the time you've done all this, the information is probably already outdated despite your best efforts. Have you ever felt less than confident with the details or the totals?

If this sounds like a familiar problem, you can use reports in salesforce.com to generate up-to-the-moment data analysis to help you measure your business. As long as you and your teams regularly use salesforce.com to manage your accounts, opportunities, and other customer-related information, you don't have to waste time wondering where to find the data and how to consolidate it — instead, salesforce.com does that work for you.

And unlike other applications where the business users often have to spend precious time relying on more technical people to build their custom reports, you can do this all by yourself in minutes, with no geeky programming. With an easy-to-use reporting wizard, you can customize existing reports or build them from scratch according to your specific needs. And then, if you want to export reports to Excel or print them, just click a button.

In this chapter, I show you how to use existing reports as launching pads to developing your own reports. This includes looking over the standard reports provided by salesforce.com, and then building reports from scratch, and also modifying existing reports to make them your own. Within a report, I take you through the different ways you can limit the report to get just the information that's necessary for creating a clearer picture of your business. Finally, because you're going to love the Reports tab so much, be sure to check out my explanation on how to keep your reports organized in easy-to-find folders as your universe of reports expands.

Discovering Reports

All your available reports are accessible from the Reports home page. With reports, you can present your data in different formats, select a seemingly infinite number of columns, filter your data, and subtotal information, just to name a few features. And like other pages in salesforce.com, you can quickly find the details. So for example, you can go from the Reports home page to a lead report to a lead record simply by clicking links.

Navigating the Reports home page

When you click the Reports tab, a list of all your available reports appears, sorted by folders. Salesforce.com comes standard with a set of predefined reports and folders (as shown in Figure 15-1) that are commonly used for measuring sales, marketing, support, and other functions.

You can't save a custom report in a standard folder. If you're an administrator, consider creating custom folders for your important functional areas that ultimately replace these standard folders.

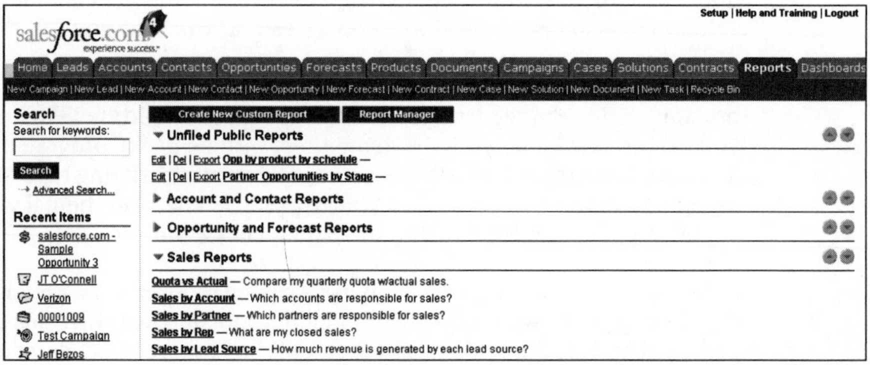

Figure 15-1:
Looking over the standard folders and reports.

From this page, you can do the following:

- ✔ Click the green arrow on the left side of a folder to hide or show a folder's reports.

- ✔ Click the gray arrows on the right side of a folder to move a folder up or down on the page. For example, if you want to see the Lead Reports folder at the top of the page, simply click its gray Up arrow to move the folder up one position at a time.

- ✔ To display the report, click a report title. Either the report appears or you see a wizard that you need to follow to generate the report.

- ✔ On custom reports, click the Edit, Del, or Export links to edit or delete a report or export its data to Excel.

- ✔ Click the Create New Custom Report button to start the report wizard.

- ✔ If you have permission to manage public reports, click the Report Manager button to organize reports.

Displaying a report

When you click a report title or run a report from the wizard, a report page appears based on the criteria that was set. For example, under the Opportunities and Forecast Reports folder, click the Opportunity Pipeline link. The Opportunity Pipeline report appears, as shown in the example in Figure 15-2. This report is one of the most-used standard reports in salesforce.com.

A basic report page in salesforce.com is broken up into two or three parts:

- ✔ **Report Options:** This section is at the top of the page. You can use it to filter and perform other operations on a report. For details on report options, see "Filtering on a Report" later in this chapter.

- ✔ **Generated Report:** This section shows the report itself. What's visible depends on the construction of the report and what you have permission to see in salesforce.com. See Chapter 17 for more details on sharing.

- ✔ **Org Drill Down:** You can use this area above the Report Options section to quickly limit results based on role hierarchy. See Chapter 17 for steps on setting up the role hierarchy.

In the Generated Report section, you can click a column heading to quickly re-sort your report by the selected column.

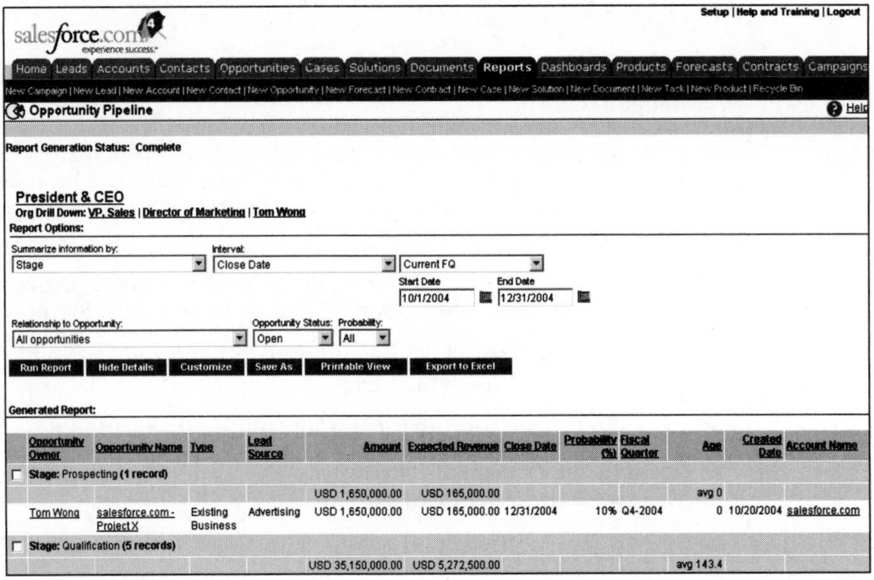

Figure 15-2:
Displaying
a report.

Developing Reports with the Wizard

Salesforce.com comes with a huge menu of useful reports, and yet they might not be exactly what you're looking for. For example, if your company has added custom fields on the account record that are unique to your customer, a standard New Accounts report doesn't show you all the information you want to see on recent accounts.

The next time you need a custom report, don't pester the IT geeks. Instead, use the report wizard to build a new report or customize an existing one.

Building a report from scratch

You don't have to be a technical guru to create a report in salesforce.com. Just make sure you can articulate a question that you're trying to answer, and then salesforce.com's Report Wizard will guide you through the steps for creating a custom report that will help you answer the question. Anyone who can view the Reports tab can create a custom report. Whether you can make it public or just private depends on permissions.

To create a report from scratch, click the Reports tab and follow these steps:

1. **Click the Create New Custom Report button.**

   The Report Wizard page appears.

2. Select the data type you want to report on, and then click Next.

You do this by first selecting the basic type of data from the drop-down list and then being more specific in the dependent list box, as shown in Figure 15-3. When you click Next, Step 1 of the wizard appears.

3. Select the radio button for the type of report that you want. You have three options:

- **Tabular Reports** provide the most basic way to look at your data in a tabular format.

- **Summary Reports** allow you to view your data with subtotals and other summary information.

- **Matrix Reports** enable you to create reports in grids against both horizontal and vertical categories. This type of report is particularly helpful for comparing related totals, especially if you're trying to summarize large amounts of data. For example, the standard report called Sales to Date versus Last Month (located in the Opportunity and Forecast Reports folder) is a matrix report that summarizes new sales by month vertically and also by close date horizontally.

4. When you're done, select the Select Columns option from the Jump to Step drop-down list in the top-right corner, and then click Next.

The Select the Report Columns page appears.

The report type that you select dictates how many of the seven possible Report Wizard steps you see and the order that they're presented in the wizard. For example, if you selected the Matrix Report radio button in Step 3 of this list, the next step out of seven is Select Groupings. But if you select the Tabular Reports radio button, the next step is Select Columns, and you have only five steps. And at any time, you can use the Jump to Step drop-down list to skip around the wizard.

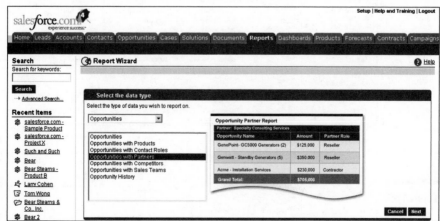

Figure 15-3:
Defining the data type for the report.

 5. **Select the check boxes for the columns that you want in your report.**

   Depending on the data type you chose, the Select the Report Columns page displays standard and then custom fields divided into sections, as shown in the example in Figure 15-4.

 6. **When you're done, select the Select Columns to Total option from the Jump to Step drop-down list.**

   A wizard page appears with the columns that can be totaled (such as currencies, amounts, and percentages) based on the columns you selected in Step 5 of this list.

 7. **Select check boxes for columns that you want summarized and how you want them summarized.**

   Salesforce.com provides you options for summing, averaging, and choosing highest or lowest values. For example, on an activity report, you could use averaging to measure the average duration of an activity, as shown in the example in Figure 15-5.

 8. **When you're done, select the Order Columns option from the Jump to Step drop-down list and click Next.**

   The wizard page appears.

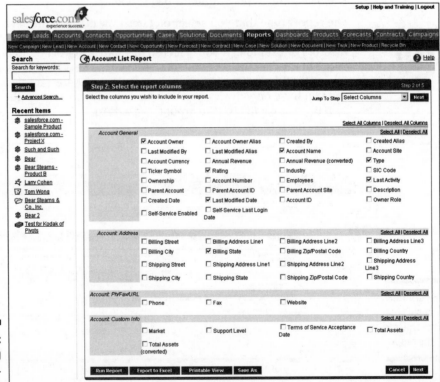

Figure 15-4:
Selecting
columns.

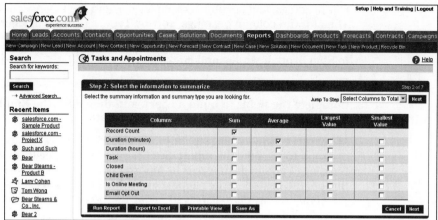

Setup | Help and Training | Logout

salesforce.com
experience success™

Home | Leads | Accounts | Contacts | Opportunities | Cases | Solutions | Documents | Reports | Dashboards | Products | Forecasts | Contracts | Campaigns

New Campaign | New Lead | New Account | New Contact | New Opportunity | New Forecast | New Contract | New Case | New Solution | New Document | New Task | New Product | Recycle Bin

Figure 15-5:
Choosing
columns
to total.

Search
Search for keywords:

Search
→ Advanced Search...

Recent Items
- salesforce.com - Sample Product
- salesforce.com - ProjectX
- Such and Such
- Bear
- Bear Stearns - Product B
- Larry Cohen
- Tom Wong
- Bear Stearns & Co., Inc.
- Bear 2

Tasks and Appointments   ❓ Help

Step 2: Select the information to summarize   Step 2 of 7
Select the summary information and summary type you are looking for.   Jump To Step [Select Columns to Total ▼] [Next]

Columns	Sum	Average	Largest Value	Smallest Value
Record Count	☑			
Duration (minutes)	☐	☑	☐	☐
Duration (hours)	☐	☐	☐	☐
Task	☐	☐	☐	☐
Closed	☐	☐	☐	☐
Child Event	☐	☐	☐	☐
Is Online Meeting	☐	☐	☐	☐
Email Opt Out	☐	☐	☐	☐

[Run Report] [Export to Excel] [Printable View] [Save As]   [Cancel] [Next]

9. **Click the directional arrows to order the columns.**

   This is how columns will appear on the report from left to right if you are showing all details.

10. **When you're done, select the Select Criteria option from the Jump to Step drop-down list and click Next.**

    The wizard page appears.

11. **Use the criteria filters to limit results on your report.**

    The standard filters will vary based on the data type you chose. For advanced filters, select fields and operators by using the drop-down lists, and then enter values, similar to creating custom views. (For help with advanced filters, see Chapter 2.)

    With advanced And/Or filters you can now create precise reports that might include complex conditions. For example, if you define strategic accounts as companies that did either over $1 billion in annual revenue or had over 500 employees plus $500 million in annual revenue, you can now generate this report. To do this, enter your advanced filters as before, and then click the Advanced Options link at the bottom of the Advanced Filters section. When the page reappears, click the Tips link located next to the Advanced Filter Conditions field. Modify your Conditions as recommended before clicking the Run Report button. (You must have Professional or Enterprise Edition.)

12. **When you're done, select the Select Groupings option from the Jump to Step drop-down list and click Next.**

    The wizard page appears.

13. **Select the columns by which your report will be grouped.**

    For example, if you want to measure the number of accounts owned by rep and subtotaled by account type, use an account matrix report. For the row headings, first sort by Account Owner, and then by Account Name. Then for the column headings, sort by Type, as shown in Figure 15-6.

14. **When you're done, select the Select Chart Type option from the Jump to Step drop-down list and click Next.**

 The wizard page appears.

15. **Complete the fields to build a chart, and then click the Run Report button.**

 Many users include this step only if they need to generate a specific chart or graph to support the report. See Chapter 16 for specific details on building charts in dashboards or reports. When you click the Run Report button, the custom report appears with Report Options at the top and the actual report data displayed under the Generated Report heading.

16. **If you want to save the report, click the Save As button.**

 A New Custom Report page appears.

17. **Complete the fields and click the Save As button.**

 Here are pointers for completing the fields:

 • Enter a title for the report in the Report Name field.

 • Type a question or sentence in the Report Question field that will help you remember the purpose of the report. For example, if you created an Opportunity by Competitor report, you might type **Who are our biggest competitors measured by opportunities?**

 • If you have permissions to manage public folders, select a folder for the report.

 After clicking the Save As button, the Reports home page appears with a link to the report under the selected folder.

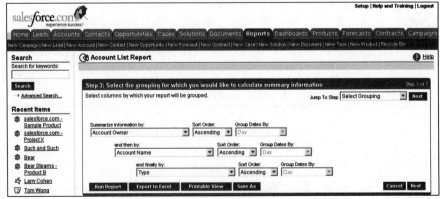

Figure 15-6: Determining the groupings.

Customizing existing reports

A fast and easy way to generate reports is to customize from an existing report. For example, if you like the standard Pipeline Report but you want to modify the columns, you can simplify work from the existing report.

To customize an existing report, go to the Reports tab and follow these steps:

1. **Click a link for an existing report.**

   The report appears.

2. **Click the Customize button.**

   A page from the report wizard appears.

3. **Based on what you want to customize, select a step from the Jump to Step drop-down list.**

   The wizard page appears based on what you selected.

4. **Modify the fields within that step to customize your report.**

   For example, if you want an opportunity report with only forecasted opportunities, select the Select Criteria option from the Jump to Step drop-down list. Then add an advanced filter, such as Forecast Category Equals Commit. (Forecast Category is the field, Equals is the operator, and Commit is the value.)

5. **Continue jumping to steps until you're satisfied, and then click the Run Report button.**

   The report appears modified based on your settings from the wizard.

6. **When you're done, click Save or Save As.**

   The Save button replaces the prior report. The Save As button saves a new one. In either case, a page appears to save the report.

7. **Complete the fields and click Save.**

   The Reports home page appears.

Filtering on a Report

Over time, you'll develop core reports that have the columns that you want in a format that makes sense to you. One of the huge benefits of reporting in salesforce.com is that you can use existing reports on the fly and apply report options to limit or reorder the report results. For example, with the standard Pipeline Report, you might want to sort by Opportunity Owner instead of Stage; look at only one region; or look at three quarters instead of one.

All those options and more are possible in seconds without having to use the Customize button. In this section, I show you how to filter your reports with tools that include the Org Drill Down feature, the Report Options section, and enhanced drill down and break out options.

Using the Org Drill Down feature

In Enterprise, Professional, and Team Editions of salesforce.com, many reports display an Org Drill Down feature that you can use to view information by users, roles, or the entire organization.

What data is accessible might be limited by your role in the organization and sharing rules, but by using the Org Drill Down feature, you can quickly analyze information specific to your teams. (See Chapter 17 for more details on role hierarchy and sharing.)

You can use the Org Drill Down feature primarily with opportunity, forecast, and activity reports. To use the Org Drill Down features, click Reports tab and follow these steps:

1. **Click a report in the Activity Reports or Opportunity and Forecast Reports folders.**

    For all but three to four reports, the report appears with a set of Org Drill Down links, as shown in the example in Figure 15-7. The titles of your links vary based on the role hierarchy set by your administrator.

    If you don't see the Org Drill Down feature, you might still see a drop-down list under the Report Options section that allows you to report on your teams. For example, on the Reports home page, click the Opportunity History Report link under the Opportunity and Forecast Reports folder. The report appears, and under the Report Options section, use the Relationship to Opportunity drop-down list to filter data on your teams (as defined by role hierarchy or sales teams). See Chapter 9 for further details on setting up sales teams.

2. **Click a link to the right of the Org Drill Down title.**

    The report reappears based on your selection, and the links above the Org Drill Down title display your current view. Notice that the links to the right of the Org Drill Down title might provide you other choices to drill down further into your team.

3. **Repeat the Step 2 as often as needed until you get your desired view.**

    Notice that you haven't changed the underlying report but just limited the view.

    If you don't see the information you expect to as you click through the Org Drill Down feature, consult your administrator. Nine out of ten times, the problem might just be that the role hierarchy is set up incorrectly or you're assigned to the wrong role.

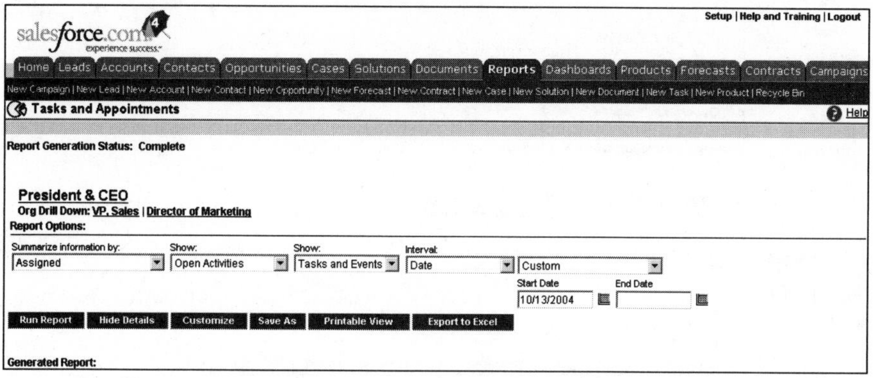

Figure 15-7:
Viewing the
Org Drill
Down
feature.

Using the Report Options section

When you open a report, it appears with a variety of filters in the Report Options section at the top of the page. By using the filters in the Report Options section, you can look at your data from multiple angles based on your needs.

The available standard filters depend on the type of report that you selected. For example, click the Lead Status link under the Lead Reports folder. The Lead Status report appears. Look over the Report Options section, and then click the Back button on your browser. Next click the Sales by Rep link under the Sales Reports folder. Notice that the standard filters in the Report Options section differ based on the type of report.

To try out the standard filters in the Report Options section by using the Opportunity Pipeline report as an example, first go to the Reports home page and click the Opportunity Pipeline link. The report appears. From the report you can do the following with the filters in the Report Options section:

- From the **Summarize Information By drop-down list,** select a field. For example, if you want to look at your opportunities by rep, select Opportunity Owner.

- From the **Interval drop-down list,** first select a date field, and then in the drop-down list to the right select a standard interval or create a custom range. For example, if you want to look at all opportunities created in 2004 to the present, you would first select Created Date, and then define the interval, as shown in Figure 15-8.

- From the **Relationship to Opportunity drop-down list,** select the scope.

- Use the **Opportunity Status drop-down list** if you want open and/or closed records.

- Use the **Probability drop-down list** if you want to limit the results by probability.

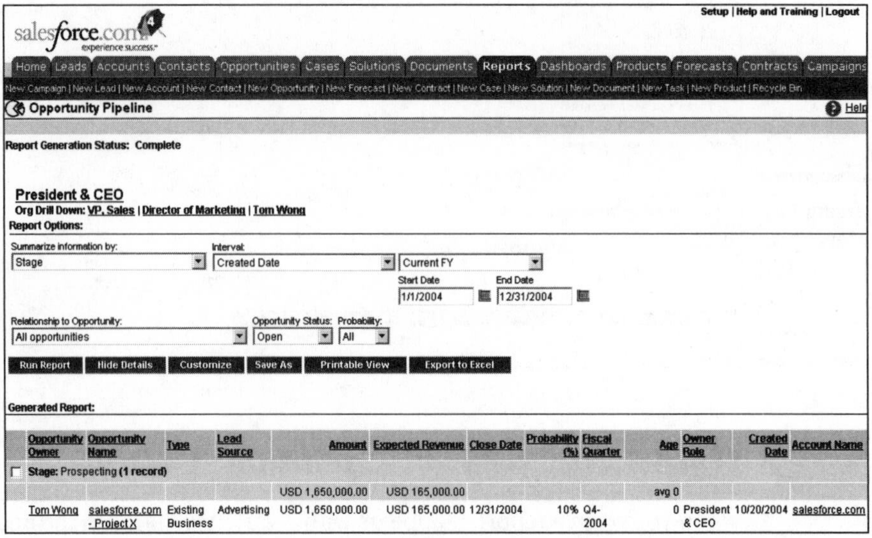

Figure 15-8:
Using the
Report
Options
section to
customize
your date
range.

At any particular time, click the Run Report button to apply your selected filters. The report reappears based on the filters you defined.

If you ultimately want to save the report, click the Save or Save As buttons and then save the report as usual. (Refer to the section "Building a report from scratch" earlier in this chapter for details on saving.)

Hiding and showing details

To see a collapsed or expanded view of your report data, use the Hide/Show Details button in the Report Options section. For example, from the Reports home page, click the Sales by Account report under Sales Reports. When the report appears, click the Hide Details button. The report reappears in a collapsed view, and the Hide Details button has morphed into the Show Details button. Now click the Show Details button, and the report expands again. By using Hide Details, you can easily view headings, subtotals, and totals.

Filtering with the drill down menu

Reports in salesforce.com now have a drill down function that you can use to select rows within a report and instantly break them down by a different field. For example, if you're reviewing an Opportunity by Rep report, you might want to select a specific rep and then sort the rep's opportunities by stage. With enhanced drill down and break out options, you can do this in just a few quick clicks.

To use the drill down and break out options (using Sales by Rep as the example), follow these steps:

1. **From the Reports home page, click the Sales by Rep link under the Sales Reports folder.**

   The report appears.

2. **In the left column of the Generated Report section, select check boxes for records you want to view.**

   If you don't see check boxes and you know you've closed opportunities in salesforce.com, select an interval in the Report Options section to see all your historical opportunities and click Run Report to view more records.

3. **At the bottom of the page, select a field from the Drill Down By drop-down list to summarize the information, if desired, and then click the Drill Down button, as shown in Figure 15-9.**

   The report reappears based on your selections. For example, if you chose the Close Month option from the Drill Down By drop-down list, your selected opportunities would be sorted by close month.

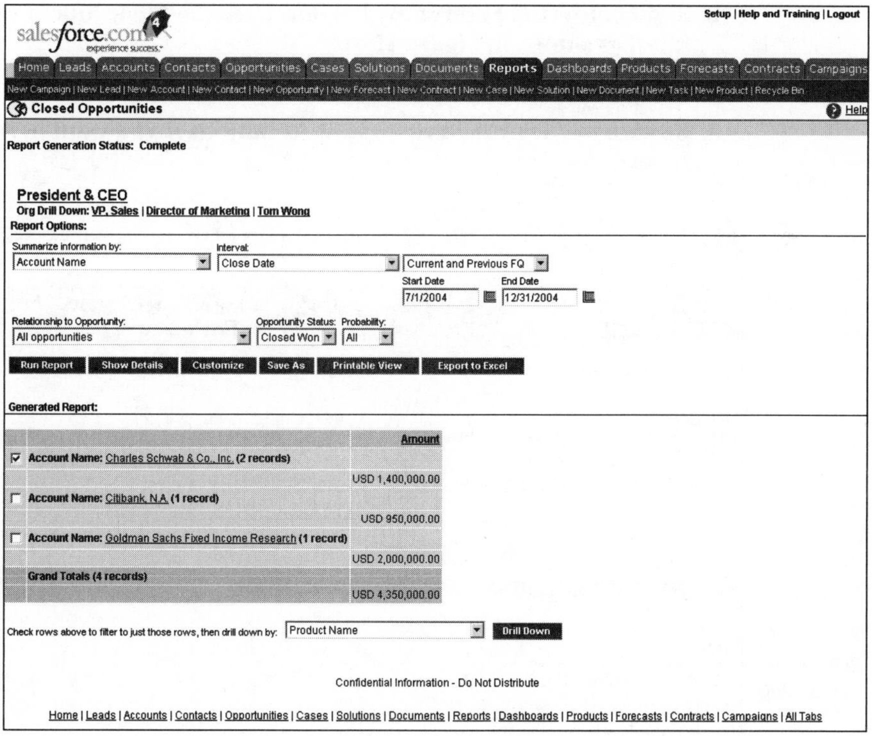

Figure 15-9: Using the enhanced drill down and break out options.

4. If you want to use the report in the future, click Save or Save As.

Then follow the normal directions for saving reports. (See the earlier section "Building a report from scratch" for saving details.)

Clearing filters

If you have reports with advanced filters, you can easily view and clear the filter to expand the results. For example, if you created and saved the test report in the preceding section, you might want to clear the filter on the selected rep(s) to see all closed opportunities by close month for all reps. The advanced filters, if any, appear just below the Generated Report header on a report page.

To clear a filter, follow these steps:

1. Click the link for a report that you've applied filters to.

The report appears, and your criteria filters are listed under the Filtered By header directly below the Generated Report header.

2. Right below the Filtered By header, click the Clear link to remove a filter, as shown in Figure 15-10.

The report reappears displaying a potentially wider universe of data.

3. Be sure to click the Save or Save As buttons if you want to save this report.

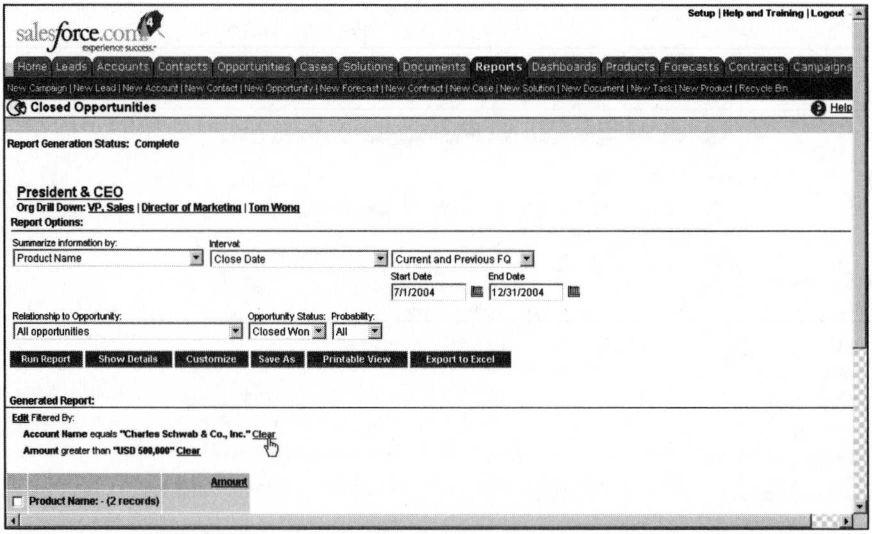

Figure 15-10:
Clearing
a filter.

You can quickly modify advanced filters by clicking the Edit link next to the Filtered By header. The Select Criteria page of the report wizard appears.

Printing and Exporting Reports

Ideally, with salesforce.com, you want to run your reports right out of the application, getting rid of that mad scramble of collecting, combining, and printing data before your next big meeting. However, sometimes you'll want to generate a report and then print it or export it to Excel. Maybe you need to run some complex spreadsheet calculations or you need to plug numbers into an existing macro template. Not a problem. Salesforce.com provides you with both of these capabilities with the click of a button.

Generating a printable view

How many times have you found a page on the Internet and printed it only to find that the printed result wasn't what it looked like on-screen? With salesforce.com, you don't have that problem. If you develop a report in salesforce.com and you like the format it's in, the printable view lets you translate the on-screen format to the printed page.

To use printable view, click the Reports tab and follow these steps:

1. **Click the link to a report to open it.**

2. **Click the Printable View button.**

   A new window opens, and you can open or save the file.

3. **Follow the steps as desired.**

   When the file opens, the report appears in Excel and in a format that's optimized for printing.

Exporting to Excel

Salesforce.com wants to rid you of your old habit of manual spreadsheet reporting. When information in salesforce.com is current, running reports in real time gives you the most accurate glimpse into how your business is doing. But salesforce.com isn't trying to eliminate your need to ever use Excel. Quite the contrary: Report functionality in salesforce.com is optimized to work with and export to Excel.

To export a report, click the Reports tab and follow these steps:

1. **Click the link to a report.**

   The report appears. You can bypass this step if you see an Export link next to a report title on the Reports home page.

2. **Click the Export to Excel button.**

   A page appears to define your settings for exporting the file.

3. **Complete the fields and click the Export button.**

   A window appears, prompting you to open or save the file.

4. **Follow the steps as desired.**

   When the file opens, the report data appears in Excel.

5. **Click Done to return to your salesforce.com report.**

   The report page reappears.

Some companies get nervous about certain users having the ability to export company data. If this is a concern and you have Enterprise Edition, you can take one precaution by using custom profiles to eliminate the ability of some users to export to Excel. See Chapter 17 for more details on creating custom profiles.

Organizing Your Reports

A word to the wise: Reports start multiplying like rabbits as you become addicted to reporting in salesforce.com. Do yourself a favor: Organize your reports from day one and lay out a process for maintaining and deleting reports.

Building folders with the Report Manager

Nothing is worse than seeing a kazillion reports under the Unfiled Public Reports folder. You start wasting a ridiculous amount of time just identifying which one is the report you want. If you have permission to manage public folders, avoid the headache and impress your peers by using the Report Manager.

With the Report Manager, administrators can create public report folders and control access to custom folders and their reports.

To use the Report Manager, click Reports tab and follow these steps:

1. **Click the Report Manager button at the top of the page.**

   The Report Manager page appears.

2. **Click the Create New Folder link next to the Folder menu.**

   A New Report Folder page appears.

3. **Type a name for the folder in the Report Folder field.**

   For example, if you want a folder for operational reports, you might name it Sales Ops Reports.

4. **Use the Public Folder Access drop-down list to determine read versus read/write privileges to the folder.**

   For example, if you select Read/Write, a user with access to the folder could save over the original report.

5. **Use the two list boxes and the Add/Remove buttons to select reports in the Unfiled Public Reports folder and move them to the new folder.**

6. **Use the radio buttons to select who should have access to the folder.**

   As with other salesforce.com folder tools, your choices amount to all, none, and selective.

7. **If you chose the Selective option in Step 6, use the two list boxes and Add/Remove buttons to highlight groups or roles and move them to the Shared To list box.**

8. **When you're done, click Save.**

   The Report Manager page reappears, and your folder is added to the Folder menu.

Maintaining your report library

Actually, what's worse than a kazillion reports under Unfiled Public Reports is a universe of reports, some of which are valuable, others of which are useless. Creating public report folders is a good first step, but you might want to apply some of these additional hints on a periodic basis:

✔ **Accurately name your reports.** You and your users can't know what's behind a report link unless you name it clearly and precisely. And if you misname a report, you either look bad or mislead people.

✔ **Consider using report numbers within your report names.** For instance, 1.1 Latin America Pipeline. By doing this, managers can refer to report numbers so that everyone's looking at the same report.

✔ **Delete unnecessary reports.** If multiple people in your company have permission to manage public reports, you might want to survey them before accidentally deleting a report. Although you won't be deleting the data, you might eliminate a critical report that involved a lot of thought. At the same time, unnecessary or redundant reports just make it harder for everyone to find what they want.

✔ **Hide folders as necessary.** If you're an administrator, you can do this globally with the Report Manager. If you're a user, you can use the green arrows on the Reports home page to hide folder's contents.

✔ **Update existing reports as needs arise.** For example, if you created an Opportunity Product Report and used an advanced filter like Product Family Equals Software, make sure that you update the report if the product family name changes. Otherwise your reports will be off.

✔ **Use clear report questions.** For example, you might use the Report Question field to summarize certain filters to your report.

Chapter 16

Seeing the Big Picture with Dashboards

Dashboards are visual representations of custom reports that you create in salesforce.com. You can use dashboards to measure key performance indicators (KPIs) and other metrics important to your business. A *metric* is simply something you want to measure (for example, sales by rep, leads by source, opportunities by partner, year-to-date sales, and so on).

What does this mean for you? If you're a sales or service rep, you can track your daily progress against attainment of goals. If you're a manager, you can easily see how reps are stacking up against each other and where you need to get involved to hit the numbers. And if you're on the executive team, you have actionable charts and graphs for strategic decision making to improve the business.

In this chapter, I share with you some tips on first planning out your strategy, and then I show you how to create dashboards. I walk you through updating dashboard properties and components. You also discover how to organize dashboards and their related reports so that you know you're looking at the right information.

Figuring Out Dashboards

Dashboards are pages in salesforce.com that are made up of tables and charts designed to help you understand important aspects of your business. Because dashboards are so critical, the following sections help you understand some basic concepts and consider your strategy before you start unleashing them on your organization.

Breaking down basic elements

You can build a dashboard with as many as 20 individual charts, tables, metrics, or gauges (each of these items is referred to as a *dashboard component*). Similar to building charts with the report wizard, components are based on reports that you create. In fact, you can click a component on a dashboard to make the underlying report appear. Here is a quick summary of the components available to you:

- **Horizontal or Vertical Bar Charts** are great when you want to depict a simple measurement with an x and y axis. For example, use bar charts if you want to create a component that displays pipeline by stage.

- **Horizontal or Vertical Stacked Bar Charts** work well when you want grouping within a bar. For example, use stacked bar charts if you want to create a chart that shows pipeline by stage and then by type (such as new versus existing business).

- **Horizontal or Vertical Stacked to 100% Bar Charts** are excellent when you're more interested in percentages than amounts. If you're comparing new versus existing business, stacked to 100% charts can help you understand what percentage of each stage was new business versus existing business.

- **Pie Charts** work just like the standard bar chart, but the data is shown as pie. (Not recommended if you're on a diet.)

- **Line Charts** are helpful if you're trying to express trends, particularly when time is part of the measurement. For example, use a line chart if you want to analyze the number of newly created opportunities by month for your entire company.

- **Line Group Charts** add a layer of complexity. For example, a line group chart could help you express the number of newly created opportunities by month broken out by region or unit.

- **Tables** create simple but powerful two-column tables. For example, use tables if you want your dashboard to show the top ten forecasted deals in the quarter in descending value. You can create tables in dashboards but not in the charting tool of the report wizard.

- **Metrics** insert the grand total of a report at the end of a dashboard label that you customize. Metrics are compelling when you want to tell a story that might require a bit more explanation. Metrics tend to work well in concert with other components. For example, if you use a pie chart to summarize opportunity by stage, you could add a metric to summarize total pipeline. Metrics aren't available in the charting tool of the report wizard.

✔ **Gauges** are useful when you have a specific measurable objective and you want to track your progress. A gauge applies the grand total of a report as a point on a scale that you define. For example, use a gauge if you want to measure actual quarterly new bookings against a quota that you define.

If you're an administrator or a user with permission to manage dashboards, you can create, edit, and organize them. Even if you don't have such permissions, you can still view them.

Planning useful dashboards

I've always said that the best way to build a system is to envision what you want to ultimately measure. Do you want to know who your top sales reps are? Would you like to understand what your best accounts are buying from you and how much? Do you wonder how long it takes to close a deal? This method of starting with the business questions you want to answer applies to your building of reports and is true of dashboards. If you're an administrator or part of the team responsible for deploying salesforce.com, consider these tips as you develop your dashboards:

✔ **Focus on your end users.** Meet with sales and marketing management and have them define to you in advance key performance indicators (KPIs) for their teams and business. Knowing this helps you customize salesforce.com and construct useful dashboards.

✔ **Create a common set of components to reflect a universal way to look at business health.** This is especially true if your company has multiple sales teams. For example, after you determine the key sales metrics for your company's overall dashboard, you can replicate the dashboard and then customize other dashboards for each sales team. By doing this, everyone in the company is speaking a common language.

Building Dashboards

To build a dashboard, you need to create your custom reports first. You also need to create public folders for your dashboard reports if you want dashboards to be viewable for other users. See Chapter 15 for all the details on creating custom reports and organizing them in folders.

Only system administrators and users with permission to manage dashboards can add, edit, and delete dashboards.

In this section, I show you how to create a sample dashboard, how to clone a dashboard, and finally I cover the steps to build a dashboard from scratch.

Generating a sample dashboard

One of the best ways to get your feet wet with dashboards is to generate a sample dashboard. Salesforce.com not only creates the dashboard for you but also builds the underlying sample reports to generate the components.

To generate a sample dashboard, follow these steps:

1. **Click the Dashboard tab.**

   Either the last dashboard that you viewed or an introduction page appears. If you get the introduction page, click the Continue button or the Don't Show Me This Page Again link in the lower-right corner to bypass the overview. If this is your first visit to the Dashboards tab, the most recently created dashboard appears.

   If you're having trouble accessing dashboards, you might not have the proper permissions. In this circumstance, consult with your administrator.

2. **If a dashboard appears, click the Go To Dashboard List link at the top left of the page.**

   A folder's list page appears, as shown in Figure 16-1.

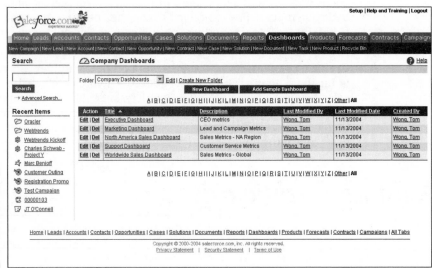

Figure 16-1:
Looking over your dashboard list.

3. **Click the Add Sample Dashboard button.**

   The list page reappears with a link to a sample dashboard entitled Company Performance Dashboard.

4. **Click the Company Performance Dashboard link.**

   The dashboard appears, as shown in the example in Figure 16-2.

5. **Click the Closed Sales to Date gauge.**

   A sample report appears entitled Closed Sales. Click the Back button on your browser to return to the dashboard.

Cloning a dashboard

You can generate a dashboard by cloning an existing one. If you envision creating multiple dashboards for different sales units with common components, you can use this shortcut and then modify the associated reports.

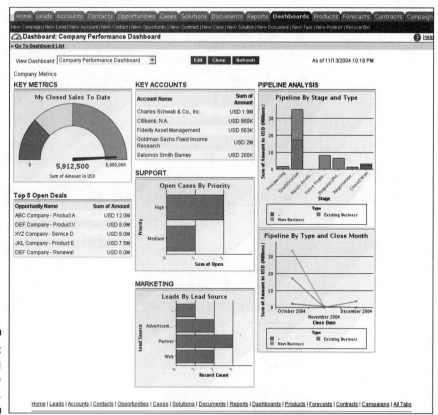

Figure 16-2:
Generating the sample dashboard.

To clone a dashboard, follow these steps:

1. **Click the Dashboard tab.**

   A dashboard appears.

2. **Use the View Dashboard drop-down list to select a dashboard you want to clone.**

   In this example, choose the sample dashboard entitled Company Performance Dashboard.

   The dashboard appears.

3. **Click the Clone button.**

   A New Dashboard page appears, as shown in Figure 16-3.

4. **Complete the required settings paying close attention to the following:**

   - Change the **Title** of the dashboard.
   - Select the **Dashboard Layout Style.**
   - Modify the **Security Settings** if necessary.
   - Alter the **Default Chart Settings** if desired.

5. **When you're done, click Save.**

   The new dashboard appears.

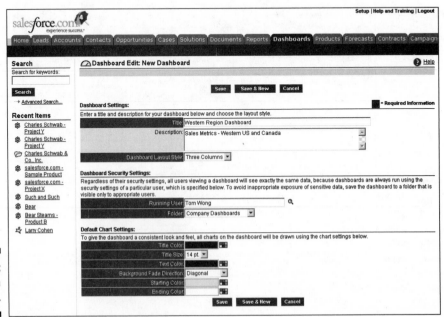

Figure 16-3:
Cloning a
dashboard.

When you clone a dashboard, you don't clone another set of identical reports. Instead, the newly cloned dashboard references the same custom reports that the original dashboard references. If you want the new dashboard to refer to different reports, see the "Editing a component" section later in this chapter.

Developing a dashboard from scratch

In previous sections, you test the waters and even generate some sample custom reports. In this section, you find out how to develop a dashboard from scratch.

To build a new dashboard, follow these steps:

1. **Click the Reports tab.**

   The Reports home page appears. You need to build your custom reports before you can develop a dashing new dashboard.

2. **Build your custom reports and save them to a public folder.**

   Dashboards that you want others to see can't use reports in your My Personal Reports folder. For purposes of this exercise, go to the My Personal Reports folder (commonly located at the top of your Reports home page) and click the following reports:

   • **Sample Report: Sales Pipeline by Stage:** Modify the Report Options to summarize information by Opportunity Owner and then Stage. Then save the report as Pipe by Rep and Stage to a public folder.

   • **Sample Report: Top Accounts:** Under Report Options, change Opportunity Status to Closed Won. Then save the report as Top Revenue Customers to a public folder.

   You must be an administrator or a user with permission to manage public reports if you want to add report folders.

3. **Click the Dashboard tab.**

   A dashboard appears.

4. **Click the Go To Dashboard List link.**

   A folder's list page appears.

5. **Click the New Dashboard button.**

   The New Dashboard page appears.

6. **Complete the settings and click Save.**

   The dashboard appears in Edit mode. See the "Cloning a dashboard" section for tips on completing the settings.

7. In the left column, click the Add Component link.

A New Dashboard Component page appears.

8. Complete the fields, as shown in the example in Figure 16-4.

- Click a radio button to select a component type. See the section "Breaking down basic elements" for details on the components. In the example, choose stay with chart.

- Enter a header, footer, and/or title. In the example, name the header **PIPELINE METRICS** and enter the title **Pipe by Rep and Stage**.

- Use the Display Units drop-down list to select the unit of measurement.

- Use the Chart Type menu to select a chart. In the example, choose Horizontal Bar – Stacked.

- Under Sort By, select the order of the bars. For example, if you want to rank the reps from biggest to smallest pipeline, choose Row Value Descending.

- If you want, enter a number under Maximum Values Displayed. For example, maybe you only want to see the top 20 reps with the biggest pipelines.

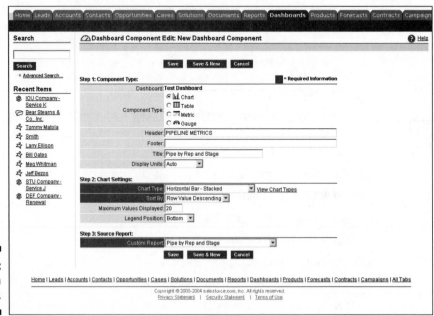

Figure 16-4:
Adding a
component.

- Select an option from the Legend Position drop-down list.

- From the Custom Report drop-down list, select the correct report. In this example, select Pipe by Rep and Stage.

9. **When you're done, click Save.**

    The dashboard reappears in Edit mode with the component displayed based on your settings.

10. **In the middle column, click the Add Component link.**

    Repeat the basic instructions from Step 8, but this time:

    - Select Table for Component Type.

    - Name the header **SALES METRICS** and the enter title **Top 10 Customers by Revenue**.

    - Sort by Row Value Descending.

    - Set the Maximum Values Displayed at 10.

    - Select the Custom Report called Top Revenue Customers.

11. **When you're done, click Save.**

    The dashboard reappears in Edit mode with a table in the middle column.

12. **When you're satisfied, click Done.**

    The dashboard appears in Saved mode.

Updating Dashboards

Over time, you might have to make changes to your dashboards, whether for cosmetic reasons or to make substantive updates. I can come up with a dozen common edits, but the good news is that updating is easy.

Editing dashboard properties

If you need to change the basic settings of a dashboard, you need to edit dashboard properties. To edit properties, follow these steps:

1. **Click the Dashboard tab.**

    A dashboard appears.

2. **Select a desired dashboard from the View Dashboard drop-down list.**

   For this example, select the sample dashboard labeled Company Performance Dashboard. The dashboard appears.

3. **Click the Edit button at the top of the dashboard page.**

   The dashboard appears in Edit mode.

4. **Click the Edit Properties button.**

   The settings page of the dashboard appears.

5. **Modify the settings as needed and click Save.**

   For example, if you want to change the background color of the charts, you would edit fields under Default Chart Settings. When you click Save, the dashboard reappears in Edit mode, and your setting changes are applied.

Editing a component

You might want to add to or change an existing component. To edit a component, follow these steps:

1. **Go to a dashboard and click the Edit button.**

   The dashboard appears in Edit mode.

2. **Click the Edit link above a component that you want to modify.**

   The Dashboard Component Edit page appears. For example, in the sample Company Performance Dashboard, click the Edit link above the component titled Pipeline by Stage & Type.

3. **Modify the fields as necessary, and then click Save.**

   For example, if you want to change it to a pie chart, select Pie from the Chart Type drop-down list, and then click Save. The dashboard reappears in Edit mode with the changes you applied to the component.

Modifying the layout

If you need to modify the dashboard layout, you can also perform this while in Edit mode, as shown in Figure 16-5.

Go to a dashboard, click the Edit button, and alter the layout. You can

✔ **Modify a column size:** Click the Narrow, Medium, or Wide links at the top of the column. All the components in the column change in size based on your setting.

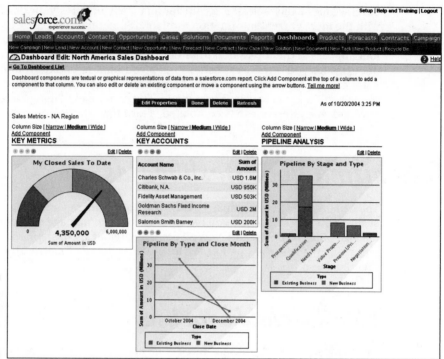

Figure 16-5:
Modifying a
dashboard
layout.

✔ **Add a component:** Click the Add Component link at the top of the column and follow the steps in the earlier section "Developing a dashboard from scratch."

✔ **Delete a component:** Click the Del link located above a component. A pop-up window appears to confirm the deletion. When you click OK, the pop-up closes, and the dashboard reappears minus the deleted component.

✔ **Rearrange components:** Click the directional arrows above a component.

When you're satisfied with your changes, remember to click the Done button. The dashboard then reappears with your modifications.

Refreshing the dashboard

Click any dashboard from your dashboard list. In the top-right corner of the dashboard, you see a time stamp starting with As Of. You can use this to let you know the last time your dashboard data was updated.

Several times a day, salesforce.com automatically updates your dashboards with the most current information available. Sometimes you can even see the page components reappearing, and a Refreshing Dashboard notification in red font appears in the top-right corner of the page. The fact that salesforce.com does this for you is quite refreshing, but if you want to update your dashboard data on your own, simply click the Refresh button at the top of the dashboard page whether it's in Saved or Edit mode. The components reappear one by one, and when the refresh is completed, a new time stamp appears.

Organizing Your Dashboards

You can organize your company's dashboards in folders and define the proper security access for users if you have permissions to manage dashboards, manage public reports, and view all data. By organizing dashboards, you can make sure that the right people are focusing on the right metrics to manage their business.

Viewing dashboard lists

Unlike most other tabs in salesforce.com, clicking the Dashboard tab doesn't take you to its home page. Instead, the last dashboard that you viewed appears.

To access your viewable dashboards, simply follow these steps:

1. **Click the Go To Dashboard List link at the top-right corner of any dashboard.**

   A dashboard folder's list page appears.

2. **Use the Folder drop-down list to select a desired folder.**

   The page for the selected folder appears with a list of available dashboards.

3. **From this list page, users, with the permissions mentioned at the beginning of this section, can perform a variety of functions that include:**

   • Click a column header to re-sort a table. (See Chapter 2 for more details on navigating list pages.)

   • Click a title name to view a dashboard.

   • Click the Edit link next to a dashboard to modify it.

• Click the Del link next to a dashboard to delete it.

• Click the New Dashboard or Add Sample Dashboard buttons to build dashboards. (See the earlier section "Developing a dashboard from scratch.")

Building dashboards folders

From a list page, you can also create and edit folders. Editing a folder is easy when you understand how to create one.

To create a folder, follow these steps:

1. Click the Create New Folder link next to the Folder drop-down list.

A New Dashboard Folder page appears, as shown in Figure 16-6.

Figure 16-6: Building a dashboard folder.

2. Type a name for the folder in the Dashboard Folder field.

For example, if you want a folder for only senior management, you might name it Executive Dashboards.

3. **Use the Public Folder Access field to determine read versus read/write privileges to the folder.**

   For example, if you select the Read/Write option, a user with access to the folder can modify a dashboard in the folder.

4. **Use the radio buttons to select who should have access to the folder.**

   Your choices amount to all, none, and selective.

5. **If you chose selective in Step 4 (the third radio button), highlight groups or roles in the Available for Sharing list box and add them to the Shared To list box.**

6. **When you're done, click Save.**

   The folder's list page reappears, and now you can add dashboards or move existing dashboards to the new folder, which I explain in the earlier section "Editing dashboard properties."

When naming folders, dashboards, and dashboard reports, consider using a standard numbering convention. You could name the senior management folder as 1.0 Executive Dashboards. Then the executive sales dashboard might be 1.1 versus the executive marketing dashboard of 1.2. Finally, the global sales pipeline report might be named 1.1.1 Global Pipeline. By using a standard numbering methodology, you can more efficiently create, clone, and organize dashboards and dashboard reports.

Part V
Designing the Salesforce.com Solution

The 5th Wave   By Rich Tennant

JUNGLE ROPE Co.

"I wouldn't qualify this one too long."

In this part . . .

Customers of salesforce.com rave about how easy it is for end users to use salesforce.com. But what I find equally (if not more) amazing is how simple it is to fine-tune salesforce.com to suit the unique needs of your company . . . as long as you understand the basic elements of the Setup, that is.

As an administrator, the Setup options available to you are extensive, regardless of what salesforce.com edition you have. In this part, I focus on the three main areas of Setup that are necessary to successfully implement and then administer salesforce.com for your end users: configuring the system, customizing the records, and migrating and maintaining your data. With system configuration, I show you how you can modify salesforce.com for the way that you want users to have privilege to data. You then discover how you can easily customize the pages by adding fields, defining processes, changing layouts, and more. Finally, I show you ways to maintain your data so it's fresh and useful for your users.

The detail in these chapters are simple enough for anyone to follow but sophisticated enough for even the largest organizations.

Chapter 17

Fine-Tuning the Configuration

*I*n earlier chapters, you discover how to add custom fields, upload documents, and create standard templates so that salesforce.com looks like it was made exactly for your business. If you're starting to think about additional ways to tweak the system so that each user only sees information pertinent to them, you've come to the right chapter.

For administrators or members of your customer relationship management (CRM) project team with the right privileges, salesforce.com allows you to easily configure your system so that users can access and share information according to your goals. Regardless of which salesforce.com edition your company has chosen, you have a variety of ways to control access and sharing of data, from system-wide sharing rules to assigning profiles. And if you have Enterprise or Developer Edition, you have industrial-strength flexibility, even to the point of field-level security. Salesforce.com can't yet enable you to leap tall buildings in a single bound, but it's only a matter of time.

In this chapter, I show you all the steps you can take (or should consider) for configuring salesforce.com, including creating the role hierarchy, assigning profiles, creating users, setting up your sharing rules, and managing groups. I also show you other methods for controlling security, which include password policies and session settings.

Figuring Out Configuration

All the things that you can change can be conveniently accessed from the Administration Setup menu of salesforce.com. If you have administrative permissions, log in to salesforce.com and follow these steps:

1. **Click the Setup link in the top-right corner of the page.**

   The Personal Setup page appears.

2. **On the sidebar, click the Administration Setup header.**

   The Administration Setup page appears with a page title that includes the edition (or version) of salesforce.com that you're using.

3. **In the sidebar, click the + buttons to expand the first three folders under Administration Setup: Manage Users, Company Profile, and Security Controls.**

   These are your basic options and the first things that you should use when configuring salesforce.com. Use the sidebar or the menu in the body of the Administration Setup page to navigate through the universe of configuration options at your disposal. (I prefer to use the sidebar because it's always visible.)

Breaking down basic elements

Before jumping into the guts of system configuration, I find it helpful to review four basic configuration elements:

- ✔ **Users:** The specific people who use your salesforce.com system.

- ✔ **Roles:** Control a user's level of access to information in salesforce.com. For example, if you are a manager of a team of sales reps, you will have read and write access to the information owned by the reps reporting to you in the role hierarchy. Each user should have an assigned role within your defined role hierarchy.

- ✔ **Profiles:** Control a user's permissions to perform different functions in salesforce.com. You must assign a profile to each user.

- ✔ **Sharing model and rules:** Defines the general access that users have to each other's data.

You use these four elements as the primary levers to deliver the proper level of access and control for your company in salesforce.com.

Planning configuration to achieve success

Put the major stakeholders of your salesforce.com solution in a room and ask them one question: "How do you envision people sharing information in salesforce.com?" More often than not, you'll get blank stares and maybe a few nasty e-mails for lobbing such a broad question.

Now, you *should* ask that question, but I suggest following it up with scenarios. Here are a couple ideas to get you started:

- ✔ Should a telemarketer be able see what the CEO sees?

- ✔ Should a sales rep be able to view data from other reps, like an opportunity record? Should one sales rep be allowed to edit another's lead record?

- ✔ Do certain groups need wider access than others? For example, does a call center team that supports all customers need more or less access than a team of sales reps?

- ✔ Does a manager require different permissions than a rep?

- ✔ Do multiple people commonly work on the same account or opportunity?

- ✔ Do you have any concerns with a fully open or completely private sharing model?

Use these types of questions and their answers to guide your configuration.

Discuss sharing issues with your CRM project team first. You should probably formulate an opinion based on what you believe would be best for your company. Take into consideration the culture, size, and type of sales organization at your company. Use this opinion to guide the specific nature of your questions.

Verifying Your Company Profile

In your Company Profile folder, you can modify many basic settings for your organization that include default time zone, language, and currencies. If you're the administrator, you can also use this section to monitor and anticipate your future needs relative to user seats.

Updating your company information

This is an easy but important step. If you're an administrator beginning your implementation, get this done before you even think of adding a new user.

To update your company information, click the Setup link in the top-right corner of salesforce.com and follow these steps:

1. **Click the Company Information link under the Company Profile heading on the sidebar.**

   The Company Information page appears.

2. Click the Edit button.

The Company Information page appears in Edit mode. You should review all the fields. Pay closest attention to verifying the accuracy of the three or four required fields in the Locale Settings section, as shown in Figure 17-1:

- Use the Default Locale drop-down list to select your company's primary geographic locale. This setting affects the format of date and time fields (for example, 09/30/2004 versus 30/09/2004).

- Select an option from the Default Language drop-down list.

- Verify that the Default Time Zone drop-down list is correctly set.

- Choose the proper location from the Currency Locale drop-down list in the event that you use a single currency. This affects the corporate currency. (You won't see this field if you set up multi-currencies.)

Don't worry, users can still modify their individual locale settings in the future.

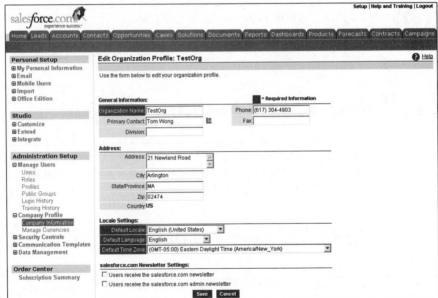

Figure 17-1: Updating locale settings on the company profile.

3. When you're done, click Save.

The Company Profile page reappears with any changes you made.

Managing currencies

If you're using Professional or Enterprise Edition, you can manage multiple currencies. If you work for a company with a global sales organization, you can allow users to manage opportunities and other records in their local currency and still consolidate reports in the corporate currency. So you could look at an individual opportunity and see that it's for ¥500,000 (Japanese yen). Then when you run an Opportunity Pipeline report, you see each individual opportunity listed with its amount in its respective currency. However, you see the grand total of the report in your base currency (U.S. dollars, for example).To manage multiple currencies, contact your salesforce.com account rep first to request it. The salesforce.com rep will notify you when the feature is available in your salesforce.com account.

To manage multiple currencies, click the Setup link and then click the Manage Currencies link under the Company Profile heading on the sidebar. The Currency page appears with an Active Currency related list and potentially an Inactive Currency related list if you've deactivated currencies already. From this page you can do the following (see Figure 17-2):

Figure 17-2: Updating multiple currencies.

Click the . . .

✔ **New button** to add a new currency. The New Currency page appears. Complete the simple fields and click Save to activate it.

✔ **Edit Rates button** to change conversion rates that relate to the corporate currency. When you're done, click Save.

✔ **Change Corporate button** if you want to change the corporate currency. On the page that appears, select a new currency and click Save.

✔ **Edit link** on a row to modify a currency's displayed decimal places.

✔ **Activate or Deactivate links** to turn on or off a currency for your users.

After you enable multiple currencies, your currency characters are changed to ISO currency codes (for example, USD instead of $). In addition, after you activate a currency, you can never completely delete the currency, only deactivate it.

Defining the Role Hierarchy

Think of a role hierarchy as the salesforce.com system's data-access org chart: If you're assigned to the role at the top of the chart, you have full access to your own data and the data of everyone below you in the hierarchy, and life is good. Unlike a typical org chart, however, it's usually less complicated and not uncommon to see a sales assistant near the top of the hierarchy because he might require access to support all the sales users (and life is not so good).

You can use the role hierarchy in salesforce.com as a primary method to control a user's access to other users' data. After you assign a role to a user, that user has owner-like access to all records owned by or shared with subordinate users in the hierarchy. For example, if you set up a hierarchy with a Sales Rep role subordinate to a Sales Manager role, users assigned to Sales Manager would have read and write access to records owned by or shared with users in the Sales Rep role.

To set up your company's role hierarchy, click the Setup link in the top-right corner and follow these steps:

1. **Click the Roles link under the Manage Users heading on the sidebar.**

   The Understanding Roles page appears, and you see a sample hierarchy.

2. **Use the View Other Sample Role Hierarchies drop-down list if you want to select a different sample hierarchy.**

3. **Click the Set Up Roles button.**

   The Roles page appears.

4. **Use the drop-down list on the right side of the page if you want to select a different view of the hierarchy.**

   Salesforce.com provides three standard views for displaying the role hierarchy: a tree view, a list view, and a sorted list view.

   When selecting a view, keep in mind that all three views allow you to perform the basic tasks related to setting up roles. Use the tree view if you have an extensive role hierarchy because you can use the plus (+) and minus (-) links to collapse or expand the tree, similar to folders. But note that the New Role button is replaced with Add Role links. Use the sorted list view if you want to re-sort the list columns.

5. **Click the New Role button.**

   A New Role page appears.

6. **Complete the fields, as shown in Figure 17-3.**

   The fields are pretty obvious, but here are some tips:

   • Type a title for the role in the Role Name field.

   • Use the This Role Reports To drop-down list to define the role's place in the hierarchy. Because the drop-down list is based on roles you've already created, add roles by starting at the top of your hierarchy and then work your way down.

   • Fill in the optional field if you want a title other than what you entered in the Role Name field to appear on reports. Otherwise, reports with the Org Drill Down features display your role names. For example, you might want the Role Name of "VP, Worldwide Sales" to appear as "Global Sales" on reports.

   • Select the Opportunity Access option that fits your company's objectives. You can provide an account owner with read/write access to related opportunities that she doesn't own, view access, or no access at all. This flexibility comes in handy in heavily regulated industries, where you might have to prevent an account executive from knowing about certain opportunities going on with her account.

7. **When you're done, click the Save button or the Save & New button.**

   If you click Save, the Roles page reappears displaying the roles and their hierarchy.

   If you click the Save & New button, a New Role page appears, and you can continue building the hierarchy. Repeat Steps 3 through 5 until your hierarchy is done.

Figure 17-3:
Adding a
new role
to the
hierarchy.

When you're constructing your hierarchy, don't confuse your actual company org chart with the role hierarchy. Role hierarchy is all about access to data to perform your duties in salesforce.com and how you want to organize certain sales-related reports. As such, hierarchies often have fewer layers than a typical org chart. For example, if your executive team will be users, you might simply create a role called Executive Team, assuming that many of those users will have similar viewing and editing privileges.

Setting Up Profiles

You can use profiles to control a user's permission to perform many functions in salesforce.com. Depending on which edition you're using, you can also use profiles to

✔ Define which page layouts a user will see.

✔ Control field-level access.

✔ Alter the tabs displayed to users.

✔ Make record types available to certain users.

✔ Secure certain login settings.

Reviewing the standard profiles

Most editions of salesforce.com come with five or six standard profiles, which can't be altered except for tab settings. Many large organizations can stick to these standard profiles and address the majority of their company's requirements related to user permissions. Oddly enough, if you have Team or Professional Edition, you can't actually view the settings on the standard profiles.

If you have Enterprise or Developer Edition, first click the Setup link in the top-right corner and then click the Profiles link under the Manage Users heading on the sidebar to see your profiles. Otherwise, here's a brief explanation of the standard profiles and how they're typically applied:

- ✔ **Contract Managers** can add, edit, approve, and activate contracts. They can also delete non-activated contracts.

- ✔ **Marketing Users** have all the rights of standard users and can perform a variety of marketing-related functions including importing leads and managing public documents and e-mail templates. If your salesforce.com edition has campaigns, marketing users can also administer campaigns.

- ✔ **Read Only** is just what its name implies. Users assigned to this profile can view data and export reports but can't edit anything.

- ✔ **Solution Managers** have all the rights of standard users and can review and publish solutions.

- ✔ **Standard Users** can create and edit most record types, run reports, and view but not modify many areas of the administration setup. If you can't create custom profiles, you would probably choose to assign sales reps to the standard user profile.

- ✔ **System Administrators** have full permissions and access across all salesforce.com functions that don't require a separate license. You would typically grant this level of control only to users administering the system or who play a critical part in configuring and customizing salesforce.com.

Creating custom profiles

If you have Enterprise or Developer Edition, you can build custom layouts that provide you greater flexibility over permissions that can be granted to users and the layouts that they see. See Chapter 18 for details on creating custom layouts, business processes, and record types.

To create a custom profile, you can start from scratch, but I suggest cloning and modifying an existing profile by following these steps:

1. **Click the Setup link in the top-right corner, and then click the Profiles link under the Manage Users heading on the sidebar.**

   The User Profiles page appears.

2. **Click the Standard User link in the Profile Name list.**

   The Profile: Standard User page appears. In practice, you can clone from any of the profiles, but by starting from the Standard User profile, you can simply add or remove permissions.

3. **Click the Clone button.**

   The Clone Profile page appears.

4. **Type a title in the Profile Name field, and then click Save.**

   The Profile page for your new profile appears.

5. **Click the Edit button to modify the permissions.**

   The Profile Edit page appears.

   Salesforce.com packs a plethora of possible permissions into a profile page. Some of those permissions aren't obvious; others are dependent on your selecting other permissions. If you have questions as you're working through the Profile Edit page, you can click the ? icon to go directly to the relevant Help documentation. In addition, if you place your cursor over the new *i* icons, located next to certain settings on the Profile Edit page, rollover text appears with tips on other settings required.

6. **Under the Tab Settings header, use the drop-down lists to determine the tab settings for your new profile. Choose from the three possible options:**

   • Stay with Default On if you want a tab to be displayed.

   • Select Default Off if you want a tab not to appear while still allowing a user assigned to the profile the choice to turn the tab back on. For example, if you created a profile for sales reps and you wanted to hide the Contracts tab but give the rep the option to display it, you would select Default Off on the Contracts field.

   • Select Tab Hidden if you want the tab to be hidden without an option to the user to turn the tab back on. For example, if your company isn't going to use cases, you might decide to hide the tab.

7. **Select the Overwrite Users' Personal Tab Customizations check box if you want to overwrite user's current personal customization settings with the settings for the new profile that you're applying.**

8. **Under the Administrative Settings header, select or deselect check boxes to modify administrative permissions from the profile.**

Most of these settings are designed for administrators, but some of these might be important depending on your goals for a custom profile. For example, if you want to build a manager's profile, you might retain permissions such as Manage Public Reports and Manage Public List Views so that managers can create public reports and list views for their teams.

9. **Under the General User Settings header, select or deselect check boxes to modify common user permissions from the profile.**

   For example, if you don't want sales reps to be able to export customer data to a file, you could create a custom profile for reps and remove the Export to Excel setting.

10. **Under the Sales Permissions header, select or deselect check boxes to modify settings that relate to the sales process.**

11. **Under the Support Settings header, select or deselect check boxes to modify permissions that relate to your customer service processes.**

12. **Under the Contracts Settings header, select or deselect check boxes to . . . you get the idea.**

13. **When you're done, click Save.**

   The Profile page reappears for your new profile.

14. **Click the View Users button if you want to assign users to the profile.**

   A list page appears where you can view, add, or reset passwords for users in the profile. See the following section to add users in salesforce.com.

Adding Users to Salesforce.com

When salesforce.com supplies user licenses for your organization, administrators can add users into salesforce.com. (See the "Setting Up Profiles" section for the scoop on viewing and modifying your company profile.) You don't have to create the roles and profiles before you add users, but I recommend doing so because Role and Profile are required fields when you're creating a user record.

To add users, click the Setup link and follow these steps:

1. **Click the Users link under the Manage Users heading on the sidebar.**

   A users list page appears.

2. **Use the View drop-down list if you want to select from standard or custom list views of your users.**

   Salesforce.com presets your views with three standard options: All Users, Active Users, and Admin Users.

3. **Click the New User button if you want to add users one at a time.**

   A New User page appears in Edit mode.

4. **Complete the fields, as shown in Figure 17-4, paying close attention to selecting appropriate Role and Profile values.**

   You can select the last check box at the bottom of the New User page if you want to notify the user immediately.

   In the event that you don't know a person's role or you haven't completed the role hierarchy, salesforce.com provides a None Specified option. Just remember to assign the user to a role as soon as possible to ensure that he or she has the right access to information.

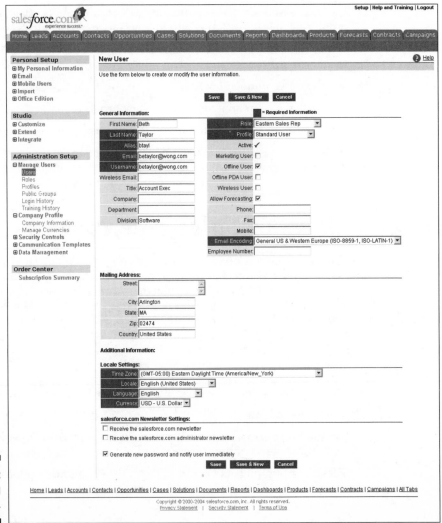

Figure 17-4: Adding a user.

5. **When you're done, click Save.**

   After you click Save, the user list page reappears.

If you're in a hurry, you can add as many as five new users at a time from one page. Just click the Add Multiple Users button from the user list page. An Add Multiple Users page appears, as shown in Figure 17-5. The only limitation is that the majority of the fields on a user record aren't displayed; if you want more complete records, you have to modify them after the fact.

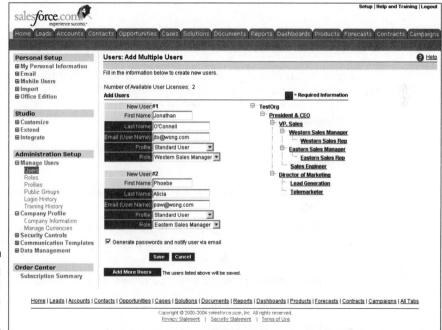

Figure 17-5: Adding multiple users.

Defining Your Sharing Model

As an administrator or member of you CRM project team, one of your biggest decisions in salesforce.com is how users will share information. A *sharing model* controls the level of access that users have to an organization's information. You can use the sharing model with the role hierarchy, public groups, personal groups, and the default access for each role to get pretty specific about what you want people to view or change. You use the organization-wide sharing model, and if necessary, public groups and expanded sharing rules in salesforce.com to configure your sharing model.

When in doubt, start with an open, collaborative sharing model, as opposed to a secretive sharing model where no one knows what anyone else is doing. (A secretive sharing model sounds like any oxymoron, right? Well it can be, because if you don't carefully think about ramifications, you could be back to where you started with giant heaps of information.) If collaboration is one of your goals, a more restrictive sharing model can have a greater potential negative impact on end user adoption. You can always change the sharing model in the future if people scream loudly enough. But nine out of ten times, the value of collaboration overcomes the initial concerns with users viewing other users' data.

Setting organization-wide defaults

The organization-wide defaults set the default access that users have to each other's data. No matter which defaults you set to the sharing model, users will still have access to all data owned by or shared with users below them in the role hierarchy.

To configure the organization-wide defaults, click the Setup link and follow these steps:

1. **Click the Sharing Rules link under the Security Controls heading on the sidebar.**

   The Sharing Rules page appears. In the event that the Understanding Sharing overview page appears, review it for tips and then click the Set Up Sharing button at the bottom of the page.

2. **Click the Edit button on the Organization Wide Defaults list.**

   The Organization Sharing Edit page appears.

3. **Select the desired settings.**

   Use the grid provided by salesforce.com (see Figure 17-6) for explanations of the different options. For example, if you want the most restrictive model, choose the following as your defaults: Private for the major records, Hide Details for Calendar, and No Access for Price Book.

4. **When you're done, click Save.**

   The Sharing Rules page reappears with your settings listed under the Organization Wide Defaults list.

Figure 17-6:
Looking
over the
options
for the
organization
-wide
sharing
model.

Creating groups

You can create public and personal groups in salesforce.com to extend greater sharing privileges. Groups comprise users, roles, or even other groups. Anyone can create personal groups, but only users with certain permissions can add public groups, which are groups that all users can see and in which they can share. (See the "Creating custom profiles" section for details on permissions.)

Public groups work in combination with sharing rules to expand sharing access to information beyond the organization-wide defaults. You can access public groups from the Manage Users heading or the Security Controls heading on the sidebar on the Personal Setup page.

To create a public group, click the Setup link in the top-right corner and follow these steps:

1. **Click the Sharing Rules link under the Security Controls heading on the sidebar.**

   The Sharing Rules page appears.

2. **Click the New button next to the Public Groups list.**

   A Group Membership page appears.

3. **Enter a name for the group in the Group Name field, and then highlight users, roles, or other groups in the Available Members list box and add them to the Selected Members list box, as shown in Figure 17-7.**

4. **When you're done, click Save.**

   The Sharing Rules page reappears with groups that you added listed under the Public Groups list.

Granting greater access with sharing rules

By using public groups, roles, or roles and subordinates, you can create sharing rules to extend access above and beyond the organization-wide defaults. For example, if your default sharing model is read only but you want a group of call center reps to have edit privileges on account records, you could do this with a custom sharing rule.

Figure 17-7: Creating a public group.

To add a sharing rule and apply it to your data, click the Setup link and follow these steps:

1. **Click the Sharing Rules link under the Security Controls heading on the sidebar.**

   The Sharing Rules page appears.

2. **Click the New button next to any of the Lead, Account, Opportunity, or Case Sharing Rules lists.**

   All four lists operate much the same but relate to different records. A sharing rules page appears for your selected record.

3. **Use the drop-down lists to define the related roles or groups and the wider access that you want to grant them, as shown in the example in Figure 17-8.**

   For example, you might create a public group for your call center team and then grant them read/write privileges to data owned by members of the Entire Organization group.

Figure 17-8:
Creating
expanded
sharing
rules.

4. **When you're done, click Save.**

   The Sharing Rules page reappears with your new rule listed under the appropriate related list.

When you add a new sharing rule, salesforce.com automatically re-evaluates the sharing rules to apply the changes. If your modifications are substantial, you will be warned with a dialog box that the operation could take significant time. When you click OK, the dialog box closes and the Sharing Rules page reappears. Use the Recalculate button on the appropriate related list to manually apply the changes.

Using Other Security Controls

Beyond the major configuration settings such as roles, profiles, and sharing model, as an administrator, you have other settings for managing the use and security of your data in salesforce.com. Those features are located under the Security Controls heading on the sidebar of the Personal Setup page.

In this section, I discuss how to manage field-level access, set password policies, and control session settings.

Setting field-level security

If you have Enterprise or Developer Edition, you have three primary ways to control access and editing on specific fields: profiles (which I discuss earlier in this chapter), page layouts (Chapter 18 covers these), and field-level settings (stay right here for the details). With field-level security, you can further restrict users' access to fields by setting whether those fields are visible, editable, or read only.

To view and administer field-level security, click the Setup link and follow these steps:

1. **Click the Field Accessibility link under the Security Controls heading on the sidebar.**

   The Field Accessibility page appears.

2. **Click the link for the type of record for which you want to view and manage field-level security.**

   A Field Accessibility page for the selected record type appears. For example, click the Account link if you want to review the security settings on account fields.

3. **Under the Choose Your View header, click the View by Fields link.**

   The Field Accessibility page for the record type reappears with a Field drop-down list.

4. **Select a field from the Field drop-down list.**

   The page reappears with a table displaying your company's profiles and the profiles' accessibility to the selected field.

5. **In the Field Access column, click a link to edit the profile's field access.**

   An Access Settings page for the selected profile and selected field appears, as shown in Figure 17-9.

6. **Select the check boxes to modify the field-level settings, and then click Save.**

The Field Accessibility page for the selected record type reappears.

Setting password policies

You can configure password policies to provide safeguards for access to salesforce.com. To set up password policies, click the Setup link and follow these steps:

1. **Click the Password Policies link under the Security Controls heading on the sidebar.**

The Password Policies page appears.

2. **Use the drop-down lists on the required fields to modify the settings, as shown in Figure 17-10.**

The fields are pretty obvious, but if you have questions you might want to consult your IT department. Many companies already have an existing set of password policies.

Figure 17-10:
Configuring
password
policies.

3. **When you're done, click Save.**

   The Security Controls page appears.

Controlling session settings

Some companies like to apply session settings as another method of preventing unauthorized access. With salesforce.com you can impose two session settings: one based on time and the other based on IP address. For example, many companies want applications to time out on a user's desktop after a set duration of time.

IP stands for "Internet Protocol" and an IP address, in its simplest terms, is the unique address for a computer accessing the Internet. So locking a session to an IP address when a user logs in is one way to try to prevent unauthorized access to your salesforce.com account.

To apply session settings, click the Setup link in the top-right corner and follow these steps:

1. **Click the Session Settings link under the Security Controls heading on the sidebar.**

   The Session Settings page appears.

2. **Use the drop-down lists and check boxes to apply your settings.**

3. **When you're done, click Save.**

   The Security Controls page appears.

Chapter 18

Customizing Salesforce.com

*I*f you're just beginning your implementation, Salesforce.com comes precon-figured with a number of common fields in simple layouts for each of the tabs. You could buy your licenses, log in, and without any customization, start using it to track your customers. So, why is it that with over 11,000 customers and growing, no two instances of salesforce.com are likely to be identical?

The answer is a key ingredient to your success: The more salesforce.com is customized to your business, the more likely your company will use it effec-tively and productively.

And with salesforce.com, customizing an application has never been easier or faster. If you're an administrator or a user with permission to customize salesforce.com, you have a universe of tools to design salesforce.com to fit the way you do business. And you don't need to be a technical wizard to make these changes. With common sense and a little help from me, you can customize salesforce.com on your own.

Salesforce.com has many customization features. I could write another book if I tried to address each feature. So instead in this chapter, I show you how to perform all the core customization options including creating fields, building in your standard processes, adding Web links, and rearranging layouts. Then for companies that have Enterprise or Developer Edition and possess com-plex needs, I show you how to develop custom page layouts, multiple busi-ness processes, and record types that link to custom profiles.

Discovering Customization

All your customization tools are conveniently accessible from the Customize menu located under the Studio heading of Setup in salesforce.com. Navigating the Customize menu is simple when you understand some basics. If you have administrative permissions, log in to salesforce.com and do this now:

1. **Click the Setup link in the top-right corner of the page.**

   The Personal Setup page appears.

2. **Under the Studio heading on the sidebar, click the Customize heading.**

   The Customize page of Setup appears, and the sidebar expands to display headings for the various tabs that can be customized. Under the Customize heading on the sidebar, you also see a couple select headings for other areas of salesforce.com (such as Workflow and Self Service), which can also be customized.

   Use the sidebar or the menu in the body of the Customize page to navigate through the universe of customization options at your disposal. I prefer to use the sidebar because it's always visible.

3. **Click the + buttons or headings that correspond to the major tabs such as accounts, contacts, and leads.**

   The sidebar expands with the different customization features available under each heading. These are all the basic things you can do when customizing a standard tab. Notice that although certain headings have more features, most of the headings have links to common customization features such as Fields, Page Layouts, Web Links, and in certain editions, Record Types and Processes.

4. **Click the Fields link under a tab-related heading on the sidebar.**

   A Fields page appears based on the selected tab heading. This easy and consistent navigation will help you through the customization.

For all you system administrators and technical gurus interested not only in customizing, but also extending and integrating salesforce.com, you should click the Studio heading on the sidebar. The Studio page of Setup appears with a big, bold title in the center named CustomForce.com. With Winter '05 release, Studio is basically being redefined and expanded as CustomForce, and this page provides you a menu of the options (some basic, some advanced) for customizing, extending, and integrating salesforce.com.

Breaking down basic elements

When diving into customization, I find it helpful to keep four basic concepts in mind:

✔ **Records** are the high-level data elements (such as accounts, contacts, and opportunities) that are stored in the salesforce.com database. Each of the tabs corresponds to a type of record. Records consist of fields.

✔ **Page layouts** is a feature that allows you to control the way a page is displayed to users. Page layouts correspond to the organization of fields, Web links, and related lists that are displayed on a detail page in salesforce.com.

✔ **Processes** is an option that allows you to build various sales, marketing, and service processes in salesforce.com that you want your reps to follow. Certain records (namely leads, opportunities, cases, solutions, contracts, and activities) each have a standard drop-down list used for defining processes.

✔ **Record Types** is a feature that allows you to offer certain business processes and subsets of drop-down lists to users based on their profiles. Not to be confused with a type of record (such as an account or contact), a record type when used with page layouts and profiles can make only some of the drop-down list values available to users within a profile.

Customizing for relevance

Prior to customizing salesforce.com, your CRM project team should conduct a series of business process reviews with functional representatives or stakeholders of the teams that will be using salesforce.com. In those meetings, not only should you map out current and desired processes, but you should ask sets of leading questions that will impact the design of fields, records, layouts, and more.

See the introductory sections of each of the tab-related chapters in this book for the types of questions you should ask. Key questions should include:

✔ How do you define your customer?

✔ What information do you want to collect on a contact?

✔ How do you know you have a qualified lead?

✔ What do you want to know about an opportunity?

Use the answers to construct a list of standard and custom fields per record that you believe should be in salesforce.com. That spreadsheet should include columns for field name, field type, field values, justification, and so on, and you should review it with your project team prior to customization.

When customizing, keep it simple at the beginning. Don't add or keep a field unless you ultimately believe that you or someone else will use it. You can always build additional fields in the future, especially if you build momentum based on early user adoption success.

Building and Editing Fields

Maybe you've heard the adage from the movie *Field of Dreams:* "If you build it, they will come." Well, when it comes to customizing salesforce.com fields, the "it" stands for "something useful and easy." The more relevant you make the record fields to your actual business, the better the user adoption batting average and the higher the likelihood of hitting a usefulness home run.

Adding fields

All editions of salesforce.com let you add fields, but some versions let you add significantly more fields than others. For example, if you have Team Edition, you can add 5 custom fields per record; with Enterprise Edition, you can create up to 250 per record.

To add a field, click the Setup link in the top-right corner of salesforce.com and follow these steps:

1. **Click any tab-related heading under the Customize heading on the sidebar.**

   The options under the selected heading appear.

2. **Click the Fields link under the heading.**

   The fields page for the selected tab appears, displaying a list of standard fields at the top and a list of custom fields at the bottom.

3. **Click the New button on the Custom Fields related list.**

   Step 1 of the new custom field wizard appears.

4. **Use the drop-down list to select the type of field (as shown in Figure 18-1), and then click Next.**

   Step 2 of the wizard appears.

5. **Enter the details and click Next.**

   Step 3 of the wizard appears. The details page varies based on the field type you selected. For example, the settings for a Text Area field are different than for a Currency field.

6. **For Enterprise or Developer Edition, use the check boxes to select the field level access and edit rights per profile, and then click Next.**

   Step 4 of the wizard appears.

7. **For Enterprise or Developer Edition, use the check boxes to select the page layouts that should include this field, and then click Save.**

   The Fields page for the selected record reappears.

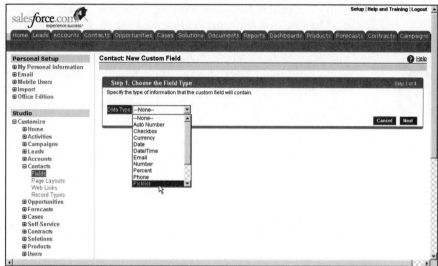

Figure 18-1:
Selecting
the type of
field to add.

Viewing and updating fields

On an ongoing basis, situations come up where you might need to update the properties of a field.

To view and update your fields, first click the Setup link in the top-right corner of any salesforce.com page and then click the Field link under a tab heading under the Customize heading on the sidebar. The field page for the selected tab appears, displaying lists of standard and custom fields. From this page, you can do the following:

✔ Click the Edit link if you want to update a field. Step 2 of the wizard appears where you can follow the steps in the preceding section on adding a field and click Save at any time.

✔ If you want to change the field type on a field, first click the Edit link and then click the Change Type of This Field button at the bottom of the Step 2 page. Step 1 of the wizard appears, and you can follow the steps in the preceding section.

✔ Click a link in the Label column to view the field and its properties.

✔ Click the Del link next to a custom field if you want to delete it.

✔ If you want to add values to a drop-down list, first click the link in the Label column and then click the New button on the Picklist Values list, as shown in Figure 18-2.

✔ If you want to replace values on a drop-down list, click the Replace link next to a field. A Find and Replace Picklist page appears. Make sure you've added the new value before trying to replace.

The Replace feature is really helpful in situations where you have existing records that have that have old values that need to be switched to new values. Take the Lead Status field, for example: You could use the Replace feature to update leads formerly marked as Unqualified and replace them all instantly with a new value called Garbage.

✔ If you want to reorder values on a drop-down list, first click the link in the Label column and then click the Reorder button on the Picklist Values list.

Figure 18-2:
Adding values to an existing drop-down list.

Replicating your key standard processes

On certain records in salesforce.com, you use a standard drop-down list to map your business processes. This feature applies to task, lead, opportunity, case, contract, and solution records.

You'll probably want to handle each of these records separately and with some careful thought. To define your standard business processes, do the following:

1. **Expand the Customize menu until you see the Fields links for leads, opportunities, cases, solutions, contracts, and activities (under the Activities heading, refer to Task Fields link).**

2. **Click a Fields link under one of the records mentioned in Step 1.**

   The fields page appears with a Standard Fields and Custom Fields related lists.

3. **Depending on the record you chose, look on the Standard Fields related list and do the following:**

   • **For task activities,** click the Status link under the Task Fields link to modify your statuses for accomplishing tasks.

   • **For leads,** click the Lead Status link if you want to redefine your lead process.

   • **For opportunities,** click the Stage link to build your sales stages with corresponding probabilities and forecast categories.

   • **For cases,** click the Status link if you want to lay out a standard process for case handling.

   • **For contracts,** click the Status link to set up your contract approval process.

   • **For solutions,** click the Status link if you want to modify your solution review stages.

   In each circumstance, a field page appears with a Picklist Values related list, listing all of the values within the process.

4. **On the Picklist Values related list, adjust your process as necessary.**

   See the previous section for details on updating picklist fields.

Using Web Integration Links

Many sales, marketing, and support teams rely on public and private Web sites and secure Web applications to perform their jobs. For example, your company might have an intranet that employees go to for a variety of reasons.

Or they might use a research Web site for market intelligence. Dependence on those sites doesn't disappear just because you roll out salesforce.com.

If this applies to you, you'll want to know how to add and update Web links in salesforce.com.

If you want to encourage your users to use salesforce.com as a one-stop shop for accessing important customer information, you can build powerful Web links in salesforce.com that connect to important Web sites or applications.

To build a Web integration link, click the Setup link in the top-right corner and follow these steps:

1. **Click any record heading under the Customize heading on the sidebar.**

   The selected heading expands.

2. **Click the Web Links link under the record heading.**

   The Web Links page for the selected record appears.

3. **Click the New button on the Web Links list.**

   Step 1 of the New Link wizard appears.

4. **Name the link and choose the link type, and then click Next.**

   Step 2 of the wizard appears. The fields are pretty obvious, but here are some tips:

   • Link Label is the how the link appears on a page. For example, if you want to create a link to your intranet, you might name the label Company Intranet.

   • Use Link Type to set whether the link is a URL or an sforce control in the sforce control library.

This book doesn't go into any detail on sforce or sforce controls. What you should know about sforce controls is the following: If your company has specific business processes not currently addressed by salesforce.com, you can use sforce control technology to build your own application in salesforce.com. sforce controls combine HTML with browser-based technologies such as Java and Active-X, so you'll need to recruit some techie geeks, if this sounds foreign. But how much time could your company save, if, for example, your reps could click a Web link on an opportunity page and immediately populate an order management form in salesforce.com? You could do that. And for additional information on sforce, you can go to www.sforce.com.

5. **Type the URL into the Link URL field and add merge fields as necessary, as shown in Figure 18-3.**

   Use the Available Merge Fields tool to select the field and then copy and paste the merge field into the Link URL where appropriate.

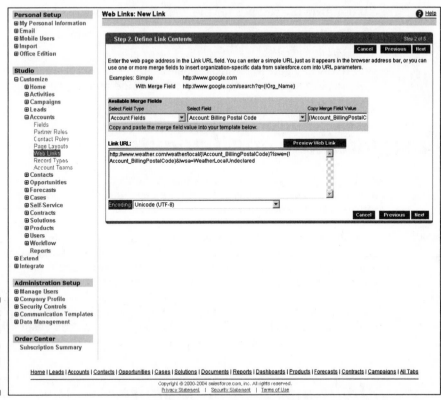

Figure 18-3:
Constructing the Web integration link.

To build Web links with merge fields, you should have some experience with URL parameters. With the right know-how, for example, you can use Web integration links to pass data to (or propagate) a Web form. If you need help, consult with salesforce.com or an experienced partner.

6. Select the encoding and click Next.

Step 3 of the wizard appears. The default encoding is based on your locale and needs to be changed only if you're passing information through the URL in a different format.

7. Click a radio button to select how the content from your Web link should be displayed in a window, and then click Next.

Step 4 of the wizard appears.

8. Complete the fields to define your window properties, and then click Next.

Step 5 of the wizard appears. If you're unsure of the properties, just accept the default settings.

9. **Confirm the settings for the Web link and click Save.**

The Web Links page for your selected record reappears, and your new Web link is listed on the page.

To display your Web links to users, you must add them to the appropriate page layout. See the later section "Modifying a page layout."

Customizing Page Layouts

Wouldn't it be great if you could take the fields on a record and rearrange them just like jigsaw puzzle pieces on a page until they fit just right? Sounds too good to be true, but with salesforce.com you can do just that and more.

With all editions of salesforce.com, you can use page layouts to modify the position of fields, Web links, and related lists on record detail pages and edit pages. While you're modifying a page layout, you can also edit field properties to determine which fields should be required or read only.

And with Enterprise and Developer Editions, you can create multiple page layouts and assign them to profiles. By doing this, you can ensure that different users are viewing just the right information to do their jobs.

Modifying a page layout

If you have permission to customize salesforce.com, you can modify page layouts at any time. I typically recommend that you create some or the majority of your proposed custom fields first before beginning to rearrange them on the layout.

To edit a page layout, click the Setup link in the top-right corner of any salesforce.com page and follow these steps:

1. **Click any tab heading under the Customize heading on the sidebar.**

The selected heading expands with links to customization options.

2. **Click the Page Layouts link under the tab heading.**

The Page Layouts page for the selected tab appears.

3. **Click the Edit link next to a page layout that you want to modify.**

An Edit Page Layout page appears. Choose from the following options to edit the layout:

- To arrange fields, links, or related lists, select an option from the View drop-down list on the right-side menu, and then click and drag fields to desired locations on the layout (see Figure 18-4).

- • To modify field properties, click one or multiple fields on the layout, and then click the Edit Field Properties button.

- • In the pop-up window that appears, use the check boxes to modify Read Only and Required settings, and then click OK as shown in Figure 18-5.

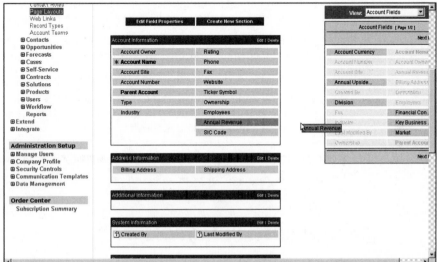

Figure 18-4: Rearranging a page layout.

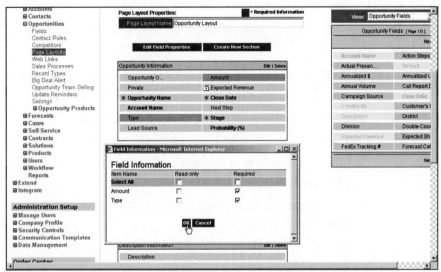

Figure 18-5: Editing field properties on the layout.

- To organize the record with sections, click the Edit link on a section or click the Create New Section button.

- In the pop-up window that appears, type a name for the section and use the drop-downs to adjust basic settings like columns and click OK.

   For example, on an account page layout, you might want to build a section named Strategic Account Planning to organize fields for account planning. When you click OK, the window closes.

- To overwrite a user's personal customizations on related lists, select the check box at the top of the Related List Section.

- To preview the layout, click the Preview button.

   A window appears with sample data displayed in the layout as you've currently modified it. In the preview window that opens, review the layout, and click Close.

4. **When you're satisfied with your layout changes, click Save.**

   The Page Layout page for your selected record reappears.

Adding custom layouts

If you have Enterprise or Developer Edition, you can build custom layouts to suit the needs of different profiles. See Chapter 17 for details on creating custom profiles. For all other editions, all users view the same page layout.

To create a custom page layout, click the Setup link in the top-right corner of any salesforce.com page and follow these steps:

1. **Click any tab heading under the Customize heading on the sidebar.**

   The selected heading expands with a menu of options.

2. **Click the Page Layouts link under a tab heading.**

   The Page Layouts page for the selected tab appears.

3. **Click the New button at the top of the Page Layouts list.**

   A Create New Page Layout page appears.

4. **Use the Existing Page Layout drop-down list to start from scratch or clone an existing layout.**

5. **Name the page layout and click Save.**

   The new Page Layout page appears.

6. **Click the Edit button and check out the steps in the preceding section if you want to modify the page layout.**

Assigning layouts to profiles

After you create custom page layouts, you can assign your layouts to profiles. By doing this, users will view detail pages based on their profile and associated page layout.

To assign layouts to profiles, click the Setup link in the top-right corner of any salesforce.com page and follow these steps:

1. **Click any tab heading under the Customize heading on the sidebar.**

   The selected heading expands with a menu of options.

2. **Click the Page Layouts link under the tab heading.**

   The Page Layouts page for the selected tab appears.

3. **Click the Page Layout Assignment button at the top of the Page Layouts list.**

   A Page Layout Assignment page appears with a list of current assignments.

4. **Click the Edit Assignments button.**

   The page reappears in Edit mode.

5. **In the Page Layout column, highlight one or multiple cells by clicking the links, as shown in Figure 18-6.**

   Use Ctrl+click or Shift+click to select multiple cells.

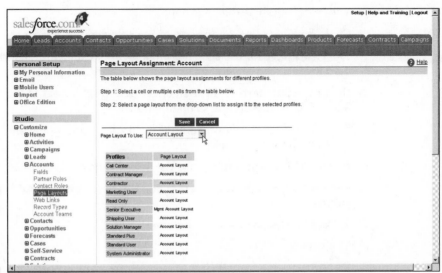

Figure 18-6: Selecting profiles for a page layout.

6. **From the Page Layout to Use drop-down list, choose the page layout that you want to assign to the selected profiles.**

7. **When you're done, click Save.**

   The Page Layout Assignment page reappears, displaying your changes.

Managing Multiple Business Processes

You can use a feature that salesforce.com calls *multiple business processes* to manage different lead, sales, support, and solution processes. This feature is particularly helpful if you have several groups of users who use a common tab (like leads) but whose processes are different. (And maybe the group leaders don't want to compromise.) For example, if your company has two sales teams that follow different sales methodologies, like Miller Heiman or Solution Selling, you can use multiple business processes and keep everyone happy.

Multiple business process features are available only in Enterprise and Developer Editions and pertain only to lead, opportunity, case, and solution records.

To set up multiple business processes, click the Setup link in the top-right corner of any salesforce.com page and follow these steps:

1. **Click the Lead, Opportunity, Case, or Solution headings under the Customize heading on the sidebar.**

   The selected tab headings expand.

2. **Click the Fields link under one of the selected tab headings.**

   The Fields page for the selected tab appears, displaying a list of standard fields at the top and a list of custom fields at the bottom.

3. **Under the Standard Fields list, click the Edit link next to the Status or Stage field to modify the drop-down list.**

   For example, on the Opportunities Fields page, you would click the Edit link next to the Stage field.

   A Picklist Edit page appears for the selected field.

4. **Review the existing values and click the New button to add additional values.**

   An Add Picklist Values page appears.

5. **Add one or more values and click Save.**

   The Picklist Edit page reappears.

6. **Review the list to verify that you have a complete master list of statuses or stages to support all business processes for that record.**

7. **Click the Reorder button if you want to change the order of the values.**

   The Picklist Edit page appears in Edit mode, and you can reorder the list.

8. **Use the arrow buttons to change the order of the drop-down list, and click Save when you're done.**

   The Picklist Edit page reappears.

9. **On the sidebar, click the Processes link under the selected record heading.**

   For example, under the Opportunities heading, you would click the Sales Processes link.

   The Processes page for the selected record appears.

10. **Click the New button to create a new process.**

    A Process Edit page appears.

11. **Choose the Existing Process, name the new process, and click Save.**

    A Process page appears, and you can select the values for your new business process.

    If you select Master as the Existing Process, you're able to choose from the master list generated from the Status or Stage field of the record.

12. **Highlight values and use the arrow buttons to modify your Selected Values list.**

    For example, if your company has a sales team that handles work orders, you could create a simple sales process, as shown in the example in Figure 18-7.

13. **Choose a Default Value from the drop-down list, and when you're done, click Save.**

    The Default Value drop-down list appears for lead, case, and solution processes but not for sales processes. The Processes page for your selected record reappears with a list of related business processes.

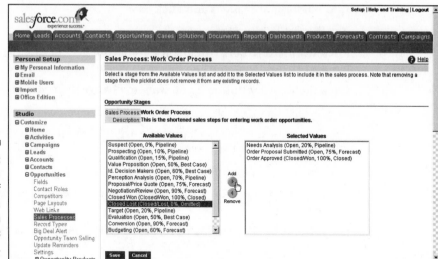

Figure 18-7:
Selecting a
subset of
values for a
custom
business
process.

Managing Record Types

If you're using Enterprise or Developer Edition, you can use record types to make subsets of drop-down lists and custom business process available to specific sets of users. For example, if you have two sales teams, one that sells into financial services and another that sells into retail verticals, both teams might share common fields on an account record but with very different values. With record types, you can customize accounts so that the same Industry field displays retail sectors for one group and financial services verticals for the other. By providing record types to your users, the big benefit is that you make common drop-down lists easier to fill out and more relevant (which is important to all companies but really important to large, complex organizations with diverse sales teams).

You can build record types to support all of the major records in salesforce.com including leads, accounts, opportunities, and so on. But before users can take advantage of the record type feature, you need to first create the record types and then assign them to profiles. The good news is that with salesforce.com's record type wizard, you can perform both actions in a series of guided steps.

Before creating your record types, check to make sure that you have added all values to a master picklist field (drop-down list). (See the earlier section, "Viewing and updating fields," for details on editing drop-down lists.)

To create a record type, click the Setup link in the top-right corner of any salesforce.com page and follow these steps:

1. **Click any tab heading under the Customize heading on the sidebar.**

   The selected tab heading expands.

2. **Click the Record Types link under the tab heading.**

   The Record Types page for the selected tab appears.

3. **Click the New button.**

   Step 1 of the New Record Type wizard appears.

4. **Complete the fields at the top of the page, as shown in Figure 18-8.**

   Most are obvious, but here are three important pointers:

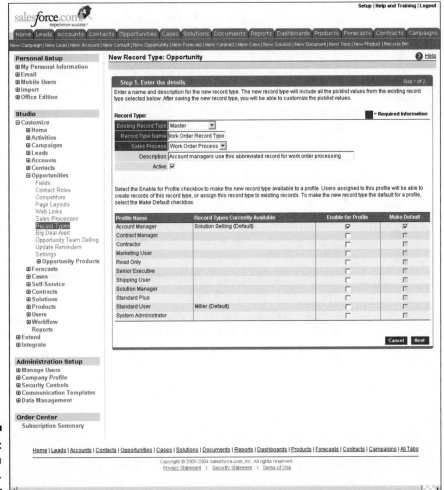

Figure 18-8:
Creating a
record type.

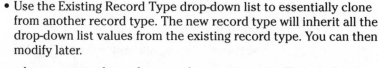

- Use the Existing Record Type drop-down list to essentially clone from another record type. The new record type will inherit all the drop-down list values from the existing record type. You can then modify later.

If you choose not to clone, the record type automatically includes the master drop-down list values for both custom and standard fields. That's okay; you can edit the drop-down lists after.

- On a lead, opportunity, case, or solution record type, select the business process from the drop-down list. See the earlier section, "Managing multiple business processes," for details.

- Select the Active check box if you want to make the record type active.

5. **Select the check boxes in the table to make the new record type available to different profiles.**

If you ever need to modify the assignment of record types to profiles, you can do this from the Record Type Settings section of a profile page. Simply click the Edit link next to a record type and follow the easy steps on the page that appears. (See Chapter 17 for details on updating profile settings.)

6. **When you're done, click Next.**

Step 2 of the wizard appears.

7. **Use the drop-down lists to select the page layout that different profiles will see for records of this record type.**

8. **When you're done, click Save.**

The new Record Type page appears with a list of the drop-down lists on the record type.

9. **Click the Edit link next to a drop-down list to modify the values.**

A Record Type Edit page appears.

10. **Highlight values in the Available Values list box and use the arrow buttons to build the Selected Values list, as shown in Figure 18-9.**

11. **Select a value from the Default drop-down list if necessary, and then click Save.**

The Record Type page reappears.

If a user will need to make use of multiple record types, remember to add the Record Type field manually to a page layout. For example, if a sales rep sells both cars and boats (and opportunity record types exist for both), providing the Record Type field on a layout allows the rep to switch a car opportunity to a boat opportunity if needed. See the earlier section "Customizing Page Layouts" for details.

Figure 18-9:
Selecting
values for a
record type.

Chapter 19

Migrating and Maintaining Your Data

*I*f you're a system administrator, often your greatest headache isn't configuring or customizing the system but getting your data in and maintaining it so that it's useful. Nothing hurts a rollout more than complaints from users that their customer data isn't in salesforce.com, that information is duplicated in several records, or that the information is wrong. And your end user adoption suffers if you don't maintain your records after the rollout. If you're not diligent, you can find yourself in the same mess that drove you to salesforce.com in the first place.

If rollout and data maintenance are giving you nightmares, use the data management tools in salesforce.com to easily import leads, accounts, and contacts. If you have in-house expertise or engage an experienced salesforce.com partner, you can migrate other critical customer data (such as opportunities, cases, and activities) by using proven third-party tools. And when your data is stored in salesforce.com, you can rely on a variety of tools to help you manage and maintain your database.

In this chapter, I first discuss your options for data import. Then I show you how to use salesforce.com tools to manage your data (including mass transferring, deleting, and reassigning data). Finally, I touch on some advanced concepts. Complex data migration and updates of data between your data sources and salesforce.com is beyond the scope of this book, but I make sure to point you in the right direction.

Understanding Your Options for Data Migration

Salesforce.com has easy-to-use wizards that step you through importing your campaign updates, leads, accounts, and contacts. If you're a system administrator or have the right profile permissions, you can perform these tasks for your users. For other legacy data that you want in salesforce.com such as opportunities, cases, and activities, you have to enter information manually or utilize a third-party ETL (extract, transform, load) tool to automatically migrate desired data into salesforce.com.

Using import wizards

Import wizards for leads, accounts, and contacts are conveniently located under the Data Management heading in the Administrative Setup section of Setup. If you're an administrator, you also see links to the import wizards in the Tools section of certain tab home pages. For example, if you want to import your company's leads, click the Leads tab and then click the Import Leads link in the Tools section. Steps and tips for each of the import wizards are detailed in relevant chapters of this book as follows:

- To **import leads,** see Chapter 4. Only a user with the Import Leads permission can perform this operation.

- To **import contacts and accounts,** see Chapter 6. Salesforce.com provides you one wizard that can take you through importing contacts and/or accounts. Individual users also have the ability to import their personal contacts and accounts.

- To **import campaign leads** or **update contacts or leads linked to a campaign,** see Chapter 13.

Investigating third-party ETL tools

Data migration is a tricky matter. I think if salesforce.com could have built wizards for records in addition to campaign members, leads, accounts, and contacts, they would have delivered it to you by now.

The good news is that several vendors now provide proven ETL or integration tools that enable you to migrate other types of records to (or from) salesforce.com and append those records where appropriate. For example, if you want to migrate your opportunities into salesforce.com, make sure that they link to the correct account records by using a unique identifier or ID. Many databases (hopefully the ones you possess) automatically generate a unique ID stored in a field for a record when it's created.

With a unique ID for an account (like ACCT-001), ETL tools can make short work of associating all the proper opportunities to the right accounts. Database experts with the proper ETL tools can pull off this wizardry and more. For example, you could link opportunities with other related records such as partners, products, and price books. Sadly, many outside databases might not have unique IDs . . . which is what can make the importing of foreign data into salesforce.com so much fun.

Without getting too technical, the experts link data by using something called the sforce API (application program interface) to enable your technical resource to access data programmatically. Sforce (`www.sforce.com`) is the platform to use to customize or integrate salesforce.com to do even snazzier things than what you can do with it out of the box. What's a platform? Think of it as a collection of rules and commands that programmers can use to get to tell salesforce.com to do certain things. To access the sforce API, you must have Enterprise or Developer Edition.

Different IT groups or partners have their preferred integration tools. Two proven solutions are the products from TIBCO and Pervasive Software. Both vendors provide tools that have built-in connectors with the sforce API to reduce your setup time. If you don't have the internal resources to help you with data migration, consult with salesforce.com, review the many implementation partners (many who have deep experience in this area), or e-mail me at `twong@clientology.net` and ask — I'll point you in the right direction.

Migrating Your Legacy Data

During the preparation phase of your implementation, you need to have a well thought out and documented plan for your data migration strategy. That plan needs to include details on objectives, resources, contingencies, and timelines based on the different steps in your plan. In this section, I discuss some of the steps that you should consider. I base these steps on my experiences, good and bad alike.

Determining your data sources

The average company I've worked with typically has some type of existing contact management tool, a variety of spreadsheets with other customer data, and often contact information living in users' Microsoft Outlook or Lotus Notes applications. (Did I mention Word documents and sticky notes?)

As you go through your preparation, assess what and how much information needs to be in salesforce.com. Here are some tips for this step:

✔ Garbage in, garbage out. Keep that in the back of your mind as you determine what goes into salesforce.com. When you move into a new home, you usually look through your old home's closets and decide what to haul with you and what to throw away. There's no point in bringing over things you know you'll never touch or look at, right? Moving data requires the same type of evaluation. Be ready to let go of any pack-rat tendencies here.

✔ Catalog the different data sources, what types of records, what range, and how many.

✔ Work with your customer relationship management (CRM) project team to determine where different information should go and why.

✔ Think about the timing and the sequence of the import. For example, many companies create user records first, then import accounts and contacts, and finally they migrate and append opportunities.

✔ Keep it simple if possible. The more complicated you make the migration, the greater the impact on your timeline. I recommend that you assess the level of effort versus the potential value of the effort.

Preparing your data

Clean it now or clean it later. I'm full of little phrases, but this is a useful idea. Some project teams like to scrub data before importing it into salesforce.com. Others prefer to bring all the records in and then utilize salesforce.com's easy data management tools to clean it up later. Regardless of when you do it, cleaning data is not glamorous work, but it's gotta be done. I think it's usually somewhere between those two extremes.

Here are a couple tips as you prepare your data:

✔ Oftentimes you might find it easiest to export data to tools such as Microsoft Access or Excel, which let you delete columns, sort rows, and make global changes.

✔ Strive for standard naming conventions. For example, if different data sources refer to accounts by different names (IBM versus International Business Machines), now is a good time to standardize naming.

✔ Edit or add fields in salesforce.com to support the migration. For instance, if your pipeline reports track margin per opportunity, you need to build a custom Opportunity field to support margin data.

✔ If your existing data source has unique record IDs, you might want to migrate those IDs to a custom field. You can always delete or hide the field at a later stage. Not only can this help you verify the accuracy of your migration, but those IDs might come in handy for integration (especially if you don't plan to shut down the other data source).

✔ Map your data columns to field names in salesforce.com. Mapping is the process of associating a field from one data source to a field in another data source so that data is imported into the right fields. For example, the Company field in Microsoft Outlook typically maps to the Account field in salesforce.com. Some system administrators even rename the column headers in migration files so that they exactly match field names in salesforce.com. Doing this minimizes the migration madness.

✔ Conform your data to fit salesforce.com standards (or the other way around). Each field in salesforce.com has certain properties that might include size limitations, decimal points, date formats, and so on.

✔ Add a Data Source column to your import file and map it to a custom field in salesforce.com. By doing this, you can defend where data came from.

✔ Wherever possible, assign the correct owners to records. If you don't have all records assigned, the owner defaults to whichever administrator is executing the migration.

✔ Gain acceptance from stakeholders of the files you've prepared. At least if you offer them the chance to review, you avoid surprises.

Testing the import

Test before you execute the final migration. Often you discover things that you missed or could improve. Here are a couple tips:

✔ Select a small sample of significant records. The more high profile the records the better — especially when reviewed by a stakeholder.

✔ Consider adjusting the page layouts to make validating the data import easier.

✔ Consider documenting your process, especially if you're using an integration tool. Most tools allow you to save process maps so you don't have to re-create your work.

Analyzing the test data results

When your test data is in salesforce.com, compare it carefully with your test file to ensure accuracy and completeness. Here are a couple tips on how to productively analyze the test data results:

✔ **Build:** Build a custom report that lets you look at the record data collectively.

✔ **Compare:** Open a record if necessary and compare it against the import file. Confirm that the record's fields show what you think they should show.

✔ **View:** Build a custom view from a relevant tab home page to see your imported data laid out in columns on a list page. For example, if you're importing contacts, build a view from the Contacts home page. You're limited to only about a dozen columns, but often this is a good way to review and share the test results with other users. Users could go to a report, but a view keeps them focused.

✔ **Validate:** Validate the data with selected stakeholders to get their feedback and support that the test data results look correct. It's not enough that you think the test import was accurate. Your end users are the ultimate test; sometimes they'll see things that you didn't because the data belonged to them.

✔ **Tweak:** Adjust your process or make changes to the import file or salesforce.com based on the results of the test import. For example, maybe you forgot to map a field or the data didn't import correctly because of a field's properties. Perhaps you forgot to add an Owner column on the import file, and you became the owner of the records. I could come up with a dozen other typical foibles, but that's why you do a test . . . so you can make modifications before you import reams of data incorrectly.

Migrating your final data

After you successfully execute, refine, and validate the test migration, you're ready to move forward with importing your file or files. (I know that's a simplification of what could be a complicated set of tasks, but the overall process is tried and true.)

Here are a couple suggestions for this step:

✔ Communicate expectations with your users. If you're cutting over from one system to another, you might have a lapse in which data must be updated prior to going live.

✔ If you have significant data, you might consider running the migration during non-working hours. Especially if the system is live for some groups of users already, this might avoid confusion.

✔ Build yourself some cushion for error. Don't try to execute the migration the day before sales training. You never know if something unanticipated might happen that prevents successful completion.

Validating your data

Similar to analyzing results of the test data (see the section "Analyzing the test data results"), when the data has been loaded, run reports to validate a cross-sampling of records to ensure accuracy and completeness. Strive for seeing perfectly imported data, but expect less than that, too.

Augmenting your data

Prior to rolling out salesforce.com, some companies take the extra step of manually or automatically updating records to wow users and drive more success. For example, I worked with one administrator who manually updated account records for major customers with up-to-date market research. By doing this, the company's sales reps immediately saw the benefits and best practices for using the salesforce.com system for managing accounts from day one.

Managing Your Salesforce.com Database

After you implement salesforce.com, you need to make sure that you create processes for periodically updating and backing up your data. If you don't, human error can lead to frustration, heartache, and hair loss. Duplicate records, dead leads, records that need to be transferred when a user leaves the company — these are just a few examples of data that needs to be updated.

Most of the data maintenance tools are accessible from the Data Management heading located under the Administrative Setup heading on the sidebar of Setup. (See Chapters 4, 5, and 6 for details on de-duplicating leads, accounts, and contacts.)

Backing up your data

If you have Enterprise or Professional Edition, salesforce.com offers a weekly export service of all your data. This service is free if you have Enterprise Edition and is available for an additional fee if you use Professional Edition.

To export your data, follow these steps:

1. **Click the Setup link in the top-right corner of any salesforce.com page.**

   The Personal Setup page appears.

2. **Click the Data Management heading on the sidebar, and then click the Data Export link under that.**

   The Data Export Service page appears.

3. **Select the appropriate export file encoding from the Export File Encoding drop-down list and select the check box if you want to include attachments.**

   If you live in the United States or Western Europe, you don't have to change the Export File Encoding selection.

4. **When you're done, click the Data Export button.**

   The Export Requested page appears. You will receive an e-mail from salesforce.com with a link to a page where you can retrieve zipped `.csv` files of all your data. You have 48 hours to download your data, after which time the data files are deleted.

5. **When you receive the e-mail entitled Your Organization Data Export Has Been Completed, click the title to open the e-mail.**

   The e-mail appears with a link to the page where you can retrieve your data export.

6. **Click the link and log in to salesforce.com if required.**

   The Weekly Export Service page appears as shown in Figure 19-1. You can also access this page through the Personal Setup page: On the sidebar, click the Data Management heading, and then click the Data Export link under that.

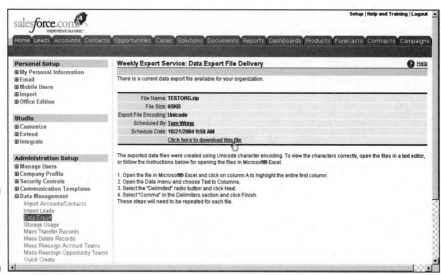

Figure 19-1: Accessing your data export file.

7. **Click the Click Here to Download This File link.**

   A dialog box appears, allowing you to open or save your zip file to a location accessible from your computer.

8. **Open the Zip file.**

9. **Open one of the export files in Microsoft Excel and click the column A button to highlight the entire first column.**

10. **Choose Data⇨Text to Columns.**

    A dialog box appears.

11. **Select the Delimited radio button and click Next.**

12. **Select the Comma option in the Delimiters section and click Finish.**

    The file reformats.

13. **Save the file in a** `.csv` **format.**

14. **Repeat Steps 9 through 13 for each file in the data export.**

Mass transferring records

A sales rep leaves. Sales territories get readjusted. You imported a file but forgot to assign records to the right owners in advance. These are just a few examples of when you might have to transfer records. Salesforce.com allows you to mass transfer lead or account records, and the two processes are very similar.

When transferring leads or accounts, salesforce.com automatically transfers certain linked records on the detail page. For both leads and accounts, all open activities transfer to the new owner. For accounts, all notes, contacts, and open opportunities owned by the existing owner transfer to the new owner.

To mass transfer lead or account records, follow these steps:

1. **Click the Setup link in the top-right corner of any salesforce.com page.**

   The Personal Setup page appears.

2. **Click the Data Management heading on the sidebar, and then click the Mass Transfer Records link under that.**

   A Mass Transfer Records page appears.

3. **Click the Transfer Accounts link or the Transfer Leads link, depending on your needs.**

   A Mass Transfer page appears with a set of filtering tools to help you search for records (see Figure 19-2).

Figure 19-2:
Finding
records for
your mass
transfer.

4. **In the Transfer From and Transfer To fields, use the Lookup icons to find the appropriate users.**

   Note that with leads, you can also transfer to or from queues. See Chapter 4 for details on lead queues.

5. **If you're mass transferring accounts, select the check boxes to specify whether you want to transfer types of opportunities, cases, and teams.**

6. **Define additional criteria to filter your search by using the drop-down lists and fields provided.**

   You do this by selecting a field in the first drop-down list, selecting an operator in the second drop-down list, and typing a value in the field. For example, if you want to transfer all of one sales rep's New York City accounts to a new rep, your criteria would be City Equals New York.

7. **When you're satisfied with your settings and filters, click the Find button.**

   The Mass Transfer page reappears with a list of results at the bottom of the page.

8. **Use the check boxes to select the records that you want to transfer.**

9. **When you're done, click the Transfer button.**

   The Mass Transfer page reappears when the transfer is complete.

Mass deleting records

If you're the administrator on various occasions you might want to or need to mass delete records. A couple typical examples include deleting dead leads and eliminating accounts that haven't had any activity. Salesforce.com allows you to mass delete leads, accounts, contacts, activities, and products, and the processes are very similar.

To mass delete records, follow these steps:

1. **Click the Setup link in the top-right corner of any salesforce.com page.**

   The Personal Setup page appears.

2. **Click the Data Management heading on the sidebar, and then click the Mass Delete Records link under that.**

   The Mass Delete Records page appears.

3. **Click one of the Mass Delete links depending on the type of record you wish to mass delete.**

   The Mass Delete page appears with a three- to five-step wizard for mass deleting. The three-step wizard is shown in Figure 19-3. Mass Delete Accounts has two extra steps based on opportunities that are closed/won or that aren't owned by you. Mass Delete Products has one extra step to archive products with line items on opportunities.

4. **Review the salesforce.com warnings in Step 1 of the wizard.**

5. **Back up relevant data by generating a report and exporting it to Excel as part of Step 2 of the wizard.**

   See Chapter 18 for details on building and exporting reports.

6. **Use the filters in Step 3 of the wizard to define criteria for the search.**

   You do this by selecting a field in the first drop-down list, selecting an operator in the second drop-down list, and typing a value in the field.

7. **Click the Search button.**

   The Mass Delete page reappears with a list of possible records at the bottom of the page. Do the following:

- • If you're mass deleting accounts, select the check box in Step 4 of the wizard if you want to delete accounts that have Closed/Won opportunities.

- • If you're mass deleting accounts, select the check box to delete accounts with another owner's opportunities.

- • If you're mass deleting products, select the check box if you want to archive products with line items on opportunities.

8. **Use the Action column to select records to be deleted (refer to Figure 19-3).**

9. **When you're satisfied, click the Delete button.**

   A dialog box appears to confirm the deletion.

10. **Click OK.**

   The Mass Delete page reappears minus the records that you deleted.

Figure 19-3:
Selecting
records for
mass
deletion.

Mass reassigning teams

If your company uses Enterprise Edition, you can create account teams from an Account detail page and/or selling teams from an Opportunity detail page. Many companies find this team definition facilitates access to data and improves collaboration. See Chapters 5 for setting up account teams.

If you use teams in salesforce.com, you can use mass reassignment tools to quickly and easily redefine teams en masse. Salesforce.com provides separate tools for reassigning account and opportunity teams. The wizards operate virtually identically but filter on account versus opportunity fields and obviously access different records.

To mass reassign teams, follow these steps:

1. **Click the Setup link in the top-right corner of any salesforce.com page.**

   The Personal Setup page appears.

2. **Click the Data Management heading on the sidebar.**

   The folder expands.

3. **Click the Mass Reassign Account Teams link or the Mass Reassign Opportunity Teams link depending on your objective.**

   Step 1 of the selected Mass *Whichever* Reassign wizard appears (see Figure 19-4).

4. **Use the radio buttons to select whether you want to add, remove, or reassign a team member, and then click Next.**

   Step 2 of the wizard appears.

5. **Search for accounts or opportunities (depending on the wizard you selected in Step 2) by using the criteria filters at the top of the page.**

   See Chapter 2 for details on setting filters.

6. **Use the fields at the bottom of the page to select information to be displayed on each column of the list, and then click Next.**

   Step 3 of the wizard appears.

7. **Use the check boxes in the Action column to select records for your team reassignment operation, and then click Next.**

   Step 4 of the wizard appears based on the operation you selected in Step 1 of the wizard.

Figure 19-4:
Selecting
your option
for team
reassign-
ment.

8. **Complete the fields to perform your operation.**

   The fields that you complete differ depending on whether you're adding, removing, or replacing a team member, but that's not too surprising.

9. **When you're satisfied with your settings, click the Add, Remove, or Replace button.**

   The Step 4 page reappears with the status of your reassignment.

10. **When you're finished, click Done.**

    The Data Management menu page reappears.

Getting Help with Complex Data Tasks

This chapter shows you some of the basic operations that you can perform to import and manage your data in salesforce.com. For many companies that have complex data needs, this might be an oversimplification. If you need help with your data, here are some resources you can turn to:

✔ Talk with your customer success manager or account rep at salesforce. com. They can help you define your needs and point you to the appropriate solution or resource.

✔ If you think you're looking for a product solution, log out of salesforce. com and go to the Partners tab of the salesforce.com public site. In the right column, click the On-Demand Marketplace link. On the On-Demand Marketplace page are links to various technology solutions that have been rigorously reviewed by salesforce.com. Click the Integration (EAI/ETL) link or the Data Services/Data Quality link for details on the partners and their tools.

✔ If you need a consulting partner with experience in executing data tasks, log out of salesforce.com and go to the Partners tab of the salesforce.com public site. In the right column, click the Consulting Partners link. On the Consulting Partners page you find lists of consulting firms, many of whom have deep experience with complex data tasks. Be sure to do your homework here including who they've worked with, the business challenge, scope, approach, and so on.

✔ On the sforce Web site, www.sforce.com, click the Community link at the top of the page to go to salesforce.com's Developer Boards. These boards are of a technical nature, but if this is what you're looking for, you might find a community of developers who have wrestled or are familiar with your data challenges.

✔ Send me an e-mail at twong@clientology.net or go to my community Web site at www.clientology.net. I have experience with a variety of complex data issues involving salesforce.com and might be able to help you define your exact needs and point you in the right direction. I'd be happy to lend a hand.

Part VI
The Part of Tens

SALES MANAGEMENT PICNIC

"Get names!"

In this part . . .

The Part of Tens is a standard for all *For Dummies* books. I use this part to highlight certain lists that deserve a special place.

Anyone can have a tough time keeping up to speed with all the feature releases from salesforce.com. In the first list, I discuss ten great productivity tools worth their weight in gold: Five are from the Winter '05 release, and the other five are super — but often overlooked — tools.

In the second list, I detail ten keys to a successful implementation. If you're an administrator, this is a must see.

Chapter 20

Ten Ways to Drive More Productivity

In This Chapter

▶ Five new features

▶ Five existing tools that you shouldn't overlook

Salesforce.com drives much of their feature updates based on their existing roadmap and requests from customers just like you. Three times a year, salesforce.com comes out with a new release of their award-winning service. Unlike traditional software upgrades, these releases are immediately available to all customers depending, of course, on which edition they use.

Also, if you've been struggling with an apparent feature limitation or you're looking to further optimize and drive productivity out of your salesforce.com solution, check out the universe of feature options currently available to you.

In this chapter, I summarize five of the hottest new features from their Winter '05 release. Then I cover five great productivity tools that you might have overlooked.

Discovering the Top Five New Features

It amazes me that with every release, salesforce.com comes out with a universe of new features and enhancements that improve an already incredible service. The Winter '05 release is no exception, and here I highlight five features that I think can make a big difference to you:

✔ **Supportforce.com Enhancements (Professional and Enterprise Editions):** Since introducing case management in Spring 2001, salesforce.com has provided the ability to integrate sales and service organizations to better satisfy customers. Over the years, salesforce.com rolled out additional enhancements for customer service functionality. If you don't currently use salesforce.com for customer service or you've deprioritized it to focus on sales and marketing, it's time you looked again. With the Winter '05 release, salesforce.com has made significant improvements, including solution categories to improve the searchability of your knowledge base; solution workflow to better manage your approval process; and a variety of case management alerts that had previously been absent.

✔ **Asset Management (Professional and Enterprise Editions):** With asset management in salesforce.com, you can now capture important information on the products and services installed with your customers whether those products are yours or your competitors. If you're a sales rep, you can use this knowledge to renew, upsell, or take away business from your competitors when the timing is right. And if you're a support rep, asset management now enables you to associate customer service issues directly with products in salesforce.com, which can help identify product quality issues and better address challenges such as return merchandise authorizations.

✔ **Opportunity Integration with Cases (Professional and Enterprise Editions):** With the Winter '05 release, cases can now be linked directly to opportunities. If you're a sales rep, this means that you can quickly initiate and/or identify service issues that relate to closed or even open deals — and if need be, get involved before it's too late. Opportunity integration with cases also helps managers to determine the level of effort and cost associated to winning and servicing deals.

✔ **Long Text Area Custom Fields (all Editions):** What seems like the smallest of things can make the biggest of differences. At long last, system administrators can create custom text area fields substantially bigger than 255 characters! In fact, the new long text area field can contain up to 32,000 characters, which will have immediate impact on reps and teams that require bigger fields to capture information such as sales planning, issue tracking, account strategy, and more.

✔ **Collapsible Page Sections (all Editions):** Depending on your customization of salesforce.com, record detail pages can get quite long. With long text area fields, I can only imagine how long some pages might become. With collapsible page sections, you can reduce the amount of scrolling and focus on the areas of the detail page that are important to you. With the click of a button, users will have the ability to collapse any section of a record detail page.

Glaringly absent from this all-star list of features are two great enhancements that I've already integrated into the chapters of this book. See Chapter 7 for details on Group Calendaring using salesforce.com's new and improved multi-user calendar view. And see Chapter 15 for tips on using And/Or Report Filters to do complex reporting.

Revisiting Five Great Productivity Tools

Few companies make use of every feature when they first deploy salesforce. com to their employees. It would be overwhelming to absorb, and you know that success is a function of end user adoption. So if you're like other CRM project teams, you tend to focus on addressing the core business objectives that often include lead, account, and opportunity management

If this sounds like you, here are five tools that I haven't addressed in earlier chapters. With these, you can substantially boost productivity depending on your objectives.

- ✔ **Custom tabs and objects (Enterprise and Developer Editions):** "Build your own CRM!" That was a key theme when salesforce.com introduced custom tabs and objects. Salesforce.com understands that certain companies have unique business needs that might not be easily addressed by the standard tabs that it offers. With custom objects, you can create your own type of record and link it to related records like accounts, contacts and opportunities. For example, if your sales reps sell into specific brands of your customer, you could create a custom object so that users can record a customer's top brands on an account related list. On a custom tab, you can create a custom object and organize its records. For example, maybe you want to create your own order management application and display it on an Order Entry tab. To build custom tabs and objects, click the Extend heading under the Studio heading in the sidebar of Setup.

- ✔ **Workflow (Enterprise and Developer Editions):** How many times have you lost business because someone forgot to do something in your sales process? With the workflow feature in salesforce.com, you can create a rule and associate it to tasks and alerts that can be assigned to different users. You can use workflow to automate certain standard processes to make sure important balls don't get dropped. For example, if your sales reps create opportunities that sometimes require special pricing approvals, you can use a workflow rule to automatically trigger alerts and tasks to finance and sales managers. To create workflow, click the Workflow link under the Customize heading under the Studio heading on the sidebar of Setup.

- ✔ **Self-service portal (Professional, Enterprise, and Developer Editions):** Help your customers help themselves. This is one method of potentially delivering great service and managing the workload in your call center. But how do you build a secure customer portal and quickly tie it in with your CRM application? With self-service portal functionality in salesforce. com, you can do this in hours rather than weeks. With recent enhancements to the self-service portal, you can actually generate a sample portal much the same way you can generate a sample dashboard. And with improved design tools, your team can ensure branding consistency with your other Web sites. To launch a self-service portal, click the Self Service Portal link under the Self Service link under the Customize heading under the Studio heading in the sidebar of Setup.

✔ **Web tabs (Enterprise and Developer Editions):** "One-stop shopping . . . one place where your sales reps can get all the information they need to manage their jobs." If you're trying to drive sales or service process improvements, that's your dream. But oftentimes, users are dependent on other Web sites, or Web applications. Web integration links might get overlooked in salesforce.com. With Web tabs, you can embed any Web resource or application into your salesforce.com solution with no coding required. And when users click the custom tab, the Web application appears seamlessly in the salesforce.com window. For example, if your sales reps set up demos through a Web application as part of their job, you can use Web tabs to access the application and save them valuable time. To build Web tabs, click the Custom Tabs link under Extend heading under the Studio heading in the sidebar of Setup.

✔ **Big deal alert (Team, Professional, Enterprise, and Developer Editions):** The big deal alert is a big deal, but often overlooked. With this feature you can trigger automated e-mail alerts to notify the right people in your organization when an opportunity reaches a certain threshold. That threshold is defined by a combination of amount and probability. If, for example, you have a professional services team that needs to get involved when an opportunity reaches a certain probability and dollar threshold, big deal alerts can notify the right people immediately without any extra work. To set up big deal alerts, click the Big Deal Alert link under the Opportunities link under the Customize heading under the Studio heading in the sidebar of Setup.

Chapter 21

Ten Keys to a Successful Implementation

In This Chapter

▶ Preparation tips

▶ Implementation tips

Several companies have rolled out customer relationship management (CRM) applications with the mistaken notion that you could buy the licenses, turn on the switch, and use the application as soon as you take it out of the box. Then these same companies look back months later and wonder why they're not experiencing the results they envisioned.

Nine out of ten times, the root cause is poor planning. Whether you're implementing salesforce.com for a single business unit, a functional group (such as marketing or service), or your entire organization, building a strong plan and then executing the plan will substantially improve your chance of success.

Salesforce.com provides you the tools and a platform to enhance your business effectiveness and productivity. What you decide to do with it is up to you. If you're involved in the rollout of salesforce.com, here are ten tips to help you successfully roll out salesforce.com.

Defining Your Objectives

Why are you implementing salesforce.com? Is it to increase sales, improve productivity, encourage collaboration, or all three? It's near impossible to implement anything correctly unless you know what you want to achieve. Use my examples of common business challenges in Chapter 1 if you need a starting point to clearly document your objectives. Then try to make your objectives even more concrete and measurable by applying specific *success metrics* to an objective. (A success metric is a numerical goal that you want to achieve, ideally within a specified timeframe.) For example, it's one thing to say you want to reduce customer service response time. It's quite another thing to define that you want to reduce response time by 20 percent by the end of the year.

Building a Team

As you might have already figured out, CRM is less about technology and more about people, human processes, and your business. Sometimes, companies make the critical mistake of assigning a system administrator to handle the rollout, but that administrator might or might not have enough business context and support to drive a CRM effort. For your company to get the most out of salesforce.com, you need to develop a team made up of critical stakeholders, project resources, and a cross-section of end users. If you're implementing salesforce.com for sales and marketing, that might mean that the team includes managers from sales, sales operations, marketing, finance, product, IT, some respected sales reps, and hopefully a member of your executive team. This doesn't have to be a huge team, nor should members expect to be involved in this project full time. But you must have people who can speak for the business and sufficient resources to get the job done.

Defining Your Scope and Prioritizing Initiatives

You can do a lot with salesforce.com, but the more complex you make it, the longer the implementation will likely take and the greater the chance you'll hit a snag. As you collect the requirements of key stakeholders, prioritize initiatives and determine what's in scope and out of scope for the initial implementation. Consider keeping the implementation limited by focusing on the major priorities. Then you can extend your initiatives by building on prior success.

Defining a Palatable Timeline

The meter starts ticking as soon as you purchase your user licenses. This is sometimes the reason that companies make the mistake of making seats available to all users even before configuration or customization has begun.

In my experience, a focused CRM project team can accomplish major milestones in an implementation within 30 to 60 days. And budget-holders can wait 30 to 60 days if the benefits justify the time spent. Make sure that you stick as close to the timeline as possible when you put a stake in the ground.

Gaining Commitment to a Plan

Building a plan isn't the hard part. Making sure that you've gained commitment from key stakeholders to the objectives, scope, timeline, and availability of resources is critical. I would try to get every stakeholder to vote *Yes* at a formal kickoff. Then do everything you can to keep personal agendas from undercutting the corporate objectives of your salesforce.com rollout.

Communicating the Vision and Plan

Rolling out or replacing a CRM solution is a big deal. For some managers and reps, this initiative can cause concerns for a variety of reasons: People get set in their ways; they think it's big brother; they assume it's going to take a lot of their time; and so on. It's important that you communicate what's in it for them and why and begin to set expectations for what you need from them during and after the implementation. This will go a long way in calming fears and gaining support and commitment. This also builds a communication mechanism for feedback and managing changes to your salesforce.com solution.

Evaluating Your Processes

How can you build something if you don't know what to build and why? You should conduct business process review meetings as key elements to your planning process. Those meetings should include a key stakeholder (or stakeholders) who can speak for his or her business and be face-to-face with the CRM project team if possible (for example, a channel sales session with the head of channel sales). By doing this, you gain further agreement to your plan and ensure that you're building a solution that meets existing or desired processes of managers and their teams.

Customizing for User Relevance

When designing records and layouts, keeping it simple isn't always appropriate. Some businesses do have complex needs. But be aware that long, complicated records can affect end user adoption. So don't build a field unless you think end users will use it, and focus your customization of the pages on relevance to your users.

Validating Your Milestones

As you accomplish major milestones (such as data migration of opportunities, configuration of role hierarchy and sharing, and customization of different records or layouts), validate your work with other members of the team who are representative of the end users. By doing this, you can make sure at key points that you're building a solution that works for your internal customer.

Building a Comprehensive Training Plan

As early as you can in the implementation process, start building a training plan. As simple as salesforce.com is to use, don't assume that users will know what to do. And don't rely solely on the generic sales training offered by salesforce.com; it might not be relevant enough to your customization. I typically recommend incorporating prerequisite classes, custom sales training, and reinforcement training in your plan as you troubleshoot problems or roll out new functionality. The key is to make sure that enough relevant training is provided so that people effectively and correctly use the salesforce.com application.

Also, be sure that your end users have personal copies of *Salesforce.com For Dummies*. Just in case.

Index